The American Love Lyric after Auschwitz and Hiroshima

The American Love Lyric after Auschwitz and Hiroshima

Barbara L. Estrin

palgrave

THE AMERICAN LOVE LYRIC AFTER AUSCHWITZ AND HIROSHIMA
© Barbara L. Estrin, 2001

First published 2001 by
PALGRAVE™
175 Fifth Avenue, New York, N.Y.10010 and
Houndmills, Basingstoke, Hampshire RG21 6XS.
Companies and representatives throughout the world.

PALGRAVE is the new global publishing imprint of St. Martin's Press LLC
Scholarly and Reference Division and Palgrave Publishers Ltd (formerly
Macmillan Press Ltd).

ISBN 0-312-23865-7 hardback

Library of Congress Cataloging-in-Publication Data
Estrin, Barbara L., 1942-
    The American love lyric after Auschwitz and Hiroshima /
by Barbara L. Estrin.
        p. cm.
    Includes bibliographical references and index.
    ISBN 0-312-23865-7
    1. Love poetry, American—History and criticism.   2. American poetry—
20th century—History and criticism.   3. Hiroshima-shi (Japan)—History—
Bombardment, 1945—Influence.   4. World War, 1939-1945—Literature and
the war.   5. Holocaust, Jewish (1939-1945), in literature.   6. World War,
1939-1945—United States.   7. World War, 1939-1945—Influence.   I. Title.

PS310.L65 E88 2001
811'.04093543—dc21   2001034820

A catalogue record for this book is available from the British Library.

Design by Westchester Book Composition

First edition: December 2001
10 9 8 7 6 5 4 3 2 1

Printed in the United States of America.

Permissions

Permission to quote from the following is gratefully acknowledged:

For Mark

Contents

Preface

[**Wittgenstein**]: I will say, posthumously, that Europe is the world's sore affliction, that you in America who have taken the best that Europe has to offer while hoping to avoid the worst are, in your indigenously American phrase, "whistling Dixie." All your God-drenched thinking replicates the religious structures built out of the hallucinatory life of the ancient Near East by European clericists, all your social frictions are the inheritance of colonialist slave-making economies of European businessmen, all your metaphysical conundrums were concocted for you by European intellectuals, and you have come now across the ocean into two world wars conceived by European politicians and so have installed in your republic just the militarist mind-state that has kept our cities burning since the days of Hadrian.

—E. L. Doctorow, *City of God*[1]

The American Love Lyric after Auschwitz and Hiroshima is about the persistence of the European construct, crystallized in the fourteenth-century *Rime sparse* by Francesco Petrarcha, in the postwar work of Wallace Stevens, Robert Lowell, and Adrienne Rich. The connections between that six-hundred-year-old poetic and "the militarist mind-state" denounced in the epigraph by Doctorow's fictional Wittgenstein form the critical nexus of the book. The seeds for this study were planted more than forty years ago when, as an undergraduate in the early sixties, I encountered Wallace Stevens guiltily, holding the *Collected Poems* on my lap and bribing myself with a poem for every ten pages of the political science text I thought I needed to master in order to be able to play some part in keeping the world from doing itself in.

While taking a few government courses at Smith College, I came to dis-

xii   *Preface*

cover that the language of politics and poetics operated on similar wave-
lengths. During the 1960 Presidential campaign, John Kennedy responded
to questions about his Catholicism by maintaining that his personal beliefs
were irrelevant because America was engaged in a struggle between the
"people of God" and the "people without God." There were the binary
divisions of Petrarchism boldly stated as political position: "them against
us" instead of "you against me." To defend "us" against the godless hordes
behind the iron and bamboo curtains, both political parties were advocat-
ing the mutual deterrence policy so firmly articulated by John Foster
Dulles under the Eisenhower administration. Build weapons massive
enough so that neither side would dare to use them: Petrarch's freezing fire
represented as defensive-offensiveness. Fight fire by not firing. There were
the Petrarchan *impossibilia* and oxymoron, overtly legitimized as military
strategy. In the face of policies that could only lead to what Stevens called
"total death" ("Burghers of Petty Death," *Collected Poems*, p. 362), I partici-
pated in the first protests against nuclear atmospheric testing in Washington
during the late fall of 1961 and the winter of 1962. The decision to abandon political science in favor of social activism freed me to study and teach
literature. The poetry books no longer had to be read on the sly. Forty years
later, the United States still follows the oxymoronic deterrence policy that
almost failed in the Cuban missile crisis, arbitrary divisions still dominate
American foreign policy, and I am still reading Wallace Stevens.

With the fall of the iron curtain, the binaries and their inherent contradictions continue to challenge the presumed safety of nuclear policies that
are as dangerous as they ever were. In late November 2000, the moratorium
on nuclear testing, guarded by the "stewardship" program of simulated
computer verifications, was challenged by scientists in Los Alamos National
Laboratory who argued, in the words of Dr. Merri Wood, a senior weapons
designer, that "a stewardship program with no testing is a religious exercise
not science."[2] In 1960, Kennedy invoked God in the name of the "we-
they" mentality of the Cold War; in 2000, Wood suggests another split—
"faith and research"—as a way of preserving the genocidal *status quo ante*.
Among the solutions Los Alamos scientists offer for maintaining deterrence
in an era of test-bans is to remanufacture new bombs that replicate the
seventies-vintage old ones. None of the proponents of testing actually
addresses the problem of what we will do with an aging and deteriorating
weapons system. Will the obsolete bombs dismantle themselves or will the
decay simply seep into the earth and the atmosphere to complicate the
other doomsday scenario—global warming?

The deterrence policy of the Cold War brings a new twist to the new millennium. Alongside bigger and dumber bombs meant not to be deployed, we have smaller and smarter bombs to outfox the other side or deadly poisons to efface the less than human "others" who are denied the right to life in the central narrative. The reintroduction of germ warfare renders the weapons of elimination identical to the metaphoric categorization of the "other" as eradicable. "Use a germ to get rid of a germ" is the inverse of deterrence which is premised on holding back what was built to be used. Release a microbe to eliminate the vermin who happen to be human or stockpile an arsenal that would be inhuman to deploy. The June 2, 1999, *New York Times* front page, for example, carried two articles describing different poles of the same problem: the first reporting the Soviet Union's failure to bury an anthrax supply so large that it "could destroy the world's people many times over"[3]; the second concerning America's inability to "devise safe storage of millions of gallons of highly radioactive waste."[4] Tiny germs and huge weapons leave behind the same poisonous detritus.

Compounding an already oxymoronic situation is the fact that existing side by side with an offense system meant never to be deployed is a defense system—with an ABM ("star wars") strategy to protect us against "rogue nations"—which most experts agree will never work. As Frances Fitzgerald reports, "between 1983 and the fall of 1999 the U.S. had spent sixty billion dollars on anti-missile research, and though technical progress had been made in a number of areas, there was still no capable interceptor on the horizon."[5] In the arms race, as in Petrarchan impasse, losing means winning. Bad love produces more poems. Failed weapons propel defense proliferation. Referring to the George W. Bush administration's plan to forge ahead with some version of the ABM, Gail Collins writes, "weapon systems, like highway construction, are on the win-win side of government. If something fails, you put out yet another contract and all the people who were happy before get even happier."[6] Yet a *defense* system so imaginary that it is named after a movie may in fact be an *offense* system so real that it will in turn unhinge the fantasized protection essential to the defense-offense balance of deterrence. If the borders between actual and imaginary villains are heightened, the borders between giant military powers and smaller nationalistic demesnes are closing down. Everyone has access to the instruments of genocide. My fear of the killer germ is identical to my fear of the atom bomb—a constant that has remained with me since the sixties: "after the war / when peace rained down / on the winds from Hiroshima Nagasaki Utah Nevada" (*Dark Fields of the Republic*, p. 64). For me, as for Adrienne Rich, peace [of mind] never "rained down." And it hasn't stopped raining.

Fourteen percent of the American military budget, twenty-five billion dollars annually, is still spent on nuclear weapons.

As we entered the millennium, the suspect "rogue" replaced, for a while at least, the Cold War "red." But under the Bush administration, the "reds" themselves are staging a comeback in defense rhetoric. Within four months of the inauguration, Secretary of Defense Donald Rumsfeld cut off "virtually all of the Pentagon's contacts with Chinese armed forces."[7] The Rumsfeld plan to "weaponize space"[8] threatens the ABM treaty and hence may instigate another arms race with the Russians. What if one of those smart bombs devised against the "rogues" is too clever by half and one of the little germs stored by those (neo-villain) "reds" becomes the unintentional fallout? Elaine Showalter has written convincingly of the links between real symptoms and imaginary diseases, chronicled by what she calls the "New Hysterians."[9] I fear, however, that against this plague—a fatality for which there are no present symptoms—there aren't enough chroniclers and there isn't enough anxiety. I think of myself as an "old hysteric" one of those "women" Yeats wrote about in "Lapis Lazuli" who wanted something drastic done to stave off "King Billy['s] pitch[ing] bomb-balls in."[10]

When I began to study the Petrarchan conventions so prevalent in the early modern poets and in the late modern work of Stevens, Lowell, and Rich, I blithely skipped over *Rime sparse* 128 because I couldn't understand why "patria mia," which sounded to me like a call to military, rather than love's, arms, was in the *canzoniere* at all. As I pursued the story of Petrarchism in postwar American poetry, I soon came to understand that the paean to nationalism in 128 sprang out of the same rhetoric and the same mechanism as the love poems.

A close reading of the binary splits in *Rime sparse* 128 suggests that there is, indeed, a connection between private love and public policy. The Petrarch who idealized Laura is also the Petrarch who spoke of "Noble Latin blood" (*Petrarch's Lyric Poems*, p. 260) as opposed to the "barbarian blood" (p. 258) that courses through the veins of the "slow northerners" (p. 260) across the Alps. Is the fixation on Latin genetic superiority in Petrarch's invocation to nationalism so very different from Himmler's injunction to be "honest, loyal, and comradely to members of our blood . . . and to nobody else"?[11]

In *The American Love Lyric after Auschwitz and Hiroshima*, I catalogue both the conscious submersion of American poets in European form and their resistance to its totalizing effect, an opposition often phrased in terms of self-immolating guilt. With the 1989–90 "Through Corralitos under Rolls of Cloud," for example, Rich turns the early Stevens "rage for order" (*Col-*

lected Poems, p. 130) into a character named "Outrage" who rails against the poet and all those who "claim protection for their own / amid such unprotection" (*An Atlas of the Difficult World*, p. 49). Though Rich was to write about, and (more than occasionally) against, Lowell and Stevens, and though Lowell wrote about Stevens, what binds these three to each other is the way, in their later poems, they keep returning to Auschwitz and Hiroshima as calamities that challenge the whole rhetoric of love. Two questions motivate these discussions: What happens to the love poem when Petrarchism and its selective protectionism of "our own" selves and their kin are seen to produce the categories of "such unprotection"? Can poets cling to the ideal they themselves shape when the "real" it produces spawns such unthinkable results?

Interviewed on CBS's Sixty Minutes five days after the World Trade Center and Pentagon bombings of 11 September 2001, Warren Buffett assured Leslie Stahl that the American economy would rebound even if biological or nuclear weapons were to be involved in the future. In the days after the terrorist attack, Americans claimed to feel simultaneously devastated by the number of casualties and inspired by reports of heroism following an event that would change life in the United States forever. But I saw no evidence that any leader was acting to do anything about the stockpiles of weapons which could render the devastation of September 11 a minor tremor in the long history of the world. The "total death" Stevens faces in his late poems, the "unprotection" Rich writes about, and the shieldless children Lowell mourns are part of (in the fictionalized Wittgenstein's terms) "the militarist mind-state that has kept our cities burning since the days of Hadrian." Acknowledging that the rhetoric impelling Wittgenstein's image of burning cities is not so very different in its sanctification of "our own" from the rhetoric driving the poetic of love, Stevens, Lowell, and Rich begin the difficult labor of recasting the divisions that shaped their poetic. To read their work in the agonizing uncertainty of our contemporary moment is to understand that "it's not enough to fear for the people we know, our own kind, ourselves."

Acknowledgments

An early version of Chapter 5 was published by *Modern Language Quarterly* 57. 1 (1996): 77–105. Substantial portions of Chapter 6 were published as "Re-Versing the Past: Adrienne Rich's Postmodern Inquietude," *Tulsa Studies in Women's Literature* 16 (1997): 345–371, and of Chapter 7 as "At Long Last First: Samuel Beckett's Colorless Cliff and Adrienne Rich's *Dark Fields of the Republic,*" *Genre* 32 (1998): 337–369. I am grateful to the readers, editors and publishers of those periodicals for their help with the original articles and for permission to reprint here.

The Petrarchan poetic I follow into the twenty-first century is impelled by a love denying impulse; yet in the writing of this book I have been sustained by a love-supported security. That base comes from Mark W. Estrin who for so many years has given me, unfalteringly and beyond desert, a fitting ballast—of wit and pleasure—to remind me, always, why the world itself matters so much. Because of his patient endurance, critical eye, and listening ear, this book is for him, again, though I know he sometimes wishes I would call an occasional amen to the agains.

I also write with two teachers in mind: Frank Murphy at Smith who introduced me to Wallace Stevens and whose impeccable taste has always spurred me to try to produce something that he might like to read; Edwin Honig, at Brown, whose unfaltering ear and gift of music taught me how much difference a poem can make.

Along the way I have been cheered and checked by my friends at Stonehill College, particularly Chet Raymo and Robert J. Kruse, my colleagues in the English Department, and the dean's office, first under the stewardship of Louis Manzo and presently with Katie Conboy at the helm. For material support in terms of publishing and summer grants, but especially because she has used her office to corroborate the links between research and teaching, Dean Conboy encourages campus scholars in innovative ways. For administrative support, I thank Elaine Melisi—the mainstay of the dean's office—for her unflinching dispatch and understanding. I am grateful as well to all the students in my courses whose questions have forced me to articulate positions and to explain ideas before I even knew what they were.

I also am appreciative of the good efforts of colleagues in the profession, especially Jackson Bryer, Jonathan Crewe and Melissa Zeiger. If I had two readers in mind as ideal literary critics, they would be Jon Quitslund, a wonderful letter-writer and fellow enjoyer of poetry, and the late Bill Readings, whose study of Jean François Lyotard remains the standard by which all subsequent work is measured.

Along the way to print I have been helped by various hands at Palgrave, the two anonymous readers, Donna Cherry, Meg Weaver, Roee Raz, Chris Cecot, and especially Kristi Long who believed in the book and whose practical and imaginative sensibility forced it into a better shape. The Rockefeller Library in Providence and the British Library in London have provided welcoming spaces and infinite resources. The Stonehill librarians have been unceasingly helpful. I am particularly appreciative of the diligence of Regina Egan who never failed to find books I needed, often at short notice.

I thank the family and friends whose conversations and queries, debates and support have been a larger influence than they know: Robin Estrin and Seamus Kelly, Abe Estrin, Anne Putzel, Sandy Rubin, Carol Nash, Arlene Berrol, Marilyn and Dietrich Rueschemeyer, Eva and Art Landy, Doris and Len Fleischer in the United States; and Merfyn Williams, Peter Pullan, Edward Brooks, Lyndon van der Pump, Bobbie and Alex deJoia, and Leslie and Tom Freudenheim in London. Memories of Tess and Charles Hoffmann, Clara Estrin, and Ella and Fred Scheuer, as well as Anne and Ernst Lieben inspired much of what is in these pages.

Introduction ~

The mind begets in resemblance as the painter begets in representation; that is to say, as the painter makes his world within a world; or as the musician begets in music, in the obvious small pieces having to do with gardens in the rain or the fountains of Rome and in the obvious larger pieces having to do with the sea, Brazilian night, or those woods in the neighborhood of Vienna in which the hunter was accustomed to blow his horn and in which, also, yesterday, the birds sang preludes to the atom bomb.
—Wallace Stevens, "Three Academic Pieces"[1]

From Bird Song to Atom Bomb

In "Three Academic Pieces," written two years after Hiroshima, Wallace Stevens off-handedly lets slip an indictment of Western culture belied by the rapturous sweep of his temporal and geographical excursuses. Arguing that the poet's desire to "beget" a world sets into motion the contradictory forces that bring it down, Stevens climaxes "yesterday's" prelude in the Vienna woods with the full orchestration of nuclear violence. The destructive mechanism, appearing to counter the high culture of poetry, painting, and music, is the logical conclusion of the original impulse. Stevens's patriarchal "begetting" results in an Ovidian and Petrarchan obviation of the woman. The excision almost goes unnoticed as Stevens glides from hunter's horn to birds' preludes and then leaps from musical song to the explosion that links poetry to war. What does Stevens intend when he collapses time, regresses to an ancient "yesterday," and then forecloses all history with the atom bomb? How does the tiny bird song bring on the monstrousness of nuclear violence?

At roughly twenty-year intervals (Robert Lowell in the seventies,[2] and

Adrienne Rich in the nineties), the three poets central to this study arrive at the same retrospective assessment and ask the same questions Stevens raises in "Three Academic Pieces." Like Stevens in that 1947 essay, all return to mid-twentieth-century catastrophe and turn against the European poetic that nevertheless structures their work. With the hindsight of an experienced destiny, they revisit the provenance of their poetic compulsions. As Rich writes, "it's not the déjà vu that kills / it's the foreseeing."[3] What "kills" (what spoils the pleasure in the Petrarchan poetic that all three use) is that *it* kills. The underside is destructive from the very beginning. The woman-denying conventions of the Petrarchan forms of love render the other-denying impulses of twentieth-century genocide culturally inevitable.

The Petrarchan tradition derived (through Ovid) from such musical "foreseeings" in the European woods offers art instead of life; biological child *and* mother are replaced by the representation. When Stevens delineates the purely masculinist pleasures of horn blowing and bird song, he follows his early modern English predecessors as they translated Petrarch's fourteenth-century poetic. But, at the end of this passage, Stevens's twentieth-century prose does not beget—with Marvell's seventeenth-century "Garden"—"other Worlds" or "other Seas"[4] as compensation for the violations it thematizes. Instead it threatens a Marvellian "annihilat[ion]" of "all that's made." Stevens's connections in "Three Academic Pieces" between ancient song and the atom, Rome and Brazil, Vienna and the New World, follow hard on the defeat of the axis powers and the close of the war through the use of that bomb. But Stevens's essay does not point to the unmitigated triumph of the civilization he locates in Vienna. Instead it connects primitive myths to a death drive.

Stevens's condemnation seems all the more remarkable because he couches it in a paean to the instinctual pleasures of metaphorical resemblance. Suggesting that poetry is as much about mass destruction as it is about artistic generation, Stevens turns to two instances of male aggression that speak to the mythic beginnings, the "yesterday," of the European poetic tradition. If Vienna is the scene of high European culture, then we need to move backward (and across the Alps) to its earliest "preludes" in Italy and to the Greek myths consolidated in Ovid and retold by Petrarch in the *Rime sparse*. Immediately before the explosion in the last moments of the quoted section, two chases allude to famous Ovidian stories that figure prominently in Petrarch's work: the hunter allied to the myth of Actaeon and Diana, where feminine revenge threatens to unhinge Petrarch's language; the singing bird intertwined with the myth of Apollo and Daphne, where masculine form provides the medium for Petrarchan

consolation. The principal story behind the poetic is based on the god
Apollo and his unappeasable love for the nymph Daphne who resisted his
advances and ran away from him until, finally, with the aid of her river god
father, she was transformed into a laurel tree. Apollo was thereby stumped.
Lamenting his impossible situation, he made beautiful music out of his
nasty loss.

Casting himself as Apollo, the fourteenth-century Italian writer, Francesco
Petrarcha, pursued his version of Daphne, the evasive Laura, and wrote the
366 *Rime sparse*, one poem for every day of the year, and an extra one for
leap year. As Apollo's laurel eventuated into the Laura of Petrarch's song,
Petrarch's musical fame mirrored Apollo's divine renown. Robert Durling
summarizes Apollo's impasse: "when the lover catches up with the object
of his pursuit, she has turned into the laurel tree" (*Petrarch's Lyric Poems*, p.
27). Durling explains sublimation in terms of that transformation. "Instead
of Laura, the lover gets (or becomes, it amounts to the same thing) the laurel of poetic achievement and glory" (p. 27). Of the laurelization complex
so persistent in the Petrarchan imitations through and beyond the Renaissance, Gordon Braden writes:

> Petrarch's extraordinary elongation of [his] frustration is echoed in almost all
> of the *Canzoniere*'s Renaissance descendants, a run of masculine bad luck so
> insistent that it becomes almost a joke, a sign of Petrarchism's monotonous
> conventionality. But jokes have their reasons and one may meditate on why
> the European lyric celebration of the feminine object of desire should begin
> with several centuries fixated on the unavailability of that object.[5]

In *The American Love Lyric after Auschwitz and Hiroshima*, I follow Stevens's
remarks about poetic origins and Braden's quip about Petrarchism's descendants as I track "conventionality" well beyond the Renaissance and the borders of continental Europe into America and the postwar era. Why did
these three American poets (who seemed to know better) so often turn to
that poetic as a medium for expressing love or, more often, the lack of it?

Stevens's connection between poetry and the bomb in the 1947 essay is
rather different from the cultural critique of his contemporary, Denis de
Rougement, in *Love in the Western World*. De Rougement writes about "the
inescapable conflict in the west between passion and marriage."[6] In the
revised edition and after having lived in postwar America for seven years,
he chronicled the conflict forward in time to include Hollywood's perpetuation of the myth of romance. His central story, that of Tristan and Iseult,
is based not on the rejection of desire by the beloved but on the interdic-

tion of a mutually held "passion" by some other, third, power, figured in the Tristan myth by King Mark. De Rougement's lovers are faced with an external impediment. Denied instead by the beloved other, the Petrarchan lover never gets that far. For de Rougement, the important element is passion and it does not make much difference whether the object of this passion is willing or unwilling to acquiesce. Thus he can equate Petrarch (who never got Laura) with Tristan (who at least had Iseult for a time). Though de Rougement also demonstrates the liaisons between generative story and fatal consequences ("what gives rise to life gives rise also to death," p. 318), the myth and its perpetuation have nothing to do with him. He merely redacts the narrative. Stevens's ambivalence toward his poetic, however, is not that of cultural critic looking on from outside but that of practicing poet returning to the site where his subject emerges, an ambivalence that goes back to the originating myths and the mechanisms through which poets establish themselves.

Collapsing the body of the mother onto the body of the resultant child—*his* work of art—Stevens's poet in "Three Academic Pieces" incorporates female generativity and does without the woman entirely. His artistic process sounds remarkably like Klaus Theweleit's description of the arrival of the nuclear age: "the first hydrogen bomb was saluted as a newly born baby boy (and Edward Teller as the mother who carried the baby; not having needed to provide an egg, only a womb for that task). The bomb is male progeny. Males give birth to wonderful explosions."[7] The desubjugation in both Stevens and Theweleit stems from a habitual pattern of narrative exclusion. As Jean François Lyotard writes of the "genocidal mentality"[8] that triggered the Holocaust and Hiroshima, "The authority of the S.S. comes out of a 'we' from which the deportee is excepted once and for all."[9]

In *The American Love Lyric after Auschwitz and Hiroshima*, I carry into the postwar context the point feminist critics have been making for the last twenty years about objectification in lyric poetry when I argue that the woman in the poem is cast in the role of the Lyotardan deportee.[10] But I also contend that, in their postwar lyrics, Stevens, Lowell, and Rich problematize that objectification and complicate feminist readings as they increasingly view the Petrarchan tradition that they inherited from their European predecessors as contributive to the cultural conditioning that codifies the desirable—and therefore the undesirable—"other." Each of the poets comes to see that the private two-partied and fictional matters of the lyric (how much damage could its purely linguistic gender repressions incur?) spill over into the larger realm of a socially dangerous norm, one that has literal and deadly repercussions. Lynn Enterline asks "why Ovid's stories about lost voices or voices that fail to effect the change they seek draw to a close only when the body containing that voice is destroyed, dismembered, or raped."[11] Her important inquiry about the links between Ovidian myth and early modern transmutations prompts me to ask whether we can't trace the "dire endings" (p. 15) of those stories to the "dire endings" on the massive scale we have seen in our own century.

Do dismembered bodies in Ovid refer us forward to the piled up corpses that are so much a part of the late-twentieth-century imago? Are these foundational stories reflections of a fundamental human desire not only fictionally to exclude the gender other but to extend the culturally embedded connection between language and act to its logical conclusion in the excision of entire peoples? Those are the questions that Stevens, Lowell, and Rich raise despite their reliance on the myths that point to such devastating conclusions. The writers in this study recognize that the inspirational breach generating the poetic "I" becomes a linguistic norm that forces the self into the expropriating form through which it, in turn, imprisons the other it presumably idealizes. Yet, even as they confront the dark truth that love words proliferate in inverse proportion to the live bodies their poems sublimate, Stevens, Lowell, and Rich still are drawn to the Petrarchan mythos. Their aim is to turn the divisions of a mutilating origin into the variation that might repair the damage language causes.

My reading extends laterally from Stevens's critically overlooked suggestion in "Three Academic Pieces" that the appropriations of poetic begetting, acts that fictionally obviate the woman, predict the violence of atomic explosions, acts that literally obviate a people. Those annulments have their roots in the beginning of representation, as something which (in Lyotard's terms) "one can only remember as forgotten 'before' memory and forgetting, and by repeating it."[12] Not only did we forget *what* we forgot, we also forgot *that* we forgot. What Stevens can't forget is how he is implicated in the Vienna woods explosions. Linking twentieth-century consequences to ancient provocations, Stevens proceeds postmodernly, as Bill Readings and Bennet Schaber define the term: "a certain return *to* past ages as a return *of* past ages, history's coming home to roost in the troubled house of modernity."[13] When he identifies those early causes in his essay, Stevens brings history "home to roost" and holds the poetic liable for the trouble in our century.

In the ensuing chapters, I measure the extent to which Stevens, Lowell, and Rich bring the forgotten other to the surface and thereby infuse accountability into their postwar poems. Recognizing what Lyotard calls "the impossible newness of the more ancient,"[14] all three first acknowledge the obviation of the other in the mythologies behind the Petrarchan poetic fueling their work. They subsequently make amends for that expulsion by bringing the missing person into the forefront, often in ways that threaten to unhinge the forms that give voice to the poem. The bomb looms in the Stevens essay as the menacing product of poetic sublimation. It appears in Lowell's work as a figure for the demonic underside of romance and in Rich as a harrowing condemnation of the poet's desire to privilege the beloved. The process for all three poets involves (as Rich writes in a recent poem) "looking backward / into this future" ("A Long Conversation," *Midnight Salvage*, p. 55) to acknowledge what in the origin leads to the destiny of the poet's present act. Of the three poets featured in the study, Rich is the most insistently subversive and the most reliably resistant to the implications of poetic marginalization, drawing on what Donna Krolik Hollenberg calls "an animating relationship to guilt that is a preparation for social change."[15] But I will argue that, in their later work, Lowell and Stevens are equally aware of the disproportionate "gigantism"[16]—the self-enlarging strategies and other-crushing mechanisms—of the forms to which they turn. When social critics like Judith Butler and Jean François Lyotard speak to and for those who were "wildly expelled"[17] in the beginning, they parallel in theory the thematic revisionism that Stevens, Lowell, and Rich enact poetically. I will therefore apply the theories of Butler and Lyotard to the work of Stevens, Lowell, and Rich as I chronicle how each of the poets remembers and reinstates *here* in the twentieth century, what is forgotten *there* in the foundational stories. Each of the writers seems aware, as Julian Barnes writes, that "the point is this: not that the myth refers us back to some original event which has been fancifully transcribed through the collective memory; but that it refers us forward to something that will happen, that must happen. Myth will become reality, however skeptical we might be."[18]

Lyric Genealogies: Poetic and Political Myth-Making

Pointing out that the mythic systems that paved the way for the Nazi "final solution" are still operative, Sande Cohen maintains that the "real fright concerning modernity is that it . . . expands in the political and social-economic spheres while in the cultural and critical spheres it is trapped by premodern belief formations."[19] Those systems function as homologous signs of "dispossession," for the sense in which premodern myths give us terms for "the continuing processes of desubjectification in our own society."[20]

The connection between the desubjectification of Jews in Nazi rhetoric and the desubjectification of women in "narratives that afford them no place, which annulled [their] existence *a priori*" ("Between Image and Phrase," pp. 180–81) does not diminish the horror of what happened in the war. Rather, the comparison focuses on the process that made it both inevitable, and, as Cynthia Ozick insists, potentially repeatable.[21] My reading is influenced by one that Ernst van Alphen applies to the paintings of Anselm Kiefer: "Not only does he make the havoc of history into the subject matter of his art but he also dissects the mythic vision as a cause of this havoc."[22]

Such linkings trace—as Stevens does in the essay—a two-way circuit to illustrate how "literature issues from, and feeds back into, the realm of history and politics."[23] In the recent "Letter to a Young Poet," Rich calls that reciprocation "ineluctable":

> Would it gladden you to think
> poetry could purely
>
> take its place beneath lightning sheets
> or fogdrip   live its own life
>
> screamed at, howled down
> by a torn bowel of dripping names
>
> —composers visit Terezin, film-makers Sarajevo
> Cabrini-Green or Edenwald Houses
>
>   ineluctable
>
> if a woman as vivid as any artist
> can fling any day herself from the 14th floor
>
> would it relieve you to decide   *Poetry*
> *doesn't make this happen?* (*Midnight Salvage*, p. 26)

When she links the poet to a woman's potential suicide—"would it relieve you to decide *Poetry* / *doesn't make this happen?*"—she immerses the forms in the element that feeds them, reversing the famous William Carlos Williams line that became the title of her *Collected Prose*: "It is difficult / to get the news from poems / yet men die miserably every day / for lack / of what is found there."[24] For the poets of this study it is not *"for lack of"* but "*because of.*" The odd word order and intrusive placement of the "any day"—in the line "can fling *any day* herself from the 14th floor"—suggest that the woman's passive-aggressive impulse is the equivalent of the poet's verbal-aggressive usurpation in the diurnal reality of the poem. If the poet can presume ownership of a woman's life with his words, the woman can take back her life with her vengeful leap and thereby beat him at his own game. She can command her physical death as easily as the poet effects her psychological erasure and preempts her selfhood. How do poems become part of the drive to destroy "vivid" lives that reached such a terrible climax in the wars of our century? What expectations does the poem build? What does its "gigantism" crush to reach those expectations?

Insisting that the poem be seen as part of what makes *politics* happen, Rich uses literature as a vehicle for exploring what went wrong, for coming to terms with atrocity, and for naming the dark underside of the culture we venerate. In their indictment of the forms she uses, her excavations counter the views of critics (such as Lawrence Langer) who maintain that art cannot compare in its scope to the accounts of those who actually lived through the events. Langer argues that the order art imposes and the necessary limitations of its formational structure are inadequate to contain the excesses witness testimony records: "All efforts to enter the dismal universe of the Holocaust must start with an unbuffered collision with its starkest crimes."[25]

Beginning with a "concrete detail" as an example of the particularity of the horror, Langer cites the testimony of a survivor of the Kovno ghetto in Lithuania against the SS officer who brutally desecrates a child's life:

> The witness was present in the room when an SS man entered and demanded from a mother the one-year old infant she was holding in her arms. She refused to surrender it, so he seized the baby by its ankles and tore the body in two before the mother's eyes.
>
> Whenever I hear a story like this . . . I try to imagine the response of those in attendance—the mother, the witness, and the killer—but even more I ask myself what can we do with such information, how we can inscribe it in historical or artistic narratives that will try to reduce to some semblance of order or pattern the spontaneous defilement implicit in such deeds. Where shall we record it in the scroll of human discourse?
>
> . . . We require a scroll of *in*human discourse to contain them, and we need a definition of the *in*human community to coexist with its more sociable partner. (105–106)

By privileging first-person Holocaust narratives over their "more sociable partner," literature, Langer's retrospective view has a prescriptive drive as well. He isn't saying "stop art" but rather proposing something like "keep the 'pristine' away from the 'inhuman discourse' of Holocaust narrative." In isolating witness testimony from literature, Langer stresses the extent to which the Holocaust was out of the bounds of any tradition. For Langer, the Holocaust has no pattern; its "spontaneous defilement[s]" lie beyond "any semblance of order" (105).[26]

Contrarily, Stevens's essay on poetry and the bomb and Rich's poem on Terezin reflect an anxiety about the "traditional forms" whose order Langer separates from mid-century reality. They ask whether there isn't something in the pattern—in the very semblance of order that we ascribe to the tradition—that abets the defilements? And, further, is there not something in the need to define by difference or to differentiate by stratification that depends on erasing those who threaten to unhinge the pattern? In light of the fact that Theodor Adorno's dictum ("after Auschwitz it is barbaric to write a poem"[27]) has silenced no poet, I suggest that Stevens, Lowell, and Rich offer an alternative, and self-directed, restraining order: "After Auschwitz, it is barbaric to write the *same* poems." A year after his often quoted but rarely cited interdiction, Adorno modified it, writing that "Perennial suffering has as much right to expression as a tortured man has to scream; hence it may have been wrong to say that after Auschwitz you could no longer write poems."[28] Adorno further argues for the lyric's "detachment from naked existence" as "the measure of the world's falsity and meanness. . . . The poem proclaims the dream of a world in which things would be different."[29] Adorno's "virgin word . . . implies a protest against a social condition which every individual experiences as hostile, distant, cold and oppressive" ("Lyric Poetry and Society," p. 214). For Stevens, Lowell, and Rich the hostile ends of war are implicated in the violative beginnings of art. There is no "virgin word," no "pristine" ("Preempting the Holocaust," 105) form. Nor is there a "less cultural question" ("After Auschwitz," p. 262) that might separate us from both the perpetrators or the victims of the war. There is nothing apart from the cultural question. We are all the products of the very excesses art promulgates. When Stevens, Lowell, and Rich identify the forces in the tradition that contribute to the atrocities, they isolate the appropriative impulse as it emerges from within the "bounds" ("Preempting the Holocaust," 106), in fact at the very start, of the "cherished" (106) forms. Echoing beyond and through Stevens's singing bird and the hunter who pursues him are the consequent Ovidian Actaeon hounded to pieces by his own dogs and the boy Adonis who, gored to bits by the boar, closes Ovid's tale of Pygmalion's dream of beauty. The last act in Langer's reality—the SS guard and his battered

child—derives from such beginnings. Believing that the Holocaust is neither "beyond historical reimagining"[30] nor excluded from literary pre-
imagining, Stevens, Lowell, and Rich assume that the myths created a
mindset that made the unthinkable feasible. The myth of the torn-apart
boy Adonis and the story of the ripped-apart Jewish baby in Langer's witness testimony are part of the same set of impulses legitimated in the can-
onization that, in turn, construes the traditions as "pristine" ("Preempting
the Holocaust," 105).

Popping Cultural Amnesia

In Petrarchan discourse, those mechanisms (or "fault lines," as Alan Sinfield
argues about early modern thinking) "run through cross-sex relations."[31]
That is why a study of gender origins becomes so crucial to a study of
political consequences.[32] In "Three Academic Pieces," the gender switches
parallel geographical crossings that involve the American writer with what
went on in Europe and temporal shifts that link the early modern to the
late modern. In *The American Love Lyric after Auschwitz and Hiroshima*, I will
argue that, after the war, Stevens still reverts to the myths (Apollo-Daphne,
Actaeon-Diana; Echo-Narcissus) that structure the six-hundred-year-old
European formula for lyric love, consolidated by Petrarch in the *Rime
sparse*. But he does so with the knowledge that the erasures behind that
poetic can no longer be regarded as simply what poems have always done
in the name of love. There is, as Vincent Pecora writes, "an inevitable link
between a dominating culture and its imaginary construction of those it
comes to dominate."[33] Such dominance, Stevens maintains in "Three Academic Pieces," also assumes mythic proliferation, not only that the nest of
enclosures has a bomb at the center but that the enclosures spill over into
the world outside poetry. Language is tainted by its repercussions.

Among the repercussions of Petrarchism is Petrarchism itself and the
extent to which it has permeated the culture to become, as Nancy Vickers
chronicles, popularized as "an ongoing discourse of love."[34] The figures of
the sought-after other pursued by the unrequited self are not just reflected
in obscure objects of poetic desire. They infiltrate all the popular media of
our times as the legacy of the *Rime sparse,* just as the *Canzoniere* revert to
the stories of Ovid, themselves retellings of the Greek myths. In the 1998
preface for an anthology of 101 Petrarchan poems to which he gives a title
(*The Handbook of Heartbreak*) borrowed from Stevens, Robert Pinsky asks
why "works of art about bad things such as loss and deprivation make us
feel good?"[35] His question is actually very similar to Adorno's presumption

about the tortured man's scream (*Negative Dialectics*, p. 361). Both functions of "perennial suffering" (p. 361), Adorno's scream and Pinsky's "bad things" find the catharsis of expression in art. When Pinsky compares the lyric to "all the violence, family strife, and catastrophic sex in Sophocles or on TV or in the Bible" (*The Handbook of Heartbreak,* p. xiii), he speaks of all art as part of a universally held and long-time tradition: the aspirin that promotes psychic numbing simultaneously as it seems to touch some deep-rooted "feeling." Heralded as a collection edited by "America's thirty-ninth poet laureate" (with an unconscious echo of Petrarch's *Rime sparse* 1, *Petrarch's Lyric Poems*, p. 36), Pinsky's anthology promotes itself as "a universal prescription . . . a must for anyone who has ever loved—and lost" (*The Handbook of Heartbreak,* back cover blurb). Pop a poem and you'll "feel" better.

If poetic talk is "pop-talk"—the currency of page, stage, screen, and music—then, as Sande Cohen suggests, the myths behind all that talk still prevail. Turning to forms that are simultaneously ancient and ubiquitous, Stevens, Lowell, and Rich inevitably ask whether the idealization mechanism in Petrarchism could have anything at all to do with the demonization mechanism of what has emerged over the centuries as a similarly "ongoing discourse" of hate? How does subject formation in a myth keep out those who, in Lyotard's terms, are not even recognized as having a right to life in the narrative formula? Is there a connection between private love and public policy?

All three poets lament their inability to detach themselves from the destructive mechanism inherent to Petrarchan poetics. In her own form-compelled voice, Rich warns her audience that the pattern of her immersion is theirs as well: "it will become your will" ("Final Notations," *Atlas of a Difficult World,* p. 57). The all-encompassing "will" exerts a threefold pressure as: the drive that compels her, the legacy she inherits from her predecessors, and the poems she will bequeath to her followers. In "An Ordinary Evening in New Haven," Stevens observes that "we fling ourselves, constantly longing, on this form" (*Collected Poems*, p. 470), characterizing his preoccupations with desire and the desirable form as "intricate evasion[s]" (p. 486). Like Rich, he maintains that the metaphoric process traps the poet (in its intrications) even as it provides deniability for its own repressions (in the evasions). Among the problems Stevens, Lowell, and Rich confront as they expose the tactics of desubjectification connected to the poetic is that the forms are seductive in themselves and because of that subversive of the very subjectivity they are supposed to enable. Their work is called into being by what Lowell identifies as the "insatiable fiction of desire" (*The Dolphin*, p. 35). His ambiguous phrasing turns the poet into a victim of both sex and form. Is the writer consumed by the fictional framework—does the formula eat him up—or by the unappeasable appetite of desire itself—the lack his form in turn infuses with the fleshed out body of the other? Stevens, Lowell, and Rich seem unable to stop framing their poems in terms of a never-achieved or a too-soon-lost-love. But, in their postwar work, they regard the poet-devouring form as suspect and their own involvement with the form as a helpless perpetuation of what they most indict.

When Stevens, Lowell, and Rich return to Petrarchism, they delineate the double bind of postmodern representation by working out of two essentially contradictory claims: (1) form and its necessary restraints both "produce" and "erase"[36] the appropriated other; (2) it is necessary to return to form as a vehicle for lamenting the loss the form produces. Judith Butler explains the simultaneous compulsion to embrace and escape forms that characterizes the ambivalence also felt by poets in this study, arguing that the "notion of the subject carries with it a doubleness that is crucial to emphasize: the subject is one who is presumed to [have] the presupposition of agency . . . but the subject is also one who is subjected to a set of rules that preclude the subject."[37] As authorizing subjects who recognize the exclusions subjectivity presupposes, Stevens, Lowell, and Rich find themselves bound by a set of rules that actually predetermines *their* subjectivity. The poet is caught, as bell hooks maintains, by the link between language and domination, both by the fact that language "takes root in our memory against our will,"[38] and by the desire to disrupt that language. While hooks invokes the 1968 poem from Rich's 1971 *The Will to Change* to illustrate how the "oppressor's language"[39] is a necessary evil eventually to be superseded, Stevens, Lowell, and Rich come to view the received forms themselves as *seductive*. It is both the desire for Petrarchan language and the desire to resist it that defines the energizing ambivalence of their postwar love lyrics.

In *The American Love Lyric after Auschwitz and Hiroshima*, I describe five principal ways Stevens, Lowell, and Rich evolve (in Butler's terms) "a strategy of opposition" that works "from within the very terms by which power is elaborated" ("How Bodies Come to Matter," 279) in order to assert a new subjectivity, one that interrogates the hierarchies of those differentiating forms to "dislodge them from [their] prior and known contexts" (*Excitable Speech*, p. 162).

First, they side with the "other" poems usually forget. Expressing a secret, or sometimes even an overt liaison with those excluded by the predetermined binaries, Stevens, Lowell, and Rich create different "others" (so evasive, so willing, or so ferocious) who compel the poets into positions that counter the usual (Apollo-Daphne / Petrarch-Laura) pairs. Following examples that can be found in the *Rime sparse* themselves, and which I will describe more fully in the first chapter, they invent a series of Lauras— closer to Mercury, Eve, and Medusa, than to Daphne—who demand different mythologies and corresponding roles for the poet—closer to Battus, Adam, and Perseus, than to Apollo.

Second, they link the creation of Petrarchan romance to their own infantile desire to incorporate the cycle of female generativity and to assign to themselves the power to make a world. Each of the poets emerges as originator of the self who introjects maternal powers. In Melanie Klein's theories (which will be applied to poems in this study), this poetic self kills the mother and then (as the old joke contends) begs mercy on the court because he is an orphan. Near the end of her 1977 sonnet series "Twenty-one Love Poems," Rich emphasizes the love-deadening need for a solitude that compels her to a poetic based on a loss propelled by her own restlessness: "I am Adrienne alone / And growing colder."[40] In her most recent book, she similarly laments the self-generated isolation of her poetic adventures: "I wanted to go somewhere / the brain had not yet gone / I wanted not to be / there so alone" ("Letter to a Young Poet," *Midnight Salvage*, p. 29). Rich's pursuit of an uncharted territory is sabotaged by her use of an exploratory vehicle that ties her to the very tradition she seeks to escape. The oxymoron of her desire for originality and plea for companionship is as old as Petrarch's invocation in *Rime sparse* 1: "Where there is anyone who understands love through experience, I hope to find pity, not only pardon" (*Petrarch's Lyric Poems*, p. 36). Her quest carries her back across the ages to the larger community of poets that has sought and found solace in the shared experience of loss. The form seems always to have been there before; the end-run cannot escape the first run: Daphne is forever frozen in flight, the poet tied to what Enterline names "the subjective condition of 'exile'" (*The Rhetoric of the Body*, p. 15). The new place is necessarily predicated on the loneliness that the old form presumes as its contradictory claim to universality.

Third, they rebel against the lyric itself by bringing in elements of other genres entirely. The impulse that starts the poem necessitates appropriating the creative energy of the mother. The impulse that stops the poem involves challenging the rules of both poetic and biological fathers. Often, as I will argue in chapter 1, Stevens, Lowell, and Rich fuse the lyric impulse with a comic one, cutting off the generational continuity of comedy with revelations of a dysfunctional family and cutting short the eternalizing encomium of lyric with a form that self-destructs. Alluding to Prospero's dismay in Act 4 of *The Tempest,* that his pageants fade into "thin air" (*The Tempest,* 4.1.150),[41] Rich works out of "thinnest air," as she "factor[s] freeze into its liquid consciousness" ("Inscriptions," *Dark Fields of the Republic,* p. 72), melting down the very comic and lyric forms that structure her poetic.

Fourth, they revise the *aubade,* that sub-genre of Petrarchan poetics, where the poet invents a woman whose complaint voices the poet's own nostalgia for the situation of loss that generates the poem. In their reinventions of this form, dating from the troubador *aube,* Stevens, Lowell, and Rich lament the "break" so crucial to the poetic even as they build bridges of return that invest the form with a new—and reciprocal—communion.

Fifth, they undermine the rigid divisions of the form by going to the center of the poem. Against the overarching claims of a love that defines itself through an exclusionary practice, all three poets choose as the point of revision the most readily identifiable element of Petrarchism: the oxymoron. As a marker, the oxymoron works inside the line—between word and word—to unhinge boundaries established at the outer edge—between self and other. Pulling the oxymoron into places it had never been before and phrasing it with opposites that had never been yoked together before, Stevens, Lowell, and Rich suggest that the defining mechanism that brings the form into being can be loosened, thrown off balance, and imploded. When they alter the nature of the beloved and renegotiate the inside and outside (as well as the past and present) of the poem, they devise a different future for the myths that have wreaked such "havoc" (*Caught by History: Holocaust Effects in Contemporary Art, Literature and Theory,* p. 7) in our century.

Lyric Work: Love and Politics in Postwar America

There have been several recent books about the connection between postwar politics and contemporary poetry.[42] These studies center "on a poetry which operates in the intersection of private and public history."[43] But, too often, when they analyze the intersection, such studies minimize the midcentury events that I maintain are so crucial to the late work of Stevens, Lowell, and Rich. Writing of the title poem in *For the Union Dead,* Kevin Stein (for example) cites Lowell's ironic allusion to the Mosler safe that "survived the [Hiroshima] blast":

> In such a world nuclear holocaust—and all the horror that conflagration implies—is viewed as apt backdrop for commercial advertisement. This

amounts to the packaging of tragedy for profit, what had become a disquieting tradition of American capitalism. For a recent example, one need only cite the media and commercial flurry surrounding the O. J. Simpson trial to underscore the point. (*Private Poets, Worldly Acts*, p. 27)

Stein's analysis reduces the tragedy of nuclear holocaust to the furor over the O. J. Simpson trial when he relegates both equally to the commodification of "tragedy for profit."[44] But I think that for Stevens, Lowell, and Rich, the postwar reckoning with the atrocities in Europe and Asia and the postwar climate that seemed to extend the possibility of genocide indefinitely into the future cannot be compared to other "flurries." Of the sense of the incomparable and incommensurable connected to nuclearization, Martin Amis writes, "All times are different, but our time is *different*. A new fall, an infinite fall, underlies the usual—indeed the traditional presentiments of decline."[45] When the repercussions of the war seeped into the consciousness of Stevens, Lowell, and Rich, it caused them retrospectively to challenge the heritage that inspired them as poets and to assign to poetry a determinative role in the "infinite fall" they were simultaneously witnessing and anticipating.

The "generic commitment"[46] that binds Stevens, Lowell, and Rich to their European heritage does not mean that their work is impelled by a desire to preserve the past as a refuge from, in Andrew Lakritz's terms, a "world that appeared to have turned against the very idea of civilization."[47] Nor is their commitment to Petrarchan poetics one which allows them to view literature, as Eric Murphy Selinger does in his history of the American love poem, as a "mode of salvation."[48] For Stevens, Lowell, and Rich, the lyric was neither (in Adorno's terms) resistant to nor "detached" ("Lyric Poetry and Society," p. 215) from the thinking that led to the war.[49] It was cathected to the very notion of "civilization." Jacques Derrida reasons:

> Nazism was not born in a desert . . . and even if, far from any desert, it had grown like a mushroom in the silence of the European forest, it would have done so in the shadow of the big trees, in the shelter of their silence or their indifference but in the same soil. . . . In their bushy taxonomy, [these trees] would bear the names of religions, philosophies, political regimes, economic structures, religious or academic institutions. In short, what is just as confusedly called culture, or the world of spirit.[50]

Because they remain within the structures of "what is confusedly called [the] culture" they found in those European forms, Stevens, Lowell, and Rich are polemically different from the self-theorizing and currently fashionable "language poets" whose "antigeneric" writing claims to "reconfigure poetry's relation to that elusive entity called the public sphere."[51] Indicting canonical white poets, published by elegant establishment presses, who work within traditional forms, Bob Perleman, for example, insists that "poetry will remain ornamental to the degree that it avoids the issues of power, history, bureaucracy, and class that theory addresses."[52] My underlying assumption is that, in their postwar poems, the "generic commitment" of Stevens, Lowell, and Rich includes the thought that the forms are worse than ornamental; they may in fact be causal, part of the cultural machinery that went so terribly awry in the twentieth century. In that regard, I theorize the relationship between the arts and politics as reciprocal in the sense that Melita Schaum means when she refers to the fictive nature of both: an "engagement with the 'unreal' makes up a large part of all social, economic, religious, and political thinking." Such a reciprocity also demands, as Schaum puts it, a redefinition of "the relationship between politics and art [so that] a clearer denominator emerges between the forces of cultural troping and the resistance or compliance of individual trope—a battle fought on the field of the image."[53] It is precisely that battle which Stevens, Lowell, and Rich wage as they simultaneously broaden the political and the poetic to tie both to linguistic subject formation and as they anticipate the theoretical revisions Butler proposes when she "consider[s] the limits of representation and representability as open to significant rearticulations and transformations."[54] To regard lyric form as dangerous is to take the process of cultural troping—the extent to which poetic images and their surrounding fictions shape our lives—seriously. Stevens, Lowell, and Rich begin their revisions by admitting that privileging "those we love" may set into motion a process of excluding those we don't, and thereby set loose (in the terms Rich invents) "such unprotection."

They follow through when they acknowledge a black hole at the root of the poetic, what Jacques Lacan specifies as the "appearance of anamorphoses," which points to "a sensitive spot, a lesion, a locus of pain, a point of reversal of the whole of history, insofar as it is the history of art and insofar as we are implicated in it."[55] Exposing the erasures behind poetic self-discovery, they demand, with Rich: "what does it mean to say *I have survived* / Until you take the mirrors and turn them outward / And read your own face in their outraged light" *(An Atlas of the Difficult World*, p. 48)? When they move beyond analysis and confess their connections to the culture that contributed to the violations they name, they also subject the poetic to the "process of abuse" ("How Bodies Come to Matter," 285) Rich hurls at the poet. "Read[ing their] own faces" in that outraged light and pitting "the legacy of humanism against itself" (285), Stevens, Lowell, and Rich hold the lyric accountable for the unthinkable.

Reading from Myth to Millennium

The anxiety-provoking border unrest I detect in Stevens, Lowell, and Rich represents a small start toward opening things up, a letting go that bypasses the conventional boundaries. Recognizing that the forms of desire are what they desire, and what they depend on for their existence as poets, they also see that the poetics of desire is problematized in the postwar period both by the fact that the massification of the slaughter of whole peoples in wars and the repression of individuals by society in peace reduces the struggle for self assertion to something tiny and futile. Why make a fuss about the lyric, so private and narrow in its audience and scope, when the spurs to sexual and societal violence from public spheres—film or television or computer games—are so much more obvious? Why indict the lyric voice when it is so often silenced by louder and more accessible media? My answer is twofold: (1) lyric binaries are the core of what those louder voices echo and enhance, the assertiveness of the "I" or the "we" over the repressed other; (2) while Petrarchan division establishes the security of what Thomas Greene characterizes as "the self's own language,"[56] its necessary power of voice, it also "harbors," as Butler writes, something which defies the "conventional boundaries" (*Excitable Speech*, p. 161) upon which the self builds its sense of control. Simultaneously as the poetic represses the other to establish the solidified "I," it also presses against its own certainties. That is why the lyric so often works against its own stratifying categories and why its boundaries can sometimes be pried open.

In the theoretical first chapter, I will link Stevens's subversions of Petrarchan idealization to the surrealist work of Alberto Giacometti. Referring to the same sculptural antecedents, Stevens's "So-and-So Reclining on her Couch" is similar in its conception to Giacometti's "La Femme Couchée qui Rêve." Like Witold Gombrowicz in the 1937 novel, *Ferdydurke,* Stevens and Giacometti challenge the exclusionary terms of art by provoking a contest in the context of the cultural hierarchies they advance, asking the same questions Gombrowicz's narrator raises:

> Doesn't all form rely on the process of exclusion, isn't all construction a
> process of whittling down, can a word express anything but a part of real-

ity? The rest is silence. And finally, do we create form or does form create us? We think we are the ones who construct it, but that's an illusion because we are, in equal measure, constructed by the construction.[57]

In their vacillation between the possibilities of invention and the probability that we are bound to a story we never invented, in their fluctuation between absence and presence, solid and space, image and word, Giacometti and Stevens (like Gombrowicz) refer to a long history of art even as they seek to undo that history. For both, the history begins in the "word" that resolves itself in the totality of what Gombrowicz calls a Hamlet-like "silence" (p. 72). As Richard Hamilton writes of Marcel Duchamp, "language is an integral part of the process that generates the image."[58] In the first chapter, I read Giacometti's work as a sculpture about language and Stevens's poem as language about sculpture. But the unease each of the artists reveals about the divisive mechanisms of "image generation" stems from two similarly based premises: first, that the mid-twentieth-century social and political crises they were witnessing had their roots in the earliest moments of myth; and, second, that the poetics of sexual evasiveness they were parodying had a good deal to do with anxieties about what was missing from the earliest moments of family life. The "no" of the Petrarchan woman's inspirational denial echoes a "no," the prohibition of the mother's perceived unresponsiveness in infancy. Both the Stevens poem and the Giacometti sculpture link the denying mother to the inaccessible *inamorata* and both suggest that something in the cultural antecedents for their art, something in the form itself, speaks to a critical *anomie* at the center of the forms of desire.

Chapter 1 ⌒

THEORIZING THE LYRIC

Little events, ordinary things, smashed and reconstituted. Imbued with new meaning. Suddenly they became the bleached bones of a story. . . .

Equally, it could be argued that it actually began thousands of years ago. Long before the Marxists came. Before the British took Malabar, before the Dutch Ascendency, before Vasco da Gama arrived, before the Zamorin's conquest of Calicut. It could be argued that it began long before Christianity arrived in a boat and seeped into Kerala like tea from a teabag.

That it really began in the days when the Love Laws were made. The laws that lay down who should be loved, and how.

And how much.

—Arundhati Roy, *The God of Small Things*[1]

The Boa-Constrictor and the Love Laws

Like Alberto Giacometti's "la Femme Couchée qui Rêve," Wallace Stevens's "So-and-So Reclining on her Couch" anticipates the anxiety that prevails in the post–World War II poetry of Stevens, Robert Lowell, and Adrienne Rich. With Ovid's story of Pygmalion and Narcissus at their base, poem and sculpture offer an entry to the psychological, theoretical, and mythological themes that I take up in the ensuing chapters. Typifying the poet's incestuous desire to make the woman into a version of the poet's self and the poet's appropriative reflex to internalize the woman's generativity, both works question the divisive tendencies of the six-hundred-year-old Petrarchan poetic that exerted such a powerful influence on Western visual arts and poetry. Playing with the connections between mother and lover, comedy and lyric, the Stevens of "So-and-So" begins an inquiry into the "Love Laws" of that poetic, laws that, as

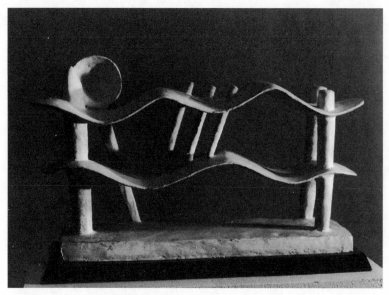

Alberto Giacometti, "La Femme Couchée qui Rêve," 1929. Alberto Giacometti Foundation, Kunsthaus Zürich. © 2001 Artists Rights Society (ARS), New York / Adgap, Paris.

So-and-So Reclining on her Couch

On her side, reclining on her elbow.
This mechanism, this apparition,
Suppose we call it Projection A.

She floats in air at the level of
The eye, completely anonymous,
Born, as she was, at twenty-one,

Without lineage or language, only
The curving of her hip, as motionless
    gesture,
Eyes dripping blue, so much to learn.

If just above her head there hung,
Suspended in air, the slightest crown
Of Gothic prong and practick bright,

The suspension, as in solid space,
The suspending hand withdrawn,
    would be
An invisible gesture. Let this be called

Projection B. To get at the thing
Without gestures is to get at it as
Idea. She floats in the contention, the
    flux

Between the thing as idea and
The idea as thing. She is half who
    made her.
This is the final projection, C.

The arrangement contains the desire of
The artist. But one confides in what has
    no
Concealed creator. One walks easily

The unpainted shore, accepts the world
As anything but sculpture. Good-bye,
Mrs. Pappadopoulos, and thanks.

Arundahti Roy writes, determine "who should be loved, and how. / And how much." After the war, Stevens, Lowell, and Rich explicitly connect those love laws to hate speech even as they acknowledge that, what Robert Pinsky calls "the sadness risked by every love or attachment,"[2] is trivialized against the immensity of mid-century devastation. But, in rendering the demarcating ethic as problematic, "So-and-So" and "Femme Couchée" identify a malaise Stevens, Lowell, and Rich intensify as, in their postwar work, they increasingly come to recognize the larger repercussions of lyric encomium.

In its critique of Petrarchan idealization, Stevens's "So-and-So" works retrospectively, alluding to a long history of violation, and, automatically, remaining within the confines of a culturally determined and already fixed design: A, B, C. In its virtual reality, the "suspension" hovers between "thing" and "idea." Drifting into abstraction, "So-and-So" gradually declines as she reclines, even in her status as object. Like Giacometti's statue, she's a surrealist joke. As artistic expression, she has no originality. At first, she's merely a "mechanism," a futuristic sex toy, or latter-day companion for the "squeaking doll" of Stevens's very early pursuit of "the origin and course / of love" in "Le Monocle de Mon Oncle" (*Collected Poems*, p. 18).[3] Alternatively, she's more stale than that, an "apparition," or ghost of something unfinished in the past, yet another in a long line of "So-and-So's." Finally, in Stevens's third try at defining her, "So-and-So" settles into being just "so-so," an "arrangement," a gentleman's agreement or object of exchange, as subject to whimsical re-arrangement as a bunch of flowers. When the speaker modifies his appellation, he also changes his own position, exorcising the haunting reminder of ancestral violation by reducing "So-and-So" to a provisional composite of scattered parts, a sculptural equivalent of Petrarch's scattered rhymes. The reduction bespeaks a lack of psychic engagement, divesting the speaker from any involvement with the woman. She's just "So-and-So," not anyone special.

In "So-and-So," Stevens brings several elements already in the tradition to the forefront, a habit he will exploit to much more serious purpose after the war. As Stevens suggests in the satiric title, the poem challenges those elements that were repressed in the original *Rime sparse*: (1) the exploitation of actual women in the formation of the poet's artistic self; (2) the tension between the passive, and "anonymous," invention the poet couches in her vulnerability and the antecedent, and familiar, woman who couches— in her generativity—as frightening maternal power; (3) the poet's artistic desire to emerge as powerful creator in the allusions to the myths of Pygmalion and Narcissus;[4] (4) the appeal of the oxymoron ("solid space . . .

motionless gesture . . . invisible gesture . . . thing as idea") as the vehicle for loosening the rigid categories of comedy and lyric, genres which the poem unhinges.

The shift in authorial position and the shiftiness in oxymoronic insta-bility indicate that what matters most is the speaker's capacity for shifting. Countering the solidity of the statue by disappearing into the space of his own unreliability, Stevens evokes the central oxymoron of the poem. The "solid space" of the sixth stanza describes the inverse relationship of art and artist and opens the poem to questions the postwar Stevens would ask of the poetic with an intensifying urgency. As the "space" exponentially impinges on the "solid," the solid gives way to abstraction. It's not just that the art kills the real women it mythologizes; it's that the authorizing poet wants nothing more than to kill the self he made in the process of invent-ing her. As much as he comes into being through art, he also wants to use that art as a vehicle for not being. And what better way simultaneously to express and to hide that desire than by representing it through an "other" whose denials, the tradition stipulates, reduce the poet to nothing? In "So-and-So," when the woman appears, the artist disappears. He is the prob-lematic "concealed creator" despite the fact that the woman's emergence facilitates the clear cut definition of a self solidified by the statue's sepa-rateness.

In a 1935 letter to Ronald Lane Lattimer, Stevens insists on his own elu-siveness: "Unfortunately, I don't have ideas that are permanently fixed. My conception of what I think a poet should be and do changes, and I hope, constantly grows."[5] Stevens's unwillingness to situate himself as a poet comes shortly after he declares himself a proponent of Mussolini's politics, a position he amplifies in a postscript: "The Italians have as much right to take Ethiopia from the coons as the coons had to take Ethiopia from the boa-constrictors" (*Letters,* p. 290). Despite Stevens's reluctance to be pinned down poetically, he has no hesitation about categorizing others politically. But his politics reflect, in ways that Stevens might not so readily admit, his poetics. The Mussolini defense parallels the hierarchical structure of the Petrarchan poem. In the construct out of which "So-and-So" is written, the poet takes over the lower order of the woman's body and places her in the higher order of the poem: just like that—woman for boa-constrictor, fascism for anarchy. Three weeks later, in another letter to Lattimer, Stevens reverses himself and sides with the under-snake. "While it is true that I have spoken sympathetically of Mussolini, all of my sympathies are the other way: with the coons and the boa-constrictors. However, ought I, as a matter of reason, to have sympathized with the Indians as against the

Colonists in this country" (*Letters,* p. 295)? Stevens turns his racist remark around but, though the reversal couches itself in an analogy that refuses to exempt Americans from the racist mindset they were so glibly castigating in their European counterparts, it nevertheless still is phrased in terms of a tightly stratified regime. Does Stevens mean his reversal? Is the shift just another "arrangement"? Are the "coons" merely a lower species the poet can walk all over and then (to make matters worse) hide himself behind the vulnerability of the walked-over other?[6] Or is this rhetorical shift just the logical extension of the poet's shiftiness and a sign of the poet's and poetry's indifference to the real women and men it treats as objects that it can merely tread underfoot? Does the poet's growth, in terms of the meta-morphic development Stevens describes in the letter, feed off a demarca-tion mechanism that enfranchises racism as it defines self and other in a rationale identical to the one that separates coons from boa-constrictors?

Finding the same pattern of racism as she rereads Stevens's *Collected Poems* in 1991, Adrienne Rich asks similar questions about Stevens even as she guiltily calls him "the 'master of [her] youth'"[7]: "How, given the sweep of his claims for the imagination, for poetry as that which gives sanction to life, his claims for modernity, could he accept the stunting of his own imagination by the repetitions of a mass imaginative failure, by nineteenth-century concepts of 'civilized' and 'savage,' by compulsive reiterations of the word 'nigger'" ("Rotted Names," p. 205)? Then Rich answers her own question: *"This is the key to the whole. Don't try to extirpate, censor or defend it.* Stevens' reliance on one-dimensional and abstract images of African-Americans is a water-mark in his poetry" (p. 205). In fact, Rich defines the water-mark of racism—"the desire to distinguish, discriminate, categorize" (p. 203)—in precisely the language we use to define the nature of Petrar-chan self-realization. The water-mark Rich identifies in Stevens is, she writes, "not only part of this poet, but of the collective poetry of which he was a part, the poetry in which I, as a young woman, had been trying to take my place" (p. 205). When she traces the water-mark, Rich argues both that it was there from the very beginning and that it seeps through to the smooth surface of the poem to reveal a decreative impulse that per-meates the poetic to which she, like Stevens, is so powerfully drawn. In implicating herself along with Stevens, Rich acknowledges that "taking one's place" means taking someone else's place, precisely the assumption behind Stevens's off-hand remark about Mussolini. In Stevens's hierarchy, the black-shirted fascists restrain "the coons," as the coons dominate the most terrible and crushing of serpents.

But the water-mark of racism is already there in the Petrarchan original. In *Rime sparse* 128, Petrarch erects rigid barriers between the Italian fatherland and the Teutonic alien territory. Using the same "we-they" divisions to castigate the callousness of the Germans across the Alps as he does to describe the cruelty of the denying Laura ("you-me") at home, he simply replaces the constructed gender of the love lyrics with a constructed genetic origin. Margaret Brose writes of the poem and its odd placement: "gendered binaries give rise to class and race hierarchies."[8] The eradicable foreigner over the border substitutes for the marginalized woman at home, as Petrarch multiplies the sometimes venomous Laura into the always hated Germans, contrasting "Bavarian treachery" (l.66) to "noble Latin Blood" (l.72), "Teutonic rage" (l. 34), to peaceful Italy ("the loveliest part of the world," l. 55), and the "green colored earth" (l.21) of the Italian fatherland to the scorched red earth of barbarian murder. The Bavarians and their genetically inferior characteristics are to the evocation of Italian nationalism what Laura and her resolutely adamant resistance are to the formation of Petrarchan identity: the necessary opposition. Like the obsession with the pure blondness of the beloved, the fixation on the polluted blood of the foreigner demarcates the ideal from evil in racially recognizable terms.

I will argue that, in their postwar poems, Stevens, Lowell, and Rich connect the hierarchical structure of Petrarchan poetics to the appropriative genesis not only of monstrous fictions but of a politics that—after the war—could no longer be thought of separately from, what Judith Butler calls, the "set of social effects"[9] that produced it and which it in turn perpetuates. Boa-constrictors, coons, and women are links in the repressive chain of signification, a chain that results in, as Butler might put it, physical or literal pain. In the same essay where she identifies Stevens as racist, Rich writes that "of the modern poets I read in my twenties, Stevens was the liberator" ("Rotted Names," p. 201). The liaisons between liberator and constrictor are centralized in the postwar work of Stevens, Lowell, and Rich as each gradually comes to understand that the very form enfranchising the *poet* and closing off the gender *other* spills over into the systems of racial othering its classifying strategies parallel.

If, in Julia Kristeva's terms, "every signifying practice is a field of transposition of various signifying systems (an intertextuality), [and the] 'place' of enunciation and its denoted 'object' are never single, complete and identical to themselves but always plural, shattered, capable of being tabulated,"[10] then the poet who is writing *now* measures, in his meters, the songs of poets who were writing *then* and the poet who is writing *here* in America has his roots *there* in European culture. David Kalstone argues, of poets (among them Lowell and Rich) who came of age after the war, that "writing poetry became firmly yoked to the English literature curriculum in ways that it had not been in the past."[11] Equally important, Kalstone writes, "was the way those same young poets reacted to (*to,* rather than *against*) their training" (*Five Temperaments,* p. 7). I will suggest that reading the postwar Stevens, as well as Lowell and Rich, changes the way we read the models by which they were "trained." Through their retrospective visioning, we come to understand how the seeds for such dangerous demarcations might have been sown. As Melissa Zeiger maintains when she compares contemporary poets to earlier ones in her study of elegy, "poems . . . [never] speak entirely for themselves; they speak in and through one another."[12] In their belated turns on the poetic, the postwar Stevens, Lowell, and Rich hold themselves accountable for the expropriations at the very beginning. Their reading back to the sources forces us to return (with them) to the original violations. Their "speaking through" renders all Petrarchan poems suspect. But, in identifying the connections between poetic creativity and appropriative behaviors, Stevens, Lowell, and Rich also seek out those elements already there that work against the seizures they name, water-marks that save the poetic from its own demarcating tendencies. Beyond their indictments is a hope that they can dissolve the rigid binaries by centralizing the element in the poetic that throws the divisions into confusion: the oxymoron.

Despite the fact that each of the poets acknowledges in terribly self-incriminating ways how much decreativity is a "key to the whole" ("Rotted Names," p. 205) of the poetic, each of the poets heightens the structural deformation that decenters that whole. As instances of the erosions that work from within the traditions they use, "So-and-So" and "Femme Couchée" enact a return to two primal scenes, that of the origin of art and of artist. What is clear in both works is that the "Love Laws" (*The God of Small Things,* p. 33) inspiring them are not so very different from the "Hate Laws" that impose their "arrangements" on the boa-constrictors. In the well-spring of the Stevens and Giacometti couches, the boa-constrictor isn't quite as subdued as Mussolini might have wished— and that's because both works call attention to the oxymoronic stain.

In each work, the venerated woman is couched to suggest two categories of earlier horizontal portraits: (1) that of (for example) Botticelli's Venus on her grassy knoll and Shakespeare's Cleopatra on Enobarbus's watery divan, where the powerful woman "floats" into view, promising an "arrangement" that, like Venus, she has already fulfilled quite openly or, like Cleopatra, she will later gratify in private; (2) that of a Modigliani "Nude," where the undressed woman—presumably in the safety of her closet—is caught, like the hapless Diana by the invasive Actaeon, in the conspiratorial "arrangement" between the originary artist in his atelier and the belated viewers in a museum. Both traditions feed on aroused libidinal expectations, rendering intimate moments fair game for, as Petrarch himself phrased it in the poetic named for him, "anyone who understands love through experience" (*Rime sparse* 1, p. 36). The Stevens of "So-and-So" and the Giacometti of "Femme Couchée" emphasize the aggression behind the exposure of intimacies that do not even belong to the artist, questioning traditions and anticipating the ambivalences that the postwar Stevens, Lowell, and Rich often make the subject of their poems. In the work of Stevens and Giacometti, the women "float" in "contention," couching desires that render the artist vulnerable as well. In both instances, it is impossible to avoid the history of art but, in both, it is also impossible to define the work of art apart from the matrix of a psychological position that resists the very representation it achieves.

The couch where the desired woman sits enthroned is also the scene of *acouchement*, the place where the desiring artist is born, a link between memory and desire that identifies the primal scene as oedipal in the sense that Yeats means: "where the crime's committed / The crime can be forgot."[13] The traditions Stevens and Giacometti joke about aren't monolithic; they're genre specific. The women they idealize take their place: as mother giving birth to the life she advances in comedy; as *inamorata,* resisting sexuality, and therefore denying life before it begins, in the lyric. With the simultaneous possibility of the lyric's obviation of male sexuality, in the "no" that impels artistic sublimation, and fulfillment of male sexuality, in the anticipated birth that completes the patriarchal demands of comic perpetuation, the woman in the couching position determines the generic characteristics of the poem. Pregnant with desire, the poet embodies his artistic aspirations in the idealized form of the representation. The woman is "born . . . at twenty-one, / Without lineage or language." Pregnant with him, the woman who precedes the artist—and therefore his representation—reduces the poet to spawn of her physical self. The poet is reborn as infant, with "lineage" but no "language." As Lowell writes, "we use identical instruments / for putting up a house and pulling down" (*The Dolphin,* p. 44). In both Stevens and Giacometti, the comic joke has a sting; the lyric paean falls apart. The house cannot be put up without thinking about the instruments that pull it down.

The violations in the Stevens poem and Giacometti sculpture play the social against the private, as the issues of lyric—with its emphasis on personal fulfillment—and the comic—with its stress on societal continuity—

reveal a violence behind the beautiful forms. The Stevens of "So-and-So" seems caught in a dependency on two genres: the lyric which "contains the desire of the artist"; and comedy which encourages the perpetuation of the race. In "So-and-So" and "Femme Couchée," the genres intersect to render each dangerous, subject to (what Jonathan Goldberg calls) "the law of genre,"[14] a law that (in their respective ironies) Stevens and Giacometti disobey.

Their rebellion returns them to their Ovidian roots in the stories of Pygmalion and his statue as a replacement for the real women he despises as well as to Narcissus and his desire to internalize the creativity of the Echo he rejects. In turn, those myths connect to the psychological theories behind this study—those of Jacques Lacan and Melanie Klein. With his anamorphic blur and her "good and bad breast," respectively, Lacan and Klein illustrate the psychological importance of the oxymoron, the poetic version of psychological indeterminacy.

In the three sections of Part I—(A) "Unsettling the Settee"; (B) "Theorizing the Mama and the Papa" and (C) "Solid Space" or Getting at the "Thing as Idea"—I will (respectively) turn to the surrealist motives of Stevens and Giacommetti, then to the psychological background for their subversions, and finally, to Stevens's actual juxtapositions of the oxymorons in the poem. In Part II, "The Petrarchan *Informe*," I will outline how Stevens, Lowell, and Rich inject different myths into their postwar work as they come to view Petrarchan form as *informe* in Georges Bataille's sense: "what form itself creates, as logic acting logically to act against itself, form producing a heterologic . . . as a possibility working at the heart of form to erode it from within."[15]

Part I

"Projection A": Unsettling the Settee

In "So-and-So" and "La Femme Couchée," Stevens and Giacometti merge parent with *inamorata*, comedy with the lyric, and mother tongue with poetic language. Since the couched woman may be the artist's beginning and end, poem and sculpture unsettle our sense of gender and genre. But the anxiety also moves the form further back, to uncover the emptiness both artists project onto the other they invent, a void made apparent in the "solid space" of the poem's central oxymoron and the sculpture's essential misalignments. In the last stanza of "So-and-So," Stevens deliberately walks away from that art and its "arrangement." Yet he leaves us wondering whom he is addressing when he steps out of the frame with the business-like "Good-bye, Mrs. Pappadopoulos, and thanks." Is Mrs. Pappadopoulos the subject of the sculpture? Or is Mrs. Pappadopoulos the muse of Stevens's insight, a ficelle[16] who offers an alternative to the art that finds its source in an (enabling) absence.

As receptive confidante, Stevens's Pappadopoulos seems to supersede the "no" of denial offered by the Laura of the traditional Petrarchan poem. She is, after all, a "Mrs." She has already said "yes." She may therefore belong, like Wyatt's Petrarchan lady in "Whoso list to hunt," to someone else, a Caesar who poses another challenge. Or, she may define herself totally outside the lyric, in the comedy that celebrates the making of a Mrs. and the success of courtship. Like all the projections in the poem, her name itself "contains" the concealed creator, the father of all forms, the papa as "rooster," answering the riddle of the chicken (poulet) and the egg (the pullet the magician pulls out of his hat when he lets loose—*Pappa-do-pou-los*—his bag of tricks). She may merely be the Mama in the domain of the authorizing Papa.

If the Mrs. includes the Mr., both as the authority for art, imposing the "law of genre," and as father to the artist, compelling the continuation of his lineage in the regime of domesticity, then the artist is haunted by both familial and artistic "apparitions." Neither the "mechanism" nor the "arrangements" are his. His work is merely the ghost of something formerly there, an insubstantial specter offering nothing of an original selfhood. The artist returns, and seems beholden, to the woman as mother even as she comes second to the father who came before her. The tripartite structure of the poem moves from son, to mother, to father in the family plot of the comedy and from artist, to *inamorata,* to poetic form in the representational story of the lyric. When they align the woman as *inamorata* of the lyric with the woman as matriarch of the comedy, Stevens and Giacometti throw both genres off, pointing to the ruthlessness of both. They loosen the forms by taking their structure less seriously and by taking their aggression more seriously.

Giving Mrs. Pappadopoulos a decidedly Greek name, Stevens may be thinking of the isle of Paphos where Pygmalion, another artist who "conceals his art," fathers a dynasty that eventually undoes the beauty he sought to attain. With that allusion, Stevens both refers to the poetic mother tongue and negotiates a return to the myths that form the basis of his poetic. In poem and sculpture, the woman is couched in representations of the father. The unnamed "So-and-So," like the unnamed statue in Ovid's original story, returns to its origin in Pygmalion. Casting the mother as mirror of such a father—as poem and sculpture both do—Stevens hints at a source that renders the artist subject to the same father of all forms, one whom Stevens calls "the concealed creator." The loosening of genders behind both poem and sculpture suspends the artist as well as the art. The couch is a nest of vipers, containing not just unresponsive parents who seem—like the Petrarchan woman—indifferent to the child but controlling forms that compel—like the Petrarchan poetic—the artist to a language that has already fixed the terms of his containment. Biologically, the father is concealed because the mother was the apparent giver of life *then*. Poetically, the originator is concealed because the poem on the surface seems the invention of the poet writing *now*. But, in fact, the poet is caught, as Frank Lentricchia demonstrates, between "patriarchy" and its genres and "patrimony" and its demands.[17] No sooner does the artist enlarge his capacity as signifier, then he is reduced to the form that also signifies him in terms of forms that came before. If the woman on the couch is exposed in her vulnerability, the artist who put her there is either strangled by the suspension, the ties that bind him to his artistic forebears, or by his dependence on his nutritive source, the ties that bind him to the family.

By nesting a form that resists the family inside a form that perpetuates the family, however, Stevens and Giacometti threaten to unhinge both. In depicting the woman as doubly symbolic, in her function as resistor and in her possession of a creative strength, both artists secretly share in her escape from family (catapulted by Daphne's resistance) and from form. (Can we locate her in this "solid space" or does she evaporate as person at the very moment we think we've stabilized her as immobile object?)

The sinister element that lurks behind Giacometti's "Femme Couchée" can be seen in two of his other works of the period. The "solid" brutalization implicit in the 1930 "Suspended Ball" and the spacey cruelty of the 1934 "Hands Holding Invisible Object" come out of the same matrix. In both the Stevens poem and the Giacometti sculptures, the connection between creation and decreation is at issue. In Stevens and Giacometti, absence suggests a suppressed violence, partly because in both works the glories of spaciness come after the goriness of breakdown, of art and families. The couching woman is slightly later than the "Spoon Woman," a work where, possibly under the influence of the later renounced André Breton, Giacometti idealizes the mother as both nurturing source and desired end. It anticipates by a few years the more famous "Invisible Object," where the woman turns away from the fullness of her maternal capacity and emerges too thin—knees locked at the source of access, hands emptied of the gift of excess. "Femme Couchée" mediates between the plenitude of the woman as absolute giver—all womb as the spoon—and the emptiness of the woman who offers not only nothing but nothingness—all unavailing in the empty hands. In "Invisible Object," the mysterious presence of the woman is closely allied with a menacing secrecy. The woman holds, or withholds, something that the man will never see. Giacometti's "Invisible Object" turns the woman into the purveyor of powers that remain hidden from the beholder, powers that she keeps to herself as a weapon to be wielded at some point in the future.

In the alternative French originals for "Invisible Object," "Mains tenant le Vide / Maintenant le Vide" ("Hands Holding the Void / Now the Void"),[18] the sculpture heightens the menace by playing with the temporal connection between mother and lover, past and future, and the spatial connection between self and other, object and viewer. The connection signals disconnection. What the woman offers—in her solidity—is her unavailability, represented by the empty space between her hands and the closed space between her legs. There are no expectations from this point forward—"maintenant le vide," the nothingness from now on—because "mains tenant le vide"—nothing was proffered way back then. The "now" of *maintenant*, like the "then" of *"mains tenant*," reflects the essential condition of loss. The denying mistress is the castrating mother, cutting off at the source, holding on to what (the artist fears) she never wanted to give. Extending her hands in a gesture that says, "look and see what I hold out to you," the woman takes away what she offers, rendering her gesture (like that of Stevens's woman) an "*e*-motionless gesture."

In Giacometti's work, that intensification is apparent as he repeats—in the 1927 head of his father as inscrutable and implacable and, in "Invisible Object," as vision of inadequate mothering—the eyes he sketched in a 1927 "head." Both maternal and paternal figures are withdrawn into themselves, one eye shut off and therefore practically unavailable to the child, one eye open and therefore potentially punitive to the child. Like the eyes in the sculpture of his father's head, the eyes of "Invisible Object" put into familial terms the missed connections of "Suspended Ball." As Rosalind Krauss writes about "Suspended Ball": "The wedge acted upon by the ball is, in one reading its feminine partner, in another, distended and sharp, it is the phallic instrument against the ball's vulnerable roundness."[19] The spatial oscillation between genders of "Suspended Ball" becomes the familial dysfunction between generations in the Giacometti family portraits. In return for what he suspects is the unreliable origin of both parents, the artist projects them as too inwardly focused (wedge) in their vision to yield to the child, too outwardly targeted (ball) in their aggression to soften to

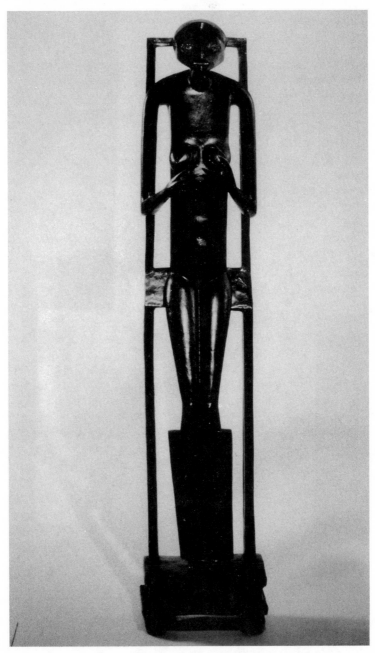

Alberto Giacometti, "L'Objet Invisible," 1934-35. Fondation Maeght–Saint-Paul. © 2001 Artists Rights Society (ARS), New York / Adgap, Paris. Photo Claude Germain.

Alberto Giacometti, "Tête," 1927. Alberto Giacometti Foundation, Kunsthaus Zürich. © 2001 Artists Rights Society (ARS), New York / Adgap, Paris.

Alberto Giacometti, "Portrait du Père de l'artiste" (plat et gravé) 1927. Alberto Giacometti Foundation, Kunsthaus Zürich. © 2001 Artists Rights Society (ARS), New York / Adgap, Paris.

the child. In all the cited instances, a sense of false hope—expressed sexually, in the teased expectation of "Suspended Ball," alimentarily in the thwarted appetite of "Invisible Object," and emotionally, in the cold affect of "la tête de mon pere"—heightens the impossibility of achieving with any other at any time the desired union. Like "Suspended Ball," the eyes retract what they offer, alternating between a wedge that disallows entry and a ball that functions as punitive weapon. The lower body gender divide of "Suspended Ball" becomes an upper body visual divide in "Invisible Object," therefore doubling the connection between gazer and gazed upon that the very idea of sculpture enacts. The eyes threaten when the roundness of the ball appears as a stone ready to jettison itself out at the beholder and as a slit that refuses to open itself to the demand of the viewer to be seen as feeling person. It's not that the eye can't see (because it is an object); it's that the eye won't see because the viewer is not capable of penetrating. We lack the very subjectivity Petrarchan art denies the woman and in that sense are turned to stone. The mother is Medusa.

If "Suspended Ball" represents aggressive objects, the eyes in Giacometti's maternal and paternal renderings suggest hostile subjects. Seer and seen are menacing. As mother, the woman of "Invisible Object" fails to sustain or even hold the child, "a Madonna of absence,"[20] in Yves Bonnefoy's terms. As lover, offering nothing, the woman evades the eye contact that might lead to the heart contact, a chain reaction also cut short in the Petrarchan tradition. In both senses, the self who projects the woman is erased. The artist emerges, as Stevens writes, "child / of a mother with vague severed arms" (*Collected Poems,* p. 438). If the Ovidian stories keep undoing the order Pygmalion established, the Giacometti story never even gets started. The denying woman in "Invisible Object" represents a dead end in the origin as well as the destiny of the family, the artist retaliating against the filially unresponsive mother with the Petrarchanly inaccessible woman. He thereby guarantees that the generations will be stopped. When Stevens returns the "motionless gesture" of the woman with the artist's "invisible gesture," he pulls back, revealing his desire to conceal his creative center in revenge for the woman's evasiveness, a withholding imputed from the inwardness of the woman's generative organs and from Ovid's story, where those organs are appropriated by Pygmalion. The "mechanism," as apogee of futuristic art, reverts to the "apparition," as ghost of the natural first cause. The arrangement of "So-and-So" couches both the compulsion for order that determines "who should be loved and how and how much" (*The God of Small Things,* p. 33) and the disordering impulse of the boa-constrictor, the origin that points to an essential desire to blur the boundaries.

Alberto Giacometti, "Boule Suspendue," 1930-31. Alberto Giacometti Stiftung.
Depositum in der Öffentliche Kunstsammlung Basel. © 2001 Artists Rights Society (ARS),
New York / Adgap, Paris.

"Projection B": Psychologizing the Mama and the Papa

Jacques Lacan describes the anamorphic blur as a return to primitivism, "something that is organized around emptiness,"[21] a visual equivalent to the perceived "solid space" of Petrarchan deferral. He discusses the baroque "play of forms" before he turns to the earlier courtly love, delaying his analysis of the twelfth-century poetic with a discussion of a device that came into being five hundred years later:

> The Baroque return to the play of forms, to all manner of devices, including anamorphosis, is an effort to restore the true meaning of artistic inquiry; artists use the discovery of the property of lines to make something emerge that is precisely there where one has lost one's bearings or, strictly speaking, nowhere. . . . At issue, in an analogical or anamorphic form, is the effort to point once again to the fact that what we seek in the illusion is something in which the illusion as such in some way transcends itself, destroys itself, by demonstrating that it is only there as signifier.
>
> And it is this which lends primacy to the domain of language above all, since with language we only have to do with the signifier in all cases. That is why raising the problems of the relationship of art to sublimation, I will begin with courtly love. ("Marginal Comments," p. 136)

Anamorphism, as Lacan sees it, is a form that points to itself as form. The empty signifier emphasizes a decreative drive, a desire to spoil even the illusion of biological evolution with the representational smudge of an unnatural and macrocephalic birth: the unpainted shore. In the sense that Lacan means, the projections in the Stevens poem and the cross sections of the Giacometti sculpture reveal an emptiness at the center. If sublimation fills in the gap through form, Stevens's projections are lines that expose the void by naming an essential coldness at the core of the self and an essential fear that at the core is the mother who rejects. This fear parallels Lacan's theory about the origins of courtly love and its connection to the belatedly anamorphic blur. Lacan skips ahead in his chronology to locate an origin that can only be identified in the blur that confounds the image. In "So-and-So," Stevens's "*un*painted shore" is doubly anamorphic. First the shore shifts with the sea so that its border is a blur; then the painting is wiped off, in a pentimento that renders the water-mark a puddle. What seems to be given is instantly taken away.

Lacan argues that the assertion of paternal power through sublimation in Freudian theory "emerges at a given historical date against the background of a visible, evident fear that she who engenders is the mother."[22]

The creativity of the father bends to the force of the mother's *procreativ-ity*. In the same way, that fear is covered over by the arrangement of "So-and-So" even as she doubles in her denials for the originally castrating mother. On the connection between *inamorata*, as creation of the artist, and Mother, as creator of the self, Lacan maintains that, in courtly love, the "object involved, the feminine object, is introduced oddly enough through the door of privation of inaccessibility" ("Courtly Love as Anamorphosis," p. 149). The nay-saying mother folds over into the denying Daphne in the Petrarchan situation, just as the sea fuses with the shore in the anamorphic vision of Stevens's poem. Lacan emphasizes how privation figures in the courtly love tradition: "Whatever the social position of him who functions in the role, the inaccessibility of the object is posited as a point of departure" ("Courtly Love as Anamorphosis," p. 149). Slavoj Žižek names that inaccessibility "the black hole . . . the mute mirror-surface"[23] of an abyssal void and argues that, for Lacan, its source is not the desired woman but the projecting self:

> Thus before we embrace the commonplaces about how the lady in courtly love has nothing to do with actual women, how she stands for man's narcis-sistic projection which involves the mortification of the flesh and blood woman, we have to answer this question: where does that empty surface come from, that cold, neutral screen which opens up the space for possible projections? That is to say, if men are to project onto the mirror their nar-cissistic ideal, the mute mirror-surface must already be there. This surface functions as a kind of "black hole" in reality, as a limit whose Beyond is inac-cessible. (*The Metastases of Enjoyment*, p. 91)

The anamorphic image signifies a lesion—an unfillable emptiness in the self—that is represented as the denying other.

And there lies the relationship to Melanie Klein who theorizes intro-spection as an explanation for the first stage in object relations. When Lacan speaks of narcissism, he uses it only in connection with idealization. But, in Kleinian theory, narcissism itself has a dark underside concerned with the other, Echo, whom Narcissus struggles to reach in recompense for his having pushed her away. The myth of Pygmalion, and the story of the creation of form to replace the hardness of the flinty woman, falls back onto the myth of Narcissus. In his desire to reach the beloved object, Nar-cissus mirrors Echo. But, in the projective identification of Kleinian the-ory, Echo already mirrors Narcissus. Inside him, her body is as inaccessible as his was to her earlier. She cannot be reached in a form to which Nar-cissus has access. The essential "arrangement" of metamorphosis is a *rearrange-*

ment that points to unavailability. Narcissus introjects Echo's initial feeling for him. Her vanishing at the beginning anticipates his disappearance at the end. Finally, only the ephemeral flower is there. At the very moment Narcissus wishes to be in a specific place, he loses his bearing and his being. In Lacanian terms, he is "nowhere" ("Marginal Comments," p. 136).

Paula Heimann explains Melanie Klein's observations about introspection in terms of narcissism by finding the links between self-love and object-love:

> According to this myth the Greeks did not believe in self-love as a primary condition and attributed to it the complex character of object-love. Whilst objectively [Narcissus] loves himself (his own image reflected in the water), subjectively he loves another person. As a consequence of his guilt for rejecting Echo, he must mourn for an unattainable (lost) object and succumb to a suicidal depression.
>
> . . . Narcissus looks into the outside world, the water, but the unconscious meaning suggested is the opposite: he looks inside himself. This element would then describe the unconscious phantasy of a (loved) object residing within the subject and this is the basis for the identification of the subject with the object which, in the manifest content of the myth, is represented by the mirror reflections of the subject mistakenly regarded as object. That Narcissus was the son of a water-nymph adds poignancy to his experience.[24]

Introspection eliminates the otherness of the other by pulling the other into the self. The only way to go on is to push the other out again, this time as the object of desire, the impulse that, in Petrarchism, places rejection at the core.

When Heimann demonstrates how Narcissus introjects Echo, she implies that Narcissus has also interiorized her love for him and distorted it, turning her into his rejecting self. Narcissus wants the water because he seeks the primal connection and its originative power. Absorbing Echo, he destroys the creative power he envies. To become the other, Narcissus must merge with the void—"mains tenant le vide"—that is the empty Echo already deprived of her generative resources. As son of a water-nymph, Narcissus internalizes the liquid fertility which was, at some never recoverable point in the past, his exclusive demesne. When Narcissus courts the other in the self, he engages what he fears, an emptiness reflected in the ever-diminishing image. The object is invisible because the subject is absent at the center. Echo is bodiless. To join her, Narcissus must lose the body that already contains her. Drowning returns him to his earlier element. In

Heimann's reading of Klein, narcissism involves the loss of Echo. Its essence is melancholia as Judith Butler defines it. "In Narcissistic love, the other contracts my abundance. In melancholia, I contract the other's absence." [25] Butler's "contraction" as bodily contagion or absorption is Klein's introjection as bodily reduction or evisceration, what Heimann identifies as a suicidal depression.

At base, then, Lacan and the Klein group meet in the space of the intro-jected object, as the first source of rejection. The inaccessible mother becomes the denying mistress. If the woman already resides in the self, then the self reflected in the poem's woman is the image of the poet's desire for self-expression. Narcissus anticipates Pygmalion. Janet Adelman writes of the "projective identification" Kleinians theorize, that "pieces of the self and its inner objects are . . . relocated with the consequence that pieces of the self are now felt to be 'out there' both controlling the object into which they have been projected and subject to dangers from it." [26] Echo's scattered voice is reflected in Narcissus's decentered body. The artist's overarchingly competitive desire is contained in the image of the unreachable woman as, in "So-and-So," the artist's desire to appropriate the function of the woman is restrained by the image of the woman whose creativity is impervious to his desire and whose "motionless gesture" spurs his retaliatory withdrawal.

As if he read Klein and Heimann, Stevens calls himself in "Esthétique du Mal": "the child of a mother fierce / In his body, fiercer in his mind, merciless / To accomplish the truth in his intelligence" (*Collected Poems,* p. 321). That mother in turn becomes "other mothers . . . she-wolves / And forest tigresses and women mixed / With the sea" (*Collected Poems,* p. 321). When the shore creature is fused with the sea, the self introjects the amni-otic fluid even as he projects the "hating woman" (*Collected Poems,* p. 454) and "bearded queen" who is the "mother [who] feed[s] on him" (p. 507). As in "Suspended Ball," the reversals produce forms that threaten the self who suspended them.

In "So-and-So," the margin moves to the center stage and the oxy-moron figures as the primal scene. The intrication at the start is what inspires Jacqueline Rose, like Žižek, to refer to a black hole and, in that ref-erence, to return to Melanie Klein:

Melanie Klein: negativity as the limit of theory or total knowledge; negativ-ity as caught up in the positive partner as much as antagonist and not some-thing to which the positive can only be opposed. The concept of negativity will not provide us with a clear account of origins (even if it affects the way that the idea of origins can be thought); nor can we place it at the distance from which it could be conceptually controlled; if it is mixed up with the positive, it ceases to be a pure entity; at the same time, the positive, implicated in its process, cannot be appealed to as the counter principle which will placate and subdue it or get it back under control (the relationships are more shifting than this).[27]

Lacan, Klein, Rose, Žižek, and Heimann get caught up in the point that turns the Stevens poem inside out: the fact that the mirror indicates a limit, precisely the place where it is impossible to tell the self from the other at the origin, the place where it is impossible to separate self from the world at the destiny. The opposites (positive-negative, self-other) fuse, "mix up," shift in the natural shiftiness of things. The standards of demarcation erode.

Stevens's term for that fusionary zone, "solid space," suggests both the threatening "mechanism" of "Suspended Ball" and the vaporous "apparition" of "Mains tenant le vide." Like "Femme Couchée qui Rêve," "So-and-So" floats in the "contention" between desire and memory. The contention exposes a history of violation that renders the love lyric, with its focus on a clearly demarcated self, and the comic form, with its emphasis on the protective enclave of family, the site of aggressive impulses masked in the passivity of the unyielding other and the negativity of the concealed creator. The relationships shift as the poet revels in his own shiftiness. In "So-and-So," Stevens identifies the oxymoronic zone that will play such a large part in his postwar redefinitions of Petrarchan form.

"Projection C": "Solid Spaces" or Getting at the "Thing as Idea"

"So-and-So Reclining on her Couch" starts to unravel with the four oxymorons central to its composition—"motionless gesture . . . solid space . . . invisible gesture . . . [and] thing as idea." The first three *impossibilia* revert to a black hole, the decreative and final "thing as idea," a metaphor that involves the subtraction of metaphor, an anti-gravitational absorption of the "solid" by the pull of amorphous "space." The "thing / without gestures" is emptied of the conflictedness real women inspire. After all, "So-and-So" is only the "idea" of her inventor. As "idea," the woman evaporates and returns to "no-thing." This see-saw motion parallels the spiral of the virtual and the visual intrinsic to Petrarchan linguistic play. In the retreat, we can no longer see what we thought we saw. Word and image disconnect. As solid entity, "So-and-So" allows us to share with the artist the universal Petrarchan sense of beauty. The standard is everyone's. The artist is us. But with the unlocalized space, we are reminded that the artist is *not* us.

When "So-and-So" disappears inside his head, the "concealed creator" retracts *from* us what he seems to have given *to* the woman: the beauty he reclaims as his own. As "idea," "So-and-So" has not yet been born. As "idea," she in fact never was. When the "thing" returns to "idea," the poet retains for himself the woman's creative capacity and his own inventive fecundity. Converting her to "his" idea, Stevens retrospectively denies her reality. She exists only as potential. The artist controls the present by withholding the future form. When nothing is hers yet, everything is still his. The artist is greater than us. All "solids" and all "things" are pulled back into his "space" and his "ideas."

The artist's elusiveness is part of the original plan. In keeping the "thing" for himself, he becomes to us what the woman allegedly is to him: unrealizable. "Get[ting] at the thing / without gestures" puts the other where (in the Kleinian sense) it originates, inside the self. While Giacometti's woman in "Mains tenant" gestures without offering anything, Stevens attempts totally to rob the woman of the power even to tantalize. While Pygmalion longs for an idea made flesh, Stevens returns all solids to "ideas." The curving of "So-and-So's" hip as "motionless gesture" outward is countered in the withdrawal of the suspending hand, the "invisible gesture," inward. In response to the woman whose body invites and repels— with her beckoning and putting off—the poet pulls back from the completed work—the suspension as disinclination: his "hide and seek" game. At both ends is the withdrawal that denies, as Stevens implies that he might never make what she might never give. "So-and-So's" lack of response (motionlessness) is met by the artist's denial of connection (invisibility). Her gesture, like the undulating folds in "Femme Couchée," is that of suggestion; she exudes a still untapped fecundity. His gesture, like the invasive phallus in the Giacometti sculpture, is one of penetration. He is there to force the question. But both gestures are stopped before they are started: hers by immobility, an inaccessibility engraved in her stoniness; his by deniability, a connection undone by secrecy. In not moving forward, she remains remote. In disappearing, he remains inscrutable. The gesture toward the other—hers in seduction, his in propagation—is undone by her rigidity and his retraction. The creator is concealed, denying his response, and the woman is congealed, locked in her potential: "so much [still] to learn." If "gesture" involves a disruption of space in terms of movement, then a "motionless gesture" turns open space into enclosed solid, locking in coldness. If a gesture denotes a progression in space—in terms of a cumulative filling in—then an "invisible gesture" implies a pulling back, a retraction into a mysterious self. The "solid space" refers outward to "So-and-So," in that she is predetermined as unresponsive, and inward to the suspending hand, in that it is genetically irresponsible. The suspension—lack of motion—results in a cutting—lack of connection. "Wedge and ball" come close to each other and immediately turn away. The "motionless gesture" refuses to give a sign as assent. In the same way, the "invisible gesture" refuses to be anything but a sign or an empty offering: "maintenant le vide; mains tenant le vide." The suspension, which is the sculpture, wavering between "yes" and "no," becomes the withdrawal, hovering between creation and demolition. The suspension itself suggests that art and its signature of denial parallels nature and its persistence in decreation. The deferral in postponement (suspension) yields to the finality of dismissal (suspension). The suspension invites the metaphor—*as in solid space*—partly because the visual illusion of the solid posits an originator denied by the empty space. When the poet retracts the supporting structure, the lady vanishes. "So-and-So" is, finally, a verbal construct. Giacometti's "Femme Couchée" similarly threatens collapse. The very *idea* of woman seems to depend on impaling male resources. As it frontally marginalizes the spoon, the penetrating phallus overshadows the female nurturing agent. Remove the support, and the waves symbolizing female fertility might just "float," like "So-and-So," in "air": "the suspending hand withdrawn." Pygmalion at the head leads to the boar at the end. Inside is the insatiable artist who eats up what he creates, "getting at" by taking back—"the thing as idea."

If sublimation covers emptiness, if at the center there is nothing, then a form which points to itself as form exposes the hole at the center—all space inside in response to the immovable other—all solid and therefore intractable outside. Finally, the whole construct disappears into an imagined sphere. Its very visual identity is subsumed by a verbal trick: "*as* in solid space." Reduced to a metaphor, it yields to an abyssal void. The solid is sucked back into the black hole of space. The female "motionless gesture" stops itself *before* it beckons, denying any maternal instinct to succor; the invisible gesture stops itself *after* it yields, disclaiming any paternal responsibility of support. The erasure of the generative body *out there* returns to the creativity of the artist *in here*: "To get at the thing / Without gestures is to get at it as / Idea." The "thing as idea" shifts the oxymoronic balance in favor of Kleinian introjection. We can never "get at" it because the artist has yet to "be-get" it. He becomes the inaccessible father and the unresponsive mother. The ambivalence of "solid space" is resolved by a denial of the world of things. "Annihilating all that's made," the "thing as idea" resembles Andrew Marvell's "green Thought in a green Shade."[28] But the oxymorons of "So-and-So" shade Marvellian greenness even darker, into the annihilative black hole of the artist's now empty centrality.

In "So-and-So," Stevens establishes both what the Petrarchan poet takes from the woman in his envy (the generativity Melanie Klein describes as her capacity to propagate) and what he really wants from the woman (the linguistic virtuosity Lacan claims her denials actually inspire). Absorbing the woman's creativity means sucking back Echo; the artist swells with her capacity to spawn. Playing up her deferrals means becoming Narcissus, gradually diminishing the self who absorbed the fecund other. Loss is what we take for granted, as a given. It is our linguistic foundation. In its most conventional form—in the figure of Apollo and Daphne—Petrarchism defines the poet in contrast to the other who denies him, the woman in her inaccessibility. The "enabling absence" which is the Lacanian "'positive condition' for the speaking subject"[29] is both dramatized—we watch "So-and-So" pull away—and psychologized—we watch the artist *inventing* the inspirational lack. "So-and-So" at once teases with her possibility for gesture and withdraws in her inability to provide support. As "So-and-So" reverts to the poet's idea, she becomes "no-thing." Through her absence, the poet retains the creative energy which, according to the poet's whim, will produce the poem.

In "So-and-So," Stevens reworks the oxymoron, exposing the generative envy in Narcissistic desire and the decreative impulses behind Pygmalion's story. By playing up the element of structural resistance at the center, Stevens reveals something that the form represses, an anticipatory menace he acknowledges as his own. That precociousness is part of the resistance mechanism to which Petrarch himself succumbed in the *Rime sparse* where he invented other Lauras based on other myths. In their postwar poems, Stevens, Lowell, and Rich increasingly turn to these alternative Lauras, siding with the "other" Petrarchan poems usually deny.

Part II

The Petrarchan "Informe": Laura's Four Selves in the Rime Sparse

These "other" Lauras defy the expectations generated by the nay-saying woman of the most typical Petarchan construct, where the poet is the pursuing Apollo and the woman the denying Daphne. And, if Apollo-Daphne is the central myth for the failure-success compact, that compact is bifurcated by the myth of Eve's Genesis 2 appearance (in *Rime sparse* 237, 181, 188, and 354), which inverts the romantic failure thought necessary to

Petrarchism, by the myth of Battus-Mercury (in *Rime sparse* 23, 105, 125, 126, 127, and 129), which decreates the poetic success figured as its essential by-product, and by the story of Perseus and Medusa (in *Rime sparse* 179, 197, and 366), which turns the poet into the monster he conquers. All of the myths thicken the texture of the Petrarchan poem to threaten the eternalizing consolation of its laurels. At various points in the *Rime sparse*, the four women—Laura-Daphne, Laura-Eve, Laura-Mercury, and Laura-Medusa—challenge what most critics see as Petrarch's exclusion of female subjectivity to: express the woman's sexual proclivities (in Daphne's denials and Eve's desire); voice the woman's creative capacity (in Mercury's inventiveness); or enact her impulse to avenge the poet who violated her (in Medusa's vindictiveness).

In four poems in the *Rime sparse*, Petrarch replaces Apollo and Daphne with Adam and Eve, and reverses the dynamics of the dyad. Instead of running away as Daphne does, the Eve of these poems faces Petrarch-Adam, meets his gaze and responds to his need for an other by being (in likeness) just that. The runaway Daphne refuses to acknowledge male desire. The stationery Eve validates it. When Petrarch imagines a Laura who returns his gaze, he cancels the frightened Daphne and the frustrated Apollo. For the brief moments of 181, 188, 237, and 354, he imagines the sexual imagination of the woman and the possibility that the construct based on denial might be replaced by a construct celebrating success. As the ensuing chapters will elaborate, Stevens refers to a responsive Laura-Eve in "The World as Meditation"; Lowell, in "The Downlook" of *Day by Day;* Rich in "For a Friend in Travail," of *An Atlas of the Difficult World.* With Laura-Eve, all three poets revise the *aubade*.

At the opposite extreme is the totally alienating Laura, the one who undermines the poetic sublimation most readers assume Petrarchism is about. This Laura invalidates poetry. If Laura-Eve preempts Adam's gaze, Laura-Mercury exceeds Petrarch's words. Her speaking is itself noteworthy. Apart from warning Petrarch in his sleep about her impending death, or defending him in a fantasy where she describes his helplessness against her beauty, Laura-alive rarely speaks in the *Rime sparse*. Occasionally she sings. Dead, she is more verbose, descending from heaven to give Petrarch a glimpse of the afterlife. Therefore the dramatic moment in *Rime sparse* 23 where she does comment on her laurelization is doubly significant. In the Battus episode, Laura speaks twice. First she forbids Petrarch's poetry; then she belittles his poetic defiance of her. Opening his breast and stealing his heart, she warns: "Make no word of this" (line 74). Like the Ovidian Mercury, she tests Petrarch-Battus, assuming "in another garment" (line 75), the role of audience for the confession she initially forbids. When she returns to her "accustomed form" (line 78) after Petrarch-Battus betrayed her to herself in disguise, she turns him into a rock and mocks his poetry: "I am not perhaps who you think I am" (line 84). Her rage is double layered: superficially over the betrayal, the mere fact of the confession; retrospectively over the portrayal, the content of the complaint.

Laura-Mercury competes in Petrarch's arena of expertise and appropriates for herself, with the heart-robbery and critical reaction, both the source of Petrarch's life and the meaning of his discourse. She takes on the poet's role, denies his power to circumscribe her, and asserts her elusiveness in terms of her exclusive control over the field that seemed, until then, the realm where only Petrarch functioned. She remains unknowable. When she defines herself as not being "who Petrarch thinks she is," her evasions annul the cognitive process that brought her into being in the first place. When she provides no rational clues to her being, she clouds herself in a mystery that annihilates all forms of knowing. Triply inscrutable, the Laura who is "not *who* Petrarch thinks [she] is" plays no assignable role. The Laura who is not *where* Petrarch "thinks [she] is" has no identifiable locus. The Laura who is not *what* Petrarch "thinks [she] is" has no tangible substance. As woman she is unreachable; as god she is abstract. Her threefold evasions deny the *who, what,* and *where* of poetic materiality. Laura-Mercury remains "airy nothing" while Petrarch-Battus is remanded to stony silence, his shape inscribed by her even as his voice is usurped by her. Stevens works toward a revisionist Laura-Mercury in "An Ordinary Evening in New Haven," Rich in "Final Notations" of *An Atlas of the Difficult World,* and Lowell in the London and New York series of *The Dolphin.* Like the Laura-Mercury of Petrarch's own text, these Lauras are simultaneously readers who critique the original and potential writers who hint at the possibility of a new or better text, one that incorporates an alternative ethos: the woman's.

The fourth woman Petrarch sets loose is Laura-Medusa, a Laura who avenges the distilling poet by turning him into her. In *Rime sparse* 366, for example, Petrarch equates himself with Medusa, admitting that, in the anamorphic image of his erratic pen, he becomes the monster who avenges him. "Medusa and my error have made me a stone dripping vain moisture" (*Petrarch's Lyric Poems,* p. 582). The instrument of Petrarch's triumph—the gift of his art—is the agent of his downfall—the revenge of the Medusa. To defeat Medusa, Perseus must mirror her. He kills the monster with her own image, and then (in subsequent battles) uses the image (again by wearing it) to kill other alleged monsters. Like Grendel "wearing God's anger,"

Perseus also becomes what he mirrors. Along with Laura-Mercury, Laura-Medusa reveals that the poetic mechanism has a stoniness at its core. When the postwar Stevens, Lowell, and Rich return to Petrarchism, it is the Medusa who most often rears her snaky head to bring out the expropriations that are at both ends of her story—in the initiating rape and in the revenge at the end. Medusa speaks in the first section of "Auroras of Autumn," in parts of Lowell's *The Dolphin,* and in Rich's "Through Corralitos under Rolls of Clouds" of *An Atlas of a Difficult World.* More than the other Lauras, Laura-Medusa alludes, in her vindictiveness, to a history of violation. For each of the poets, this last Laura expresses the political repercussions of such violations. Substituting (with greater frequency and intensity than Petrarch ever did) their versions of Laura-Mercury, Laura-Medusa, and Laura-Eve for the predictable Laura-Daphne, Stevens, Lowell, and Rich begin to elide the boundaries between self and other. That breakdown in turn tends to blur the social and racial binaries implicit in the poetic. And it is in the social realm that Stevens, Lowell, and Rich mean to subvert the Petrarchism to which they so often turn.

If the psychological underpinnings of their poetry establish a point where Jacques Lacan intersects with Melanie Klein, the political basis for their work might be assessed around Jean François Lyotard's questions about erasure and Judith Butler's recent conclusions that the very "ordering regimes" that determine who is erased are, paradoxically, the only means we have to "compel the terms of modernity to embrace those they have traditionally excluded" *(Excitable Speech,* p.161). In writing of the Nazi determination to efface European Jewry, Lyotard cites a postwar indifference to the "massification of slaughter" that occurred during the war:

> Nazism does not only say "thou shalt kill," but also "Let them disappear so that we may appear." But what is extinguished by our contemporary totalitarianism is the very inquietude of appearance and disappearance.[30]

Lyotard here describes how—after the war—the full picture of what happened faded from view just after he names the mechanism for what happened an erasure which worked toward the clarity of Nazi self-definition. In Lyotard's phrasing ("let them disappear so that we might appear"), genocide seems a logical extension of the way poetic language bypasses the woman's literal body in order to establish the virtual reality through which the poet comes linguistically to be.

But there is a further element connected to the knowledge that the instrument of self-empowerment is so often based on disempowering the other. When Stevens, Lowell, and Rich explore the terms of their Lyotardan "appearance," they suggest that the initiating cut—the fertile lack that generates the Lacanian sense of poetic being—is not clear cut. As Butler maintains when she moves beyond Lacan, "power not only *acts* on a subject but in a transitive sense, *enacts* the subject into being. . . . Where conditions of subordination make possible the assumption of power, the power assumed remains tied to those conditions but in an ambivalent way; in fact the power assumed may at once retain and resist that subordination" (*The Psychic Life of Power*, p. 13). If Petrarchan form is considered as a power—a pre-existent set of determining instruments—then the poetic both offers a means to assume the "I" who speaks in a poem and a vehicle to challenge the originative power it presumably absorbs. Ambivalence or ambiguity becomes the prevailing trope, a loosening that ultimately changes the bind. Instead of erasure, Stevens, Lowell, and Rich opt for obscurity of the oxymoron; instead of a self distinct from the other, they opt to become the other, through the alternative Lauras—Mercury, Eve, or Medusa—that so often appear in their poems. On both counts, the blur is all.

In the ensuing chapters, I will focus on those serial or short poems illustrative of the cycle central to the *Rime sparse* schematics: Stevens's "Auroras of Autumn," "An Ordinary Evening in New Haven," and "The World as Meditation"; Lowell's London and New York sequences in *The Dolphin* and diurnal peregrinations in *Day by Day;* Rich's "Through Corralitos Under Rolls of Cloud" of *An Atlas of the Difficult World* and "Inscriptions" of *Dark Fields of the Republic.* Like the *Rime sparse,* these poems are based on a pattern of temporal hope and deferral that (with its daily or even hourly vicissitudes) underscores the thematics of erasure. If Petrarch retold the story of Apollo and Daphne in the saga of his persistent pursuit of the denying Laura, so Stevens, Lowell, and Rich find within the framework of such a fiction a way to catalogue their compulsions and to write their resistance. Imagining the unimaginable as something that has already happened, they free poetic language to speak, as Edgar does in *King Lear,* "what we feel, not what we ought to say" (5.3.323).[31] Their reconfigurations are possible only after each of the poets has obeyed what Edgar calls the "weight of [these] sad time[s]" (5.3.320) and the terrifying consequences of "going on" with a craft so perversely allied to the marginalization of the other over the centuries that it could foster, in our own, a spirit utterly removed from the love ostensibly inspiring it.

Written in 1947, Stevens's "Auroras of Autumn" comes out of the "weight" of the sad realities revealed in the aftermath of World War II. In it, the victimized woman speaks the revenge of the violated Medusa, her voice sounding a "knock like a rifle-butt against the door" (*Collected Poems*, p. 414) of the secure house of the American Petrarchan poem. The poet of "Auroras of Autumn" opens the door of that house to see "an Arctic effulgence flaring on the frame / Of everything he is. And he feels afraid" (p. 417). My discussion of Stevens begins with his postwar fear that the Petrarchan frames shaping his sense of "everything he is" as a writer are structurally related to the conflagrations, "the gusts of great enkindlings" (p. 413), the war unleashed.

Chapter 2 ∽

"FORM GULPING AFTER FORMLESSNESS": PETRARCH'S RESISTANT LAURAS IN STEVENS'S "AURORAS OF AUTUMN"

Speculating that the horrors exposed in the aftermath of World War II "triggered" the 1947 "Auroras," Charles Berger reads it as a last gasp of civilization: "when the books are about to burn, the values they radiate are brightest."[1] But Berger projects a too optimistic Stevens. If Hiroshima and the Holocaust prompted the poem, Stevens seems to be saying that the cultural roots of books and bomb are the same. The values they radiate explode. The nihilism of the opening image—"this is where the serpent lives"—represents the long-seated cultural malaise Stevens reveals in "Three Academic Pieces." James Longenbach calls the apocalypse in this poem "an unveiling of what we already know."[2] I would go one step further than Longenbach to argue that the poem in fact chronicles how *what we know* (the whole of Western culture) led into *what we did*. For the Stevens of "Auroras," the war was a consequence of that culture, a serpentine evolution of its original violations.

The exposé in "Auroras" involves a section of "Three Academic Pieces" where Stevens links the serpentine *animus* for revenge to the narcissistic desire for resemblance. Explaining the metaphoric impulse, Stevens refers immediately to Narcissus and then (as he does in the birdsong–atom bomb link) turns the reference sour by alluding—unexpectedly—to Medusa:

> Narcissus did not expect, when he looked in the stream, to find in his hair a serpent coiled to strike, nor, when he looked in his own eyes there, to be met by a look of hate, nor, in general, to discover himself at the center of an inexplicable ugliness from which he would be bound to avert himself. On the contrary, he sought out his image everywhere because it was the principle of his nature to do so and, to go a step beyond that, because it was the principle of his nature, as it is of ours, to expect to find pleasure in what he found.[3]

While Stevens sets up Medusa only to replace her with what Narcissus "expected" and in fact achieved, a Kleinian reading of the passage would find a preliminary danger behind the pleasure principle. The readers need to bypass the Medusa before they even can get to Narcissus. And, once there, the mere mention of Narcissus brings in Echo and Narcissus's tragic end. Why does Stevens talk about a story that describes a punishment for what happens to those who like resemblance too much and why does Stevens put Medusa and her story (a myth that also propagates killing mirrors) *first*? When Narcissus searches the stream, he replaces Echo, the woman whom (in Kleinian introjection) he has already absorbed, with Medusa, the woman "coiled to strike." Ovid's Kleinian Echo shrinks backward as Narcissus reaches toward her image in the water; Stevens's Medusa is positioned to spring forward and let loose the full force of her menace. In the essay, the nostalgia of narcissism is replaced by an uncoiling that will produce the anticipated retaliation as an imminent strike, and a recoiling that opens to an initial usurpation. In his wishing, Ovid's Narcissus projects Echo's look of love out again. In his dread, Stevens's Narcissus is met by a "look of hate." "At the center" is the "inexplicable ugliness" of the repressive self. The voice of "Aurora's" opening moments comes from that Medusan center. In "So-and-So," Stevens's shifting oxymorons expose the faulty gender dynamics of the Petrarchan formula. In "Auroras," Stevens reverses genders, loosens the categories, and then reveals oxymorons that are even more puzzling than those of "So-and-So." He exposes the poem to both Laura-Medusa and Laura-Mercury.

In cantos I–V, Stevens imagines Laura-Medusa—the other who petrifies the self; in canto VI, he projects Laura-Mercury—the other who invalidates the poem. Those poet and poem defying women become the *medium* through which the poet speaks his doubt. In the first five cantos, Laura-Medusa and her annihilations prod him into the self-cancellations typical of one kind of Petrarchan oxymoron that—like the Malevich "white square"—sinks anamorphically into obscurity. In canto VI, Stevens gravitates toward the pulsating movement in a second type of oxymoron, one which turns inside out, as the words invert each other like a Marcel Duchamp rotorelief.[4] Stevens's poetic effects in the sixth canto operate on the "beat of desire" (*The Optical Unconscious*, p. 216), rotating in a pulsation—"wave on wave, / Through waves of light" (*Collected Poems*, p. 416)—an in and out movement that vocalizes the visual effect of the rotorelief and dramatizes the finding and losing attendant to the infinite deferral of Petrarchan poetics. Through the Medusa of the first five cantos, the "I" is wiped out. But through the Mercury of the sixth canto, he is forced to reverse himself and feel, as the woman does, afraid. The *technique* Stevens uses to convey his unsettling poetic in the after-shock of Hiroshima is painterly, as he switches from the anamorphic annihilations of Suprematist abstraction in the first five cantos to the dizzying motions of surrealist rotorelief in the sixth canto.

In the first five cantos of "Auroras," Stevens works through the woman's retaliations as she annihilates all expectations of comfort in self and family. Inserting the horror of "Three Academic Pieces" into his own picture, Stevens opens with Laura-Medusa and projects a series of doubles that calls the original into question. In the sixth canto, Stevens introduces the Laura of *Rime sparse* 23 who, by abstracting herself, takes back the energy the poet has confined to his form. Challenging the sign rather than the substance, the sixth canto illustrates, as Laura-Mercury does, an evasiveness that heightens the fear of—rather than a pleasure in—form. If the woman is monstrous, and if she mirrors the man who invented her, then the poet is implicated (through Laura-Medusa) in the monstrosity he represents and (through Laura-Mercury) in the monstrosity of representation itself.

Laura-Medusa and her doubling subtract the self we think we like. Laura-Mercury and her evasions deconstruct the forms we think express us. The "Auroras" women retaliate against the history of the male gaze, reverting the line of vision to their own matrix: "the eyes fix on us." Medusa's look turns men to stone, as they are "fixed" by her retaliatory fixation. Like Malevich's "white square," the first five cantos render old securities blank, suggesting differences and then erasing them. In canto VI, the "palm-eyed . . . wild wedges" (p. 416) link the writing hand (in the palm) to the vanishing vision (in the eye), as the peek-a-boo of the "hand" first blocks the "eye" and then opens to it, just as the rotorelief first holds back and then pushes its center forward. One image effaces the other in anamorphic revision. In the spirals of its abyss, "Auroras" exposes the missing link repressed in the Petrarchan poem. Opening to the voices of alternative Lauras, Stevens confesses that the poet is the origin of the crimes he perpetuates.

Medusan Doubling: "This Is Where the Serpent Lives"

Standing at the water's edge, the Narcissus of "Three Academic Pieces" sees the snaky monster instead of the head he covets. In "Auroras," Stevens speaks as the monster, substituting her voice for his. The mirrors in the poem reverberate with the original violations. The first canto consolidates several Ovidian myths. Echo comes back as Medusa. The indian in the glade fuses with the flecked animal he hunts. The Actaeon-deer let loose by the hunter of "Three Academic Pieces" slithers into Perseus's snake. Canto I sets up the anamorphic sense of decreation by projecting a series of enclosures that begins with a "nest," works its way through "fields" and "hills" and "tinted distances" (p. 411) and results in a sense of foreclosure: "form gulping after formlessness" (p. 411). The remarkable unravellings of "form gulping after formlessness" (p. 411) produce a spiral, a serpentine abyss that connects the productions of desire to the devolutions of abstraction. "Gulping after" signifies the boa-constrictor as hungry for supportive sustenance (still always denied) yet uncomfortable with its sublimating appropriations (still always regretting). Desire (gulping after, in the chase) is a consequence of a previous Kleinian introjection (gulping after, once the other is swallowed). But form carries with it a two-fold nostalgia for formlessness. As soon as the form takes its expected shape, the self can only be regarded in relationship to the denying other it invents. Solace is never attainable. Formlessness emerges desirable again as the "I" longs to regress to the state of infantile dependency, where the self is attached to, and shaped by, the originating parent. But such an other is never sustainable. Cantos II-V unravel the safety of parental harbor as well. In those cantos, the family is dismembered. In canto I, the poet is unmade by the other he trapped in his representation:

This is where the serpent lives. This is his nest,
These fields, these hills, these tinted distances,
And the pines above and along and beside the sea.

This is form gulping after formlessness,
Skin flashing to wished-for disappearances
And the serpent body flashing without the skin.

This is the height emerging and its base
These lights may finally attain a pole
In the midmost midnight and find the serpent there,

In another nest, the master of the maze
Of body and air and forms and images,
Relentlessly in possession of happiness.

This is his poison: that we should disbelieve
Even that. His meditations in the ferns,
When he moved so slightly to make sure of sun,

Made us no less as sure. We saw in his head,
Black beaded in the rock, the flecked animal,
The moving grass, the Indian in his glade. (pp. 411–412)

The erosions in the first canto result in the doubling of myths—Medusa
and Perseus / Actaeon and Diana—which in turn leads to the cycle of
revenge implicated in those myths: the body's dismemberment in the
Actaeon story; the body's petrification in the Medusa story. The first order
to disappear is that of gender. Is Perseus, wearing the shield, the invincible
male or the avenging female? The "this" of the opening line only points to
where the serpent is, not what it is. The hiss is hers, the bodilessness his.
But sound mixes things up further, rendering the body unlocatable, the
voice unrecognizable. The *this* is a *hiss*, as the snake's body becomes all
tongue, its insistent sound an expression of its force as signifier of male
identity in phallic representation, its persistent wriggling, a resistance to the
form that representation has traditionally given women. There is no form;
there is only the desire to disrupt form. The serpent undoes the past until,
at the end of the first canto, the male hunter of the Actaeon story turns
into the female deer he pursues. Snake and woman, deer and woman,
hunter and hunted: all merge. Once gender is de-stabilized, the old boundaries break down. As the voice distorts the gender identifications of male
and female, so it disrupts the geographical order of topographical demarcations. When mountain turns into sky and sea fuses with land, the speci-
fying functions of demonstrative pronouns (*there*, *this*, and *that*) are as
ambiguous as Medusa and Perseus. The "look of hate" ("Three Academic
Pieces," p. 79) in those eyes undoes everything.

The complicated deixis redefines "form's relationship to the eye"[5] by
resituating the eyes that discern and determine form. The *this* is what Mary
Arensberg calls a "pronoun in obvious search for its subject."[6] In its wriggling *out*, the snake represents bodilessness as a replacement for body, confusing the circle of the egg with the wriggling *in* of the sperm and
suggesting that beginnings and ends are merely other versions of the
anamorphism that turns Perseus into Medusa:

Or is this another wriggling out of the egg,
Another image at the end of the cave,
Another bodiless for the body's slough? (p. 411)

This smashes the determinism of sexual difference as it unwinds the circle
of the egg into a line with an "end," and unseats linguistic reality by dis-

torting the connection between the past and the future represented by consecutive spatial indicators (*that* and *there*). Breaking down signs, particularly in the way it causes the male serpent and its observers to founder, the femaled voice revels in its own distortions. If *this* is uncertain, its observers are "no less sure." *This* is not another wriggling or image of a self-perpetuating self. *This* is something reformed by what it formed: revenge as mimesis. In "Auroras," the lines evaporate into air as the poetic line-maker, or originator of language, surrenders his power.

Since the snake has its tail in its mouth, the reader uses "tips" from the end of canto I to decode the opening *this*. In the final verses, the compression is repeated yet again as the deer hunter (the indian in his glade) merges with the flecked animal he pursues. Deer, snake, rock, and indian form links on the same undulating chain:

> This is his poison: that we should disbelieve
> Even that. His meditations in the ferns,
> When he moved so slightly to make sure of sun,
>
> Made us no less as sure. We saw in his head,
> Black beaded in the rock, the flecked animal,
> The moving grass, the Indian in his glade. (pp. 411– 412)

The phrase, seeing "in his head," suggests an exchange between hunted animal and hunter, another version of the Diana/Actaeon myth where the victimized victimizes his pursuer by making him feel what she felt. The flecked animal appears as the Actaeon/deer in his glade. The *locus amoenus* (and the glade's circle of safety) is reduced to a slither (the blade of grass) as the indian emerges: first, spotted deer (animal) and, finally, moving grass (vegetable). Figure and ground become indistinguishable. Out of the mangrove swamp of the snake and its ferns, the currency of exchange "made us no less sure," since wearing the snake skin means seeing through the snake's head. In the snaky frame, the man reflects the woman's apprehension, just as, in the Actaeon myth, the deer-Actaeon trembles with Diana's fear.[7] Revenge as sensitivity. At the moment of articulating power, the serpent decreases cultural transcription. The pursuer ("the indian in his glade") fades into the pursued ("the flecked animal") as spatial demarcators are compressed. The act of seeing "*in* his head" negates the material body and the mastery that constructs the maze. Like Petrarch-Actaeon in *Rime sparse* 23, the indian feels himself "drawn from his own image" (*Petrarch's Lyric Poems*, p. 66). He becomes what he pursues. Everything seems a signifier without an antecedent subject. "*This* is where the serpent lives, the bodiless." Since *that* is annihilated by the serpent's poison and *there* is rendered speculative by the serpent's mastery as Ur-namer, what is left for *this* but its position as objectified other? The end of the canto returns to the opening as the bodiless serpent drifts from glade to sky. If *that* sets up the spiral of seeing (naming the maze) and *there* destroys sight by overseeing (mastering the maze), *this* becomes a spiralling—"*this* is his nest"—and an unspiralling—"form gulping after formlessness." Stanzas 3 and 4 similarly elaborate unhingings:

> These fields, these hills, these tinted distances,
> And the pines above and along and beside the sea.
>
> This is form gulping after formlessness,
> Skin flashing to wished-for disappearances
> And the serpent body flashing without the skin. (p. 411)

This pluralizes as landscapes multiply into "*these* tinted distances" of fields and hills. Then *this* narrows again as the annihilative impulse ("form gulping after formlessness") is writ large. The nest swamps the difference, engulfing the landscape and rendering it a seascape. The image of the flood continues in the "gulping after" and the "flashing to" so that the shining body becomes the land both before and after the wave of the sea. The inundating waters first absorb and then erase the landscape. Form pursuing formlessness is Actaeon hunting Diana. Form regretting formlessness is Actaeon torn apart by his own dogs. Visualizing the sea as a skin involves calling the movement of the waves deciduous. Such a view traces a decreative cycle that keeps skinning and unskinning the land, as the seasons keep lapping against the shore of the year. Nothing is solid when temporal opposites (the seasons of fall and spring) and spatial poles (the boundaries between earth and sky) coalesce.

What is left after the "wished-for disappearances" is precisely what is left in the malice of Medusa's "look of hate": the woman's psychological resistance couched as spatial and temporal unlocatability. When Medusa "looks," she transforms the "look" of what she sees. Wearing the shield, Perseus becomes Medusa. Slithering out of the line of male vision, the serpent redefines the definer and resituates the origin of sight:

> This is where the serpent lives, the bodiless.
> His head is air. Beneath his tip at night
> Eyes open and fix on us in every sky. (p. 411)

Fixed by Medusa's gaze, we have no recourse of escape. As the end of the first canto spirals round to the beginning, the snake turns out to have a head of air. We are spotted by eyes whose source we cannot locate and fixed by an unfathomable "other." We are both immobilized, as Petrarch was in the rock, and unhinged, as Perseus was in the shield. The Petrarch of *Rime sparse* 366 is identified by his error. But his error is the wandering and the haphazard repressions of his own way of imaging. He is stuck in the maze of the self. In "Auroras," the *this* is remote, unrecognizable through anything it projects (its head is air) and unyielding in what it portends; we are held fast by the multiple eyes that mold us by their gaze. From all those eyes, there is no escape for us. The *there* of our mastery is fused to the *that* of our memory. With the family in cantos II–V, both are consigned to oblivion. In canto II, Stevens describes a movement into the anamorphic obscurity that—like a suprematist painting and an oxymoron—works by eliminating contrasts at the very moment that they seem most necessary for stabilization. When the snake and the glade merge in canto I, spaces lose their localizing boundaries. When recent white fades into earlier whitenesses in cantos II–V, the "disordered mooch" does away with temporal demarcators as well. Cantos II–V dissolve the illusion of family; parents never protect the child.

Orphaning the Family

Linguistic and psychological control are threatened with extinction in canto I. In cantos II–V, the represented returns to rebut the patriarchal myth of hermitage and family. Heard now as wind, the disquieting air of canto II reduces "what we felt was sure" (p. 412) to "a motion not a touch" (p. 413). The blazing oxymorons in the family section ("frigid brilliances . . . gusts of great enkindlings . . . the color of ice and fire and solitude," p. 413), one each for cantos III, IV, V, work toward cancellation. Following through on the disappearances of the first canto the oxymorons in the family poems render linguistically the "unpresentable" forms the Russian suprematists represented visually. As Jean François Lyotard argues, such abstractions are not pure or even innocent forms; the matrix of their avoidance still alludes to the inadmissable:

> [it] present[s] something but negatively. It therefore avoid[s] figuration or representation; it [is] "blank" [blanche] like one of Malevich's squares; it will make one see only by prohibiting one from seeing; it will give pleasure only by giving pain. [It will allude] to the unpresentable through visible presentations.[8]

A form that "avoids figuration," the white square signifies erasure even as it hints at something whited out: an "intricate evasion," as Stevens calls it in "An Ordinary Evening in New Haven" (p. 486). The foreground undoes the background and the background cancels the foreground. The moment of seeing reverts to a moment of loss. One item displaces the other. The shown hints at the not shown: the repressed. The movements in the second canto produce contradictions that are the oral equivalents of the visually anamorphic Malevich square in Lyotard's example. The stillness suggests movement and movement results only in stillness. The sign creates and cancels itself. The identifying demarcator disappears. Its simplicity belies the complicated violations the presumed innocence of its whiteness covers over.

The second canto starts a process of erasure that emphasizes the relativity (and hence the lack of stability) of relatives:

It is white,
As by a custom or according to

An ancestral theme or as a consequence
Of an infinite course. The flowers against the wall
Are white, a little dried, a kind of mark

Reminding, trying to remind, of a white
That was different, something else, last year
Or before, . . . (p. 412)

When the thematics shift temporally backward, with the twice repeated "remind," the whiteness of the past bleeds into the whiteness of the present, the way (when it pushes itself into prominence), the background of the Malevich square cancels the foreground it displaces. Reminding—calling back to mind—eliminates all difference as yesterday overtakes today and so ceases to exist as the past. One year merges with another and one generation eats the next. There is no "white / That was different," no pleasure apart from this pain. Thus, there never was "something else" before. The present is indistinguishable from what preceded it, and everything returns to the indifference of the distant mother. The oxymorons in the second canto—with their "frigid brilliances" (p. 413)—drift, as the first canto did, in a sequence of "disappearances" that leaves nothing solid. The "infinite course" is toward nothingness, whiteness reduced to the blankness of unresponsiveness: "maintenant le vide."

Bidding farewell to hermitage, mother, and father, the serpent voice announces the dissolution of all security. Everything is at the mercy of the controlling sky. The reversed perspective of the starry connaissance turns earthly knowledge into an idea of the stars:

> The house is evening, half dissolved.
> Only the half they can never possess remains,
>
> Still-starred. (p. 413)

As the airy eyes of canto I "fix on us," so the earthly house of canto III falls victim of the stars, fated by their destiny. Everything dissolves as difference vanishes. Only the elusive heavenly half stays in control. To be "still-starred" is to be perpetually under the orbit of those eyes and therefore always objectified by their light. To be "still-starred" is also to be completely immobilized by someone else's gaze, distilled by the stars. Medusa prevails. The relativity dissolves relatives, turning mother and father into ice sculptures easily melted by the fiery stars. Protection is a chimera. No resistance. No backbone. No bodies. Whiteness retracts into the emptiness of blankness. The retaliative snake determines everything:

> Boreal night
> Will look like frost as it approaches them
>
> And to the mother as she falls asleep
> And as they say good-night, good-night. Upstairs
> The windows will be lighted, not the rooms.
>
> A wind will spread its windy grandeurs round
> And knock like a rifle-butt against the door.
> The wind will command them with invincible sound. (pp. 413–414)

When the evening dissolves into night, its presence is felt as coldness, the mother's kiss remanded to frost bite. The frost on the grass emerges yet another version of the indifferent and heavenly coldness: "Boreal night will look like frost." The whiteness on the surface of the sky reflects the frost on the surface of the ground. Starry cold mirrors frosty ice. The "infinite course" leads to erasure. There are no protective barriers. Frozen in stillness, earthly life is shaped by a heavenly design. Fate, in its distant and inaccessible chamber, determines our beings.

With the "rifle-butt against the door," the wind snakes its way into the house, taking away all semblance of comfort and safety. No sun warms the earth because the stars are still. Unmoving in their orbit, they are unmoved by human need. If the windows (and not the rooms) are lighted, then they are yet other mirrors of the stars, the heavenly eyes determining—starring once again—the earthly prospect. In back of the mirror is an essential emptiness, the Lacanian "mute mirror-surface . . . a limit whose Beyond is inaccessible."[9] The windows reflect the snaky origin in the sky. The scopic power of the snake in the first canto becomes horoscopic in cantos II, III, and IV, its prognostications climaxing in the familial tragedy of V. Feeding back to the heaven what it feeds them, the mirror replaces the nurturing mother. The children now see in her only replicas of their own helplessness. Penetrating where the stars can't go, the wind knocks "like a rifle-butt against the door" (p. 414). The gestapo invasion renders the mother ineffectual. As the wind spreads, the maternally protective barrier fails. The wind dissipates the mother's "good night, good night" into bad and impenetrable night; the command violates mothers and children. Like the starry mirror, she remains unavailing. Lulled by her own lullaby, the guardian falls asleep at the watch.

In the frost and lighted window of canto III, the earth visually reflects the icy stillness of the stars. In canto V, the star crossings become the vanishing prospect of self-canceling auditory echoes. The musicians are windbags, dubbing at tragedy:

> What festival? This loud, disordered mooch?
> These hospitaliers? These brute-like guests?
> These musicians dubbing at a tragedy,
>
> A-dub, a-dub, which is made up of this:
> That there are no lines to speak? There is no play.
> Or, the persons act one merely by being here. (pp. 415–416)

A reverberating drum, the mirroring sound plays back the starry connaissance so that the dubbing or naming is yet another futile gesture that erases (like the rifle-butt) the articulate play. "There are no lines to speak." The dub is a backward bud, an autumn answer to incipience, another rebuttal (a repetition of the "rifle-butt") of filial expectation. "A-dub a-dub" suggests "rub-a-dub," the way Medusa emerges Perseus and Perseus (in "Three Academic Pieces") fades into Narcissus who finds Medusa instead of the missing body of Echo. Rub-a-dub wipes out the body. When the end folds back to the beginning, erasure is included in the rub. The drum beat reduces language to "disordered mooch"; tragedy drifts into nursery rhyme, the "tale of a tub" governed by the tail of the snake. For the submerged Narcissus of the boreal night in canto III, canto V offers a hollow Echo. Like the mirror that lights the windows and not the room, the play has no human center, its sound only empty wind. "Merely by being there," the persons "act one" because they are still-starred, their presence an absence of self, as they, like Laura-Medusa's rock, are "stilled" there, playing their parts in a star-crossed tragedy they cannot control. Like Perseus' anamorphic armor, the echoes of "a-dub" reflect the snaky image and reverberate with the opening hiss. No parent shields the child.[10] The rifle-butt of canto IV is repeated yet again in the dubbing of canto V, as the patriarchal order smashes security. In the Nazi invasion of home, in the nuclear obliteration of hearth, "there is no [room for] play." The "disordered mooch" links linguistic chaos to mass murder. "Brute-like guests" violate all notions of home and hearth. In cantoVI, however, the poet acknowledges that he is the source of the annihilation and desolation the first five cantos chronicle.

Palming off the Poem

Canto VI ends by summarizing the oxymorons of the earlier poems ("frigid brilliances [p. 413] . . . the color of ice and fire and solitude" [p. 413]) in the "Arctic effulgence" (p. 417) of the final stanza. But something happens in the course of the poem to cast the oxymoron differently. The first five cantos demolish the enclosures of family and home: "form gulping after formlessness." In the sixth canto, the container includes what the earlier oxymorons preclude. The room becomes roomier. The oxymorons reiterate the annihilative force of the *this* in canto I and then render the hiss in "this" harmless:

> This is nothing until in a single man contained,
> Nothing until this named thing nameless is
> And is destroyed. (p. 416)

In canto VI, *this* emerges both all-encompassing and all-consuming, an already accomplished devastation ("*this* is nothing") and a still-to-be-experienced feeling ("*this* is nothing *until*"). In the Petrarchan ethos, "until" refers to a deferral that actually means "never." Here, "until" suggests that the deferral might first be reversed and then overcome, as the "single man" contains and feels what the appropriated "other" felt. Instead of infinite postponement of a never-to-be realized union, there is the imminent collapse of demarcation. "Namelessness" annuls the appropriative process. Canto I demolishes the mind. Canto VI builds on the senses. Instead of thinking *for* the other, the canto demands that the poet feel *as* the other. The sixth canto suggests that, as abstractions, the opening annihilations are both easily dismissable (*"this* is nothing") and impossible to ignore (*"this* is nothing until in a single man contained"). The elsewhere Stevens identifies in canto VI has its roots in the nowhere Petrarch uncovers in *Rime sparse* 23. As signator who erases sign, Laura-Mercury appears in *Rime sparse* 23 to challenge the poet who invented her and undo the name he called her. She presents the unpresentable as herself. When Laura speaks in *Rime sparse* 23, she unhinges the defining forms even as she petrifies the poet. Similarly, in canto VI, the scholar feels "afraid" (p. 417) of his own formulations. But his fear is a beginning, not an end. While in cantos I-V, the representational matrix is annulled, in VI it is reversed, as the poet feels what the woman feels. Like the rotorelief, the images in the center of canto VI protrude and recede with a speed that blurs boundaries. But, unlike the opening oxymorons, which cancel each other out the way the Malevich square does, the opal and the theater of canto VI project a sequence of pulsating stages as the oxymorons flow into each other. The new image suggests interchange rather than annihilation.

The canto moves outward to the clouds and colorless cold and then inward to the opal and its firey circles. The transformations are unending and the voice revels in the lavishness of change:

It is a theater floating through the clouds,
Itself a cloud, although of misted rock
And mountains running like water, wave on wave

Through waves of light. It is of cloud transformed
To cloud transformed again, idly, the way
A season changes color to no end,

Except the lavishing of itself in change,
As light changes yellow into gold and gold
To its opal elements and fire's delight,

Splashed wide-wise because it likes magnificence
And the solemn pleasures of magnificent space.
The cloud drifts idly through half-thought-of forms. (p. 416)

In canto I, the determining head is air; in canto VI, the head is first rock, then theater, then man, as each suggests its own unimagining and nevertheless persists in its own being. As rock, the theater is flooded by the ocean—mountains running like water—or obscured by the air—mountains misting into clouds. When the firmament falls into the ocean and wave of light fuses with wave of the sea, one becomes the other. First, the misted rock emerges an opal element, an iridescence that suggests an earthly eye in fire that is at once self-effacing (splashing) and self-enlarging (wide-wise). The fire ignites itself (in flame) and waters itself down (in splashing). The wave contains the fire as it reflects the sun, including the solar flame in the fiery foam. The movement is exhilarating—lavishly self-reflexive—"fire's delight." With the "splash," the water first reaches into the sky and then mirrors the sun. The vertical traversing of distances then suggests a circle, as the movement in the "wide-wise" closes up geographical and horizontal distance as well. Canto I focuses on the impulse to avenge the appropriating self. Canto VI offers an alternative to the discursive practices that fuel such eventuations. Rather than seizing the resources of the other, the self absorbs the feelings of the other, as sea becomes sun and rock becomes sky.

The formulative eye restructures the picture: first, in the wavy light; second, in the shining opal element; third, in the alternative map of wide-wise (an inversion of side-wise, that recharts the perspective from heavenly to earthly even as it acknowledges *wissenschaft* in the wisdom of the hyphenated wise); and, fourth, in the half-thought-of-forms that connect the clouds and their random shapes to man and his purposeful design. Those four inchings toward the imagined possible flesh out a theater of abstraction that, like Konstantin's airy theater in *The Sea Gull*, moves beyond the forms of patriarchal and matriarchal convention:

> The theatre is filled with flying birds,
> Wild wedges, as of a volcano's smoke, palm-eyed
> And vanishing, a web in a corridor
>
> Or massive portico. (p. 416)

Not an empty stage, the theater is filled, the container simultaneously a trap for the flying birds and a vessel to which they lend shape (as "wild *wedges*"). But, as oxymoronic *wild* wedges, the birds provide earthly answers to the stilling stars of the first five cantos. They threaten the theater, the wedging shaken by their wildness, and they stabilize it, their wildness restrained by their wedging. Like the opal element, the birds pulse in and sweep out, moving from convex to concave, prodding the building into collapse by flying out, keeping the theater afloat by wedging in. A "web in a corridor" describes the matrix of an interior labyrinth, the female womb; the "massive portico" protudes like an appendage, the male member. In the self-canceling oxymorons of cantos I-V, the representations point to an essential absence. In the inverting oxymorons of canto VI ("wild wedges" and "opal element"), one form contains the other and then releases it, as wildness collapses the wedges, fire splashes in the lubricated opal, and water runs away with the reflected sun. The destabilizing mechanism keeps pointing to the fragility of forms, the thin tissue of "a *web* in a corridor." The defining mechanism includes collapse in its structure. In cantos I-V, erasure is all. In canto VI, the fluctuation is all. In cantos I-V, the other disappears, leaving nothing. Blankness presides. In canto VI, the other reappears. Wildness reigns. The movement between the web and the portico is as sexually suggestive as the Duchamp rotorelief, the physical throb yielding one gender to the other.[11] In the rapid pulsation of in-out, the undecidability between him and her depends on the flux, the third term that throws expectation off. While canto II laments "the motion" that is "not a touch" (p. 413) because it signals the anomie of detachment, canto VI fleshes out the "motion," rendering it the source of connection that first challenges the demarcating mechanism and then, by a process of inversion, overrides the binaries and their arbitrary divisions.

As there are four earthly answers to the annihilating *this*, so there are four earthly interpretations of palm-eyed that (like a peacock's feathers) point to the possibilities for fusion: first, the introduction of the palm, as sublimation (like the Petrarchan laurel) for peace instead of battle; second, the multiplicity of the many leaves within the many leaves, depicting the interior of the web again; third, the linguistic link of eye and hand (in the palm-eyed), cementing the connection between the male gaze in the eye and the male pen in the palm. The man "contains" his vision of the woman in the palm of his hand and then releases it in the writing that frames her yet again even as (in the nest-like web of the palm) the man returns to his origin in the woman; fourth, the Christian metamorphosis and the palmed triumph of Christ's ascent that could not occur without his prior emergence from the female womb. All four variations posit earthly foils to the firmament. The birds, whose upward motions defy the gravitational push of starry fixation and whose downward leanings deny the heavenly appeal of the starry romance, mediate the spheres. Order reverses and unhinges itself. Wedges now. Wildness later. Woman now. Man later.

If the first canto yields to outer space, the sixth canto results in framed spaces—the theater, the opal, the single man—localizing abstractions as oxymorons and preparing for the changed perspective of the concluding

Marcel Duchamp, Corollas, 1953. The Museum of Modern Art, New York. Gift of Rose
Fried. © 2001 The Museum of Modern Art, New York. © 2001 Artists Rights Society
(ARS), New York / Adgap, Paris / Estate of Marcel Duchamp.

sequences. Annulling the *this* in the *"this* is nothing," the serpent voice of canto VI cancels its own cancellations, burning down the house of the single man while confessing that the drama cannot exist apart from the house or context of the cultural representations it resists and the thinking it ruptures. Canto VI articulates the conundrum that, like Stevens's "the absence of the imagination had / Itself to be imagined" (p. 503), insists that Laura-Mercury and Stevens's serpent only come into being through the discourse they subsequently challenge. Since containment signals a holding and a restraining pattern, the single man who "contains" includes the resistance Petrarchism represses. The containment incorporates the annihilative impulse of the woman's evasiveness and puts off its effect. If the man *contains* the resistance mechanism, he restrains it and, hence, renders it nothing. If the man *contains* the impulse that spurs resistance by sharing it, he includes resistance and therefore obviates the need for violence. The resistance can only become nothing when the man fears his own inventive capacity, imagines being imagined, and begins to feel like a woman. The wildness that threatens is a reaction to the shaping wedges:

> This is nothing until in a single man contained,
> Nothing until this named thing nameless is
> And is destroyed. He opens the door of his house
>
> On flames. The scholar of one candle sees
> An Arctic effulgence flaring on the frame
> Of everything he is. And he feels afraid. (pp. 416–417)

If *this*—the female impulse to resist representation—is felt by the man, then the named thing—the female image invented by the man—is no longer capable of inciting fear. Only when the artist destroys the impulse to create an other from his self and contains his desire to name an other in his own image can the threat of revenge cease. As the formerly imagined woman becomes, in turn, the imaginer of the man, Stevens's scholar sets in motion the terrifying spiral of his own objectification. In the Arctic effulgence, he sees both: (1) his ephemerality as designator, or namer, of others; and (2) his vulnerability as "named thing" in someone else's schema.

The paradox describes the central question. Can the feeling poet (the man who understands the restrictive containment of representation) continue to write? Facing head on the issues of mid-century anguish, the scholar sees "an arctic effulgence flaring on the frame / Of everything he is." The fires of Europe are burning in his own house. Framing itself is called into question as the poet feels the effects of his compulsions. Beginning as an outward turning and a floating toward nothingness, the section ends with an inward burning and a deliberate conflagration. *This* is nothing until a single man sees it and *this* is nothing when a single man contains it. The Medusa of canto I is nothing in herself when the Perseus of canto VI wears her anger on his shield, when he becomes she. For that exchange to occur, the scholar of canto VI needs to absorb Laura-Mercury's abstracting impulses and—with her—challenge the forms he invents. Canto VI twice doubles the inversion, moving from wind, to eye, to wind again, as the arctic effulgence flares, sets to fire by wind, an essentially uncontainable energy. The temporal marker becomes a psychological marker: "And he feels afraid" (p. 417). The scholar fears the repressive impulse in himself, his need to keep inventing the forms of his own deformation. *This* is nothing until the scholar imagines it. Petrarch feels compelled to invent the Laura who annihilates him. Stevens is reduced to the serpent who neutralizes poetry. The self-denouncing self acknowledges the "other's" resistance as an impulse it shares. Felt by the man, that resistance renders the woman's insistence on taking him over unnecessary and hence nothing. With her, he feels afraid. He feels what she felt. Differences vanish as the oxymorons melt into each other, "mountains running like water . . . wave on wave through waves of light." The frigid and annihilating "stillnesses" of cantos I-V give way to the pulsing circularity of canto VI.

Reversing the "looking relations" by yielding a head for the eyes, canto VI revitalizes the telling relations, finding a vehicle for its tale in the story of the scholar: "this is nothing until in a single man contained" (p. 416). The scholar of the sixth canto comes to understand the reality of the "other" whom he repressed in his anxiety to "realize" himself. When the single man fears his own inventive capacity and when he fears representation itself, he contains and therefore subdues the need for revenge. He stops the acquisitive process he started. The explosion of the fissionable device can only be prevented at the outset, as if Einstein foresaw what theoretical physics could produce, or as if Oppenheimer understood, before it began, what the Manhattan project could unleash.

With the prophecy that "this is nothing until in a single man contained," Stevens repalms the poem, reasoning that the deconstructive vision is the inevitable result of the constructions language enables. But he also stresses that the cosmic explosions of the poem can only be understood when they are felt by a "single man" and when what happened *over there*, to the many men devastated by the war, stirs a feeling of fear *here at home* in the single man left seemingly untouched by the war. To call the buttresses of the building "wild wedges" is to acknowledge the divisiveness implicit in creativity and to understand that the artistic process may instigate a cycle that includes its own destruction. The "named thing" insists on "namelessness" in the same way as Laura-Mercury persists in abstraction. In breaking the boundaries of the discursive, the imagined "other" renders the wedges of poetical or theatrical constructions "wild." The poet takes on the snake skin, which he sheds again. Cantos I–V end in the "disordered mooch." The "wild wedges" of VI suggest that the explosive impulse is only provisionally containable. The wedges support the defining form but the wildness threatens to unhinge all containers. Like "the web in the corridor," the wedges are diaphanous, finally revealing the repressive self at the origin. But by exposing the repressiveness, the wedges also release the wildness underneath, a wildness that presages and prepares for change.

As Petrarch becomes petrified when he hears Laura-Mercury, so the scholar of one candle sees an arctic effulgence "flaring on," both illuminating and exploding, the frame. *This* is nothing until it is felt and *this* is nothing after it is cancelled out in the Arctic effulgence. If *this* is the resistant present, *that* the definable past and *there* the locatable future, *until* both suggests anteriority (a time before destruction) and subsequentiality (the possibility that something exists apart from the exploded construction and that projects a difference somewhere on the horizon). "Namelessness" is the prelinguistic stage and the openings that occur after the old terms are deconstructed. "Namelessness" therefore presupposes a different symbolic order. Its essence is undecidability, a state not prescribed by the formula. It anticipates the return of the forgotten and so includes what was missing from the original.[12] "Until" leaves a wedge at the opening and therefore presupposes that, at the end, the repressed other might "wildly" return. "Until" implies that the presumed end with its namelessness actually comes before the beginning and the "named thing." It therefore opens to a new sequence, one that evolves when everything seems over and one that might be "expanded to describe," in Judith Butler's terms, "those who were not permitted into the interlocutory scene of the public sphere."[13] Such a telling is possible when the scholar imagines being imagined and when the self fuses with the other he "wedged" into or kept out of the form. Wildness becomes the beginning as well as the end when it signifies a loosening of the boundaries, an opening to a prelapsarian time, the *wilderness* of a not-yet-charted territory, before form and its theatrical structures came into being.

Acknowledging fear, the representer incorporates the represented's impulse to fly away. When he contains the impulse and becomes the theater temporarily holding the birds, he admits that he is beset by the ambivalence the birds express in the moment when their wildness exceeds their wedging. The self contains and then issues forth the other through invention; but the other also "contains," and effectively restrains, the self through its potential to explode or exceed the invention. The exploration begins with what the scholar of one candle sees "flaring on the frame / of everything he is" (p. 417). How can he see what is "flaring on the frame" if he is inside it? To "see" is to objectify the self as the image of the inflaming namer and to project the self into the situation of the gazed upon excluded other. It is to invert the images and to move with them. When he becomes the image, the containing man acknowledges that the "other" feels afraid. But he also dissolves the barriers of signification that separate self from other simultaneously as he opens up the border between "this is nothing" and "this is nothing until." The borderland saves him in the end, the wedges only a temporary answer to the wildness and the threat of collapse. But the extent to which the wedges contain the wildness suggests the force with which they touch on an originary excitement, just as the extent to which the wedges restrain the wildness is a measure of, and an admission to, their repression. Turning the inside out, Stevens invests the oxymoron with the energy of the other. Moving introspectively and retrospectively at once, he establishes the poetic rotorelief as the metamorphic matrix.

Blazoning the Palm

When the poem arrives at the last canto, it returns to a beginning and projects innocence as something that might still occur:

> An unhappy people in a happy world—
> Read, rabbi, the phases of this difference.
> An unhappy people in an unhappy world—
>
> Here are too many mirrors for misery.
> A happy people in an unhappy world—
> It cannot be. There's nothing there to roll
>
> On the expressive tongue, the finding fang.
> A happy people in a happy world—
> Buffo! A ball, an opera, a bar.
>
> Turn back to where we were when we began:
> An unhappy people in a happy world.
> Now, solemnize the secretive syllables.

Read to the congregation, for today
And for tomorrow, this extremity,
This contrivance of the spectre of the spheres,

Contriving balance to contrive a whole,
The vital, the never-failing genius,
Fulfilling his meditations, great and small.

In these unhappy he meditates a whole,
The full of fortune and the full of fate,
As if he lived all lives, that he might know,

In hall harridan, not hushful paradise,
To a haggling of wind and weather, by these lights
Like a blaze of summer straw, in winter's nick. (pp. 420–21)

Trying out various possibilities in the canto as alternatives to his first proposition, "an unhappy people in a happy world"—with (respectively) "an unhappy people in an unhappy world . . . a happy people in an unhappy world . . . a happy people in a happy world"—Stevens dismisses each alternative: the first as altogether too miserable (too many mirrors); the second as too anthropomorphic (too many projections); the third as too trivial to yield poetic material (too easy a joy). Returning to the Petrarchan position with the denied and empty self in an indifferent and capacious world, Stevens needs to go back to something earlier than his own immediate proposition. Does "turn[ing] back to where we were when began" (p. 420) mean when we began the canto or when we began the poem? Does Stevens locate his beginning in language as Petrarch (with one pulsating thrust backward) or in the woman as Laura (with one pulsating thrust inward)? The ambiguous beginning implies that it might be possible to reimagine (as Laura-Mercury does in her abstractions, as the rotorelief does in its convolutions) the relations. Since we don't know what then or there are and since we're uncertain about where we began, we can't be sure what here and now are. The "ancestral theme" (p. 412) of erasure in the self-canceling oxymoron is replaced by a relaxation of the demarcating mechanism even as the connective link names the poet as repressor. "Turning back to where we began," the poet "meditates a whole" and so negotiates to include the repressed other in the poem. "Turning back" to his beginning, the poet acknowledges his origin in the woman.

The final "as if" of "Auroras" recalls the initial "this is where the serpent lives" and circles back to the snake "meditating" (p. 411) in the ferns and the snake mastering the maze to pose yet another hypothesis. Finally, the amorphous *this* of canto I is localized as *this extremity*, as outer reach reasserts the human form. The apogee or climax of the poem is figured in the apogee or climax of the body, extremities as fingers and toes. The poetic hand and metric foot are part of "this contrivance," this mechanism of reader reading and writer writing, a spiral that reverts to the beginning of Laura reading Petrarch writing her. The situation of utterance (this extremity) becomes the text that fuses mechanism with mechanic, poem with poet, and imagined with imaginer to offer an alternative discourse. The fusion suggests an anticipation—a blaze of summer straw melting down winter's nick (winter summerfied, summer winterfied) and a memory—a remnant of summer caught in winter's throat (winter thawed, summer remaindered). If canto I begins with a head of air, the last canto proposes another container, the huge head of the seasons, and another headlessness, pursuant to the annihilating blaze of summer straw. Summer is internalized in an easy image ("like a blaze of summer straw in winter's nick," 421) that is casual, not catastrophic, flippant, not sibylline: almost accidental: a straw. The possibility for melting even the rock of winter sustains the poem. The possibility for humanizing the shape of winter sustains the poet.

When the fire moves inside the discourse, it threatens to annihilate the containing form. A blaze of straw can melt down the frost-bite of winter. But the summer's straw is anticipatory as well as retaliatory. Winter eventually turns into summer. The finale of Shelley's autumnal poem, "Ode to the West Wind," is similarly "if winter comes can spring be far behind?"[14] As poetic blazon, the fire's light illuminates difference. As summer blaze, its excess undoes its own representation. The blaze renders summer straw and winter's nick oxymoronic. When the straw melts the nick by obscuring its solid borders, the whole configuration changes. Caught in a moment of poetic arrest, Stevens's image still moves toward the skinlessness that undoes it. The instrument of salvation merges with the instrument of conflagration. Like Petrarch's evasive Laura-Mercury, the blazon acknowledges the woman's abstracting impulses. But as an ideational state, its potential skinlessness suggests that the critical unmasking is still ahead, somewhere spiraling out of the "contrivance" the imagined poet makes of the woman's idealized body.

Stevens's final image equalizes the genders, temporarily postponing the terrifying immolations of the poem's initial usurpations. For the moment, the nick of male voice "contains" the female flame "Auroras of Autumn" so powerfully lets loose. But the boundary breaking impulses of resistance are nevertheless fully and threateningly present. The end of the poem pulls out yet another oxymoron as the poet acknowledges his origin. In that light, "form gulping after formlessness" seems an expression of comic relief, an almost cartoon ("Pop-eyed") recovery of a hero's rescued selfhood in the "nick" of good timing. The hero swallows his pride to emerge the female impersonator of male voice. But the gulp also represents the Petrarchan lover's desire to hold the wind in a net, the almost fatal pursuit of the poet's evasive love. The lump in the tragic hero's throat for the other he can't have produces the repressed Petrarchan sigh, "the gulp after," or the swallowed tears, of the sublimating love poem.

"Auroras of Autumn" chronicles both the unavoidable absurdity of the poetic ethos and the inevitable resistance it instigates. But that resistance remains part of what follows. Working through Petrarch's early modern "unsettling" images and bringing them into the post-Hiroshima age, Stevens's final vision includes the repressed memory of the violations that initiated the Medusan revenge in cantos I through V and the Mercurial evasions in cantos VI through X. Half memory, the summer straw is also half anticipation. The "hissing" flame in winter's nick of canto X echoes the icy "this" of canto I, its melting (of the boundaries between past and future, male and female) auguring a poetic still to come.

In its deferral of Petrarch's Ovidian transmutations, "Auroras" corroborates Stevens's presumption that the songs poets sing are, indeed, "preludes to the atom bomb" (*The Necessary Angel*, p. 76) even as its isolation of the accusatory women Petrarch depicts in the Laura-Medusa of *Rime sparse* 366 and the Laura-Mercury of *Rime sparse* 23 is an acknowledgment of Stevens's complicity in the ongoing generic constrictions he identifies. In the "hall" of the "harridans"—through the anamorphic doubling of Laura-Medusa and the complicated labyrinth of Laura-Mercury—the poem points a guilty finger at the poet. But, in the haggling, the poet changes places with the other, alternating movements so that the "hall" of the poem becomes the woman's space as well. The hiss is hers as the rotorelief turns inside out, suggesting the ways in which an expropriating poetic can be recast. In the "wild wedges" of canto VI, the poet acknowledges how flimsy his structures are, how they can barely contain the other they hold. It is the "wildness" that forces the representational issues in VI. And, in X, it is the blaze of the woman's rebellion that melts the icy nick, recodifying the binaries of the inherited frame. The "hiss" of resistance is there at the end as well in the implied sound of the summer straw as it strikes against and so melts winter's icy nick. The meltdown in turn does away with the barriers between summer and winter, self and other, through which Petrarchism structures differences. Since "nick" implies both the act of cutting and the cut place, the straw of summer carves its space in, and already casts its imprint on, the wintry discourse. As cutting agent, the "summer straw" signifies the meltdown it will effect. Turning the discourse around, it follows the pattern of temporal reversals—remaining as insistent reminder, anticipating as missing agent—to signal the eventuation of the repressed other into the narrational frame. Moving the discourse away from the "hushful [Biblical] paradise" (p. 421) where Adam was the namer of all things to the "hall harridan," where the discursive space includes the woman, Stevens recognizes a back and forth that dislocates all the old orderings of first and last. When he forces the deconstruction of the "wild wedges," and opens himself to a "haggling in hall harridan," he loosens the boundaries of, and suggests alternatives to, the repressions instigated by his own poetic materializations.

It is the "haggling" from within the generic material in "Auroras" that gives the reversal meaning. Those re-locations could only be imagined because the poet implicates himself there in the representational crimes he uncovers. In "An Ordinary Evening in New Haven," Stevens returns to the disputed territory once more, as he includes the history of evasions in the incriminated discourse, naming himself as the usurper in the beginning and making room for the usurped woman at the end. Only in "An Ordinary Evening," Stevens ventures one step further than in "Auroras" and imagines the woman as a writer who, overriding the confining strictures, recasts "the handbook of heartbreak" (*Collected Poems*, p. 507) in her own image.

Chapter 3 ∽

"THE INTRICATE EVASIONS OF AS": HISTORY'S DUPLICITIES IN STEVENS'S "AN ORDINARY EVENING IN NEW HAVEN"

History is the poisoned well seeping into the ground-water. It's not the unknown past we're doomed to repeat, but the past we know. Every recorded event is a brick of potential, of precedent, thrown into the future. Eventually the idea will hit someone in the back of the head. This is the duplicity of history: an idea recorded will be an idea resurrected. Out of fertile ground, the compost of history.

Destruction doesn't create a vacuum, it simply transforms presence into absence. The splitting atom creates absence, palpable "missing" energy.

— Anne Michaels, *Fugitive Pieces*[1]

The Poisoned Well of Petrarchan Form

In the course of "Auroras of Autumn," Stevens comes to "feel afraid" of his own appropriations, the violations that resulted in the explosions "flaring on the frame / Of everything he is" (p. 417). In "An Ordinary Evening in New Haven," Stevens acts on those fears. His project is to find "the thing apart" (p. 465) from the "thing as idea" (p. 295) he relished in "So-and-So Reclining on her Couch." Abandoning the frame with its "apparition[s]" (p. 295) of repressed seizures and "mechanism[s]" (p. 295) of poetic determinism, the Stevens of "An Ordinary Evening in New Haven" struggles to work out an alternative to the oxymoronic "solid space" of the earlier poem. He finds it by redefining the reality of the "solid":

It is not in the premise that reality
Is a solid. It may be a shade that traverses
A dust, a force that traverses a shade. (p. 489)

In order to get to the newly interpreted real at the end, Stevens begins with an attempt to break free from "the origin of a mother tongue" (p. 470) he inherits from the patriarchal language of "th[e] form[s]" (p. 470) of desire, with their "inescapable romance" and "inescapable choice / of dreams" (p. 468). The "romance" of the "romance" looms in its infinite deferrals. Satisfaction is always just beyond reach. The inescapability of the "romance" lies in the attraction of its repertoire of culturally prescribed dreams. "The form[s]," so inevitably coming to hand, preclude choice.

In an essay written in the same year as "An Ordinary Evening in New Haven," Stevens praises the French artist Marcel Gromaire, for releasing himself from the tyranny of received forms and artistic fashion. Stevens's phrasing, however, moves into the political as he argues that Gromaire produces an art "directement social."[2] Defining Gromaire's artistic originality in terms that suggest an ideological independence, Stevens fuses artistic and social mechanisms: "Being rebellious is being oneself and being oneself is not being one of the automata of one's time" ("Marcel Gromaire," p. 250).[3] In "An Ordinary Evening in New Haven" Stevens, like Gromaire, denounces the narcissistic pleasures of the readily available poetic, its "mirror," its "lake of reflections in a room / [its] glassy ocean lying at the door" (p. 468). Calling the poetic incrementally frightening and overwhelming (as he founders from mirrors, to lakes, to oceans), Stevens resists the reflective temptation and reduces it to the derivative and almost atavistic instinct he characterizes in the essay: "the day's great common flocks and herds and shoals of things alike" ("Marcel Gromaire," p. 250). The thrice repeated bestiality of "flocks and herds and shoals"—birds and beasts and fish—relegates the desire for resemblances, in the robotic alikeness of things, to a less than human instinct, at once animal and mechanical, simultaneously bullying and repressive. Stevens's sense of the "automata" in "An Ordinary Evening" returns industrial, political, and artistic systems to their roots in the perilous Vienna woods of "Three Academic Pieces." But, against the pressure of such entanglements, the Stevens of "An Ordinary Evening in New Haven" finds that "being oneself" is not as easy as it seems. He cannot stop himself from relying on the inherited forms of "alikeness" in the artistic automata of Petrarchism. Rebelling is not just a matter of wanting to turn away. The formula, massive and monolithic, is programmed to be used and the poet is programmed as user. Stevens acknowledges the expressive force of the automaton in "So-and-So" when he refers to the "concealed creator" behind the "mechanism." But Stevens's resistance is more politically ambitious in "An Ordinary Evening," not just concerned with the isolated artist juggling his familial and amorous ambivalence.

With the hindsight of his postwar malaise, Stevens renders New Haven "a banlieu" (p. 504) of Europe and therefore interchangeable with the old havens and their baggage.[4] As Stevens writes in "One of the Inhabitants of the West," "so much guilt lies buried / Beneath the innocence of autumn days" (p. 504). "An Ordinary Evening" exhumes what is repressed in the leaves of a New Haven autumn, turning them over to expose "the horrid figures of Medusa" (p. 504) impressed beneath the surface of the forms he can't escape. Like that of "Auroras of Autumn," Stevens's rebellion in "An Ordinary Evening" identifies: (1) the connections between the "automata of one's time" and the repressions of the past, best illustrated by the surreal appropriations of XII, where "statues / are like newspapers blown by the wind" (p. 473); (2) the deep-rooted and manipulative desire to conceal the repressive instinct that Stevens confesses in "the intricate evasions of as" (p. 486) in XXVIII; and (3) the repressed self and appropriated other whom he allows to eventuate naturally—rather than explosively—in the "less legible meanings of sounds" and "the little reds / Not often realized" (p. 488) of XXXI. In "Auroras," Stevens unhinges the oxymoron through the pulsations of rapid-fire and spontaneous interchangeability. With the last canto of "An Ordinary Evening," Stevens turns the oxymoron into a series of deliberative and voluntary actions. Following the ebb and flow of the universe, the final oxymorons thrust both the excluded other and the repressed self onto the poetic foreground to reveal the "less legible meanings . . . the inner men / Behind the outer shields" (p. 488).

"An Ordinary Evening in New Haven" centers on a "never-ending meditation" (p. 465) to find the "thing apart" (p. 465) from what came before, a quest that keeps turning back to the oxymoronic condition symptomatic of the Petrarchan mode, "the handbook of heartbreak" (p. 507) Stevens finds so compelling. The more the poet seeks, the less able he feels to find an alternative. The escape route emerges a no-exit maze, an "and yet, and yet, and yet" (p. 465), as Stevens puts it in the third line of the poem. The process of contradiction—the "yes, but" in "and yet"—is so suffused by the overpowering drive of the form—the "still another" in "and yet"—that rebellion merely catapults the poet backward, to his original self. The oxymoron is all consuming and all compelling. The multiple planes of Petrarchism disallow the "plain version" (p. 465) partly because the very terms of refutation are built into the original poetic. For Stevens, as for Anne Michaels in the epigraph, history is infinitely repetitive and inevitably confining, "duplicitous" because the past is always duplicated. Unhinged from their moorings in another place or time, the bricks that built the supposed old havens of Europe[5] are not only repeated in the architecture of New Haven but lurk as potential weapons in the twelfth canto, an arsenal so powerful that an entire city is defined in terms of an "idea that will hit someone in the back of the head."

In canto XII, when the statues fly "like newspapers blown by the wind" (p. 473), the ideas that generate "solid space" are dangerously thickened. Pliable newspapers stiffen into marble statues; statues give up their foundations and float into space. Space solidifies as newspapers harden into bricks. Detached from their moorings, statues emerge lethal weapons. Weighted down by their resemblance, newspapers strike back as well as fly away. In canto XXVIII, when modern art, with its naturalistic impulse, reverts to older forms and their religious imperatives, the poet uncovers the acquisitiveness of both. At the very end, in XXXI, when Stevens works the oxymoron differently and when he opens the poetic to other players, the form finally seems free enough to allow for the small opening—the "dust" and "shade"—that might make a huge difference. Whereas, in XII, the poetic impulse is toward the representational "more," and in XXVIII it compounds itself and expands toward a geographical and historical "more," in XXXI Stevens settles for "less": "It is not in the premise that reality / is a solid" (p. 489). But this new "premise" appears only after the statues and newspapers of XII, the "intricate evasions" (p. 486) of XXVIII, and the "visibility of thought" of XXX (p. 488) are seen to explode, with the "fire-foam" (p. 488) of XXXI, into the still finer oxymoron, " a shade that traverses / A dust, a force that traverses a shade" (p. 489). In "An Ordinary Evening in New Haven," Stevens works through the duplicities of history by making manifest the self-destructive mechanism that is simultaneously miniscule, "a dust," and potentially explosive, "a force."

The new agents Stevens names at the end are possible partially because, in the course of the poem written in very traditional tercets, he renders the oxymoron so surrealistically that it exposes the mechanism as simultaneously bizarre and dangerous.[6] The "concealed creator" (p. 295) of "An Ordinary Evening" seems a "wizard of Oz" gone beserk. In XII, he pairs politics and love. The statues of the idealized past merge with the newspapers of an all-too-real present; in XXVIII, he doubles the doubling mechanism itself when, in "the intricate evasions of as" (p. 486), he pulls back to the serpent of Genesis 3 and the impulses of imperialist self-aggrandizement. The oxymorons function as commentaries on the appropriative tendency of lyrical ambition. In XII, the oxymoron renders the simile phantasmagorical: statues fly; soft newspapers stiffen into dangerous projectiles. In XXVIII, the oxymoron doubles itself into a definition of simile, indicting metaphor as self-aggrandizing, and situating it as inextricably human. But, in XXXI, the oxymorons appear as actions ("evoking . . . practicing . . . tearing . . . up") that resist the closure and automata of the form.

The Reverberations of a Windy Night—Canto XII

Charles Berger writes that "An Ordinary Evening in New Haven" is both "a superimposition onto the scene of New Haven of all the destruction in the war" and an expression of the sense of "sheer survival."[7] Berger's reading presupposes a Stevens bent on peace and recovery "from war and the anxieties it spawned" (p. 83). In his view, "An Ordinary Evening" does not "concern itself much with memory for the poem searches out a 'new resemblance of the sun.'" (p. 91). While I think, with Berger, that "An Ordinary Evening" is philosophically a postwar poem, I will argue that the quest in the poem—to replace the "giant" (p. 465) of the past with a "recent imagining of reality" (p. 465)—fails precisely because cultural memory cannot so easily be exorcised. The twelfth canto summarizes the failure of the quest as Stevens begins with the plain version—"the poem is the cry of its occasion" (p. 473)—and ends caught in the net of the form and formulae he inherits from his Petrarchan forebears. The most devastating moment in the twelfth canto is the point of vision "when the marble statues / Are like newspapers blown by the wind" (p. 473). In the ethos of "So-and-So," it seemed possible to revert to "the world as anything but sculpture." In the world of "Ordinary Evening," the impeccable whiteness of marble folds into the sullied blackness of newsprint: the world of everything *as* sculpture. Nothing escapes the immobilizing instinct. Yet nothing is stable enough to remain firmly planted.

Unhinged from their roots in the past, statues merge with contemporary representations. Marble statues are the newspapers of the past, valorizing specific events and their perpetrators. If statues become "like newspapers blown by the wind," then the events they commemorate feed into and are absorbed by those recorded by the tabloids of the day. Both the fixtures and the ephemera are subject to the same volatility. As temporal oxymorons, marble statues and newspapers are oppositional, statues dedicated to the newsmakers of the past, newspapers identifying the celebrities who eventuate into statues. But, as spatial oxymorons, they brush against each other, newspapers celebrating the fame that commissions statues, statues in turn canonizing the newspaper record. Not only are monuments self-consuming. In their potential impact, they consume others.

In canto XII, an Ovidian Narcissus is involved with the "reverberations" of the second stanza and an Ovidian Apollo with the "burnished" leaves of the fourth stanza. Those are the two poles of the canto. Narcissus reverts to Echo in the "reverberations" of the first half. Apollo implants himself forward to Daphne in the "burnished" leaves of the second. The two myths are also connected to each other, as the shine in the Apollonian allusion of "burnished" flashes back to the mirrors of Narcissus and the "reverberations" in the earlier stanza anticipate the echoes of Apollonian song. The past is always present, although the first line insists that the poem belongs only to the moment of its writing:

> The poem is the cry of its occasion,
> Part of the res itself and not about it.
> The poet speaks the poem as it is,
>
> Not as it was, part of the reverberation
> Of a windy night as it is, when the marble statues
> Are like newspapers blown by the wind. He speaks
>
> By sight and insight as they are. There is no
> Tomorrow for him. The wind will have passed by,
> The statues will have gone back to be things about. (p. 473)

As "the cry of its occasion," the first stanza does away with the past. The occasion is now, "as it is / Not as it was." But that wrenching gets complicated in the second stanza when the cry volumes out to the ambiguous "reverberation." Is reverberation reflective only of the moment of utterance echoing into the indefinite future, or does it also resonate with voices of the past repeating history as an infinite incantation of an originary violation? Does "as it was" haunt "as it is" despite the disclaimer?

When Stevens renders "statues . . . like newspapers," he emphasizes the sound of the wind hurtling the statue as weapon against the self (unhinged as projectile, coming toward him now) and as the already deadened self (calcified as the projection of his earlier destructive tendencies). The potential crackling noise of newspapers coincides with the remembered visual image of the statue and it does so, through the reverberation, at the very moment when sound and sight fuse. Narcissus sees Echo in himself, as the flickering remnant of his fading light parallels the faint volume of her repeated call. The accidental whirlings become conscious hurlings. Creative energy cannot be seen as separate from the destructive impulse. The sexual icon of the statue merges with the political icon of the newspaper to suggest their interchangeability and to indicate the connection between the forces that generate the discourses of love and war. Through the introjected Echo, Narcissism reflects a sense of the past that translates the present moment into the language of the already iterated. As flimsy artifacts, the newspapers recall the attenuation (the Echo-like remnants) into which the solid statues will eventuate.

In the next section, the image of Apollo implants itself in Daphne so that the "burnished" trees in their rootedness and immobility contain the transforming energy of the sun and the shifting influence of light. The "burnishing" reflects a slippage in the Petrarchan roles, a mirroring that allows Apollo to take over Daphne despite her escape. As Giuseppe Mazzotta writes of such shifts in the *Rime sparse*: "Petrarch casts himself in the role of Apollo and, in the same breath, casts Laura as the sun."[8] The flickering of the leaves is both the faintest sound created by the wind (the woman who evades the nets) and the last squibs projected by the sun (the Apollo who pursues with nets). The "whirling away" is a "whirling *around.*" The past comes back to haunt the present. The tales of Narcissus, Echo, Daphne and Apollo are compressed into each other. The "burnishing" rustles with Echo even as it reflects Narcissus and his sad story.

If the first stanza closes off *is from was*, the other stanzas surrender *is to was*. Having fused statues with newspapers, the speaker slowly begins to enact the connection between area—a region designated by sight—and aria—the region formulated in song. And it is in that sense that Stevens annuls the poem as the "cry of its occasion." "Sight" is always "re-vision"; sound is always echo: the poem as "reverberating" materialization and cry of past occasions. The tree contains song, not just as Shakespeare describes in "Sonnet 73": "bare ruin'd choirs where late the sweet birds sang"[9] but as an endlessly repeated chorus.[10] The "sweet birds" are not silenced. They "s[i]ng preludes to the atom bomb" ("Three Academic Pieces," p. 76). Their "late" singing is always belated. Their "sweetness" secretes a sour afterlife. The choirs are "burnished" with Apollo's desire for song, as the reverberations "echo" Narcissus's desire for himself. The empty space "flickers," casting light and sound as memory, anticipating a recovery that is itself the source of dread:

> The mobile and the immobile flickering
> In the area between is and was are leaves,
> Leaves burnished in autumnal burnished trees
>
> And leaves in whirlings in the gutter, whirlings
> Around and away, resembling the presence of thought,
> Resembling the presences of thoughts, as if,

> In the end, in the whole psychology, the self,
> The town, the weather, in a casual litter,
> Together, said words of the world are the life of the world. (p. 474)

If the single statue merges with the multiple newspapers, so the first song, Apollo's lament over Daphne, anticipates all future songs, the whirlings as multiple as leaves, their potential messages too innumerable to count. One poem is all future poems, as one leaf is refigured in the next leaf that carries the genetic markers of the previous one. The buried old in the new troubles the surface of the reverberations. The "burnishings" age the leaves before they even bud. "Whirlings away" return to "whirlings around" in the "area between is and was," partly because the inevitable cycle of nature returns leaves to trees and partly because the aria is swallowed up by the chorus: the individual becomes the whole. Spring is therefore not consoling. Replacement precipitates effacement. Multiplication is inevitably followed by subtraction. The cycle of nature presumably reasserts the leaves in the innocence of their moisture. But, despite their newness, the leaves are already products of the sun's heat, as the laurel could not be without Apollo. Apollo "burnishes," his heat sucking dry the liquid energy he precipitates. The image of separation—the litter in the streets—is already, and alas, the vehicle (litter as a means of transportation, and litter as a whole new brood) of rebirth. The "casual litter" is the causal Apollo, as he reconstitutes the tired leavings of the years before. In the "litter," the last, dwindling and discarded, remainder resurfaces as the first, tiny and much heralded, new arrival. When the leaves are "burnished" in the trees, Apollo seems embossed on Daphne, the leaves already charred by the sun.

The measure of time is light and the leaves shining in the trees reflect their source in the sun. What takes place over time transpires in space as well. The trees rooted in the earth are acted on by the sun. Daphne is changed by Apollo, as Apollo moves too close: "The point of vision and desire are the same" (p. 466). What we see *now* is what we wanted *then*. Yet the imagined closeness in itself precipitates separation in the same way as leaves inevitably fall from trees. "Burnishing" fuses with "flickering." The final flourish of the immobilizing instinct spreads its tentacles around the first sign of a new mobility, equating the paralyzing stillness of the frozen statue with the repetitive chords of unstillable song. The "gutter" becomes the connecting conduit and the path to the sea that then joins the laurel leaves to the inscribed Echo, just as the whirling wind reinscribes the whirlpool of Narcissus. The mobile and immobile flickerings of light join the currents of the ocean to the wind in the sky.

In canto XII, the connection is as much between the whole and the part, the tree and the leaves, as it is between the *now* and the *then*. The pluralizing possibility—the leaves whirling in the gutter and away from individuation—becomes a contemporizing construct, one that forces the connection between this moment and all previous ones. The leaves resemble the presence of thought, the nowness of the moment, and the presences of thought, the many ghosts of the past. Union produces a stifling claustrophobia; separation hints at a void hollowed out by the sepulchral overflow. If statues and newspapers merge, so do former thoughts besiege the present. Nothing is quite singular and nothing is quite now. The "casual litter" becomes, triply, the remnant of what was, the vehicle that connects, and the manifestation of multiple births. The laurel through which Daphne escaped Apollo is the vehicle that reflects him, as the leaves "burnished" and brought to life by the sun are eventually blackened by it. Daphne is first imprisoned in the laurel and then relegated by the song to the flight that propels her straight back into immobility. Apollo resumes his original quest in the songs that commemorate her as never-realizable. The songs first set Daphne in motion again and then trap her as a figure rooted in deniability. The cycle inevitably confirms the projections of an annihilative desire. The whirlings "around and away" both release the leaves from the tree and render them—like Daphne—victims of the forces through which their identity is lost. The mobile and immobile flickering, the shade between "is and was," is the moment of undecidability in the oxymoron that binds Echo to Narcissus in the "reverberations" and Apollo to Daphne in the "burnishings."[11]

The Inevitable *"Of"*ness of *"As"*

The twelfth canto ends up trapped in the *causal* litter of the originating linguistic bind. The twenty-eighth canto begins with another art and another appetite, starting in the visual mode of naturalism,[12] Picasso's "Mother and Child, 1905" with its tin plate and her *"misericordia,"* and falling back on the other-worldly ambitions of Renaissance painting and its verbal equivalent in, say, Spenser's *Faerie Queene* with its "heavens . . . hells . . . [and] longed-for lands." The "casual litter" of the twelfth canto is repeated with a casual example in the twenty-eighth: "Bergamo on a postcard," as mailings become part of the habitual detritus. New Haven is a belated Bergamo and the postcard image carries not just Europe's exotic romance but its wartime aftermath. As Roland Barthes writes, "I observe with horror an anterior future of which death is the stake. . . . In front of the photograph of my mother as a child, I tell myself: she is going to die: I shudder . . . *over a catastrophe which has already occurred.*[13] Perusing the postcard in New Haven, Stevens transfers Europe's "catastrophe" and its biblical roots into the American foreground and the contemporary scene. And he complicates the process even further by melding political ambition with amorous excess, pointing to the desired woman behind Christian expansiveness and the guilty woman of old testament transgression. Mary hovers over the first half, Eve, over the second. The canto shuffles between periods; early modern enthusiasm lapses into late modern depression. Raphael's Mary holding the fat baby anticipates, in her vacant spirituality, Picasso's woman in her self-absorbed *anorexia,* just as David's masculine and grandiose psalms are mirrored inversely in the tin plate and long-bladed knife of a feminized *misericordia.* The late modern "shudder" is already there at the beginning:

XXVIIII

If it should be true that reality exists
In the mind: the tin plate, the loaf of bread on it,
The long-bladed knife, the little to drink and her

Misericordia, it follows that
Real and unreal are two in one: New Haven
Before and after one arrives or, say,

Bergamo on a postcard, Rome after dark,
Sweden described, Salzburg with shaded eyes
Or Paris in conversation at a café.

This endlessly elaborating poem
Displays the theory of poetry,
As the life of poetry. A more severe,

More harassing master would extemporize
Subtler, more urgent proof that the theory
Of poetry is the theory of life,

As it is, in the intricate evasions of as,
In things seen and unseen, created from nothingness,
The heavens, the hells, the worlds, the longed-for lands. (pp. 485–486)

While the twelfth canto reverts to Ovidian metamorphosis, the poles of the twenty-eighth canto are Biblical, as Stevens wavers between David's

Pablo Picasso, "Mother and Child (Acrobats)," 1905. Staatsgalerie Stuttgart. © 2001 Estate of Pablo Picasso / Artists Rights Society (ARS), New York.

(Ed.ᵐᵉ Alinari) N.ᵒ 258. FIRENZE – R. Galleria Pitti. La Madonna detta del Granduca. (Raffaello Sanzio).

Raphael (1483-1520), "Madonna and Child," Palazzo Pitti, Florence, Italy, Alinari/Art Resource, New York.

psalms (the *misericordia* and their hint of new testament forgiveness) and Genesis 3, and its unforgiving sentence.[14] When Stevens refers to the psalms, he includes those where David, repenting Bathsheba, seeks (and in some way presumes) God's forgiveness. David's abjection catapults him into the euphoria of "the heavens, the hells, the longed-for lands" of Christian dominion as David prefigures, and grants himself, Christ's pardon. When David woos God in the *misericordia* (the fifty-first psalm), he already mouths the grace he seeks, just as the Petrarchan poet invents (and therefore in some way already possesses) the sought-after other. Genesis 3 looks back to punish overarching desire and to render sin unredeemable. David "looks ahead" to what he desires, assuming a forgiveness his present sinfulness would seem to preclude.

The painterly tradition of Mary and Christ confers a grace the artist accepts from the tradition as a given, just as David asks God for a deliverance that he will requite with the tribute he already enacts:

O Lord, open thou my lips
And my mouth shall show forth thy praise. (Psalm 51)

From the nothingness of his despair, words will flow, if the prayer for opening is granted. But the opening is already forged as the psalmist in anticipation utters the praise he claims only God can enable him to sing. The self-aggrandizing psalmist confers upon himself the flowing words he asks God to give, as the self-referring Petrarchist already produces the poem and woman he desires. Having annexed the divine power he allegedly still invokes, David passes himself off as deprived. If the self already contains the other, then the represented other is always missing from the scene. Poor David. Poor poet. In Picasso's mother and child, the absence of response is figured by the empty and narcissistic self-enclosing gestures, as child and mother hug their hollow bodies, and as the draping sweep of clothes calls attention to the utter emptiness underneath. The undernourished child turns away in response to the mother's inward turning. Picasso's painfully thin mother and child are twentieth-century inversions of the fullness of the Madonna and child in a Raphael painting. Renaissance spirituality becomes Picasso's unresponsiveness. As Jeremy Gilbert-Rolfe argues about the blank expression: "The face signifies by refusing to signify."[15] Empty Mother. Vacant child.

In the twenty-eighth canto, absence produces a religious appetite abetted by cultural memory. Picasso's image suggests that the clasping instinct and its self-sustaining rage for incorporation belie the impassivity in the expressions of mother and child. For Stevens, the isolationism of the incorporative gesture impels the immensity of the land grasp at the end: the "heavens, the hells, the longed-for lands." In the twelfth canto, the sexual appetite keeps flickering to reproduce "said words of the world." In the twenty-eighth canto, spiritual hunger still yields the fertile lack of other mythlogies. With the image of mother and child, the language of the new art reiterates the central iconography of the Christian experience. Our expectation includes memory. In the twelfth canto, Apollo enters Daphne ("leaves burnished by the sun") and locks her into his obsession. In the twenty-eighth canto, the inward taking is presumed as a given.

When "real and unreal are two in one" (p. 485), the privately felt need justifies global acquisition. Lyric gives way to epic. "Longed-for lands" in the actual world parallel the heavens and Hells in the Biblical world. As the Petrarchan poetic incorporates real women, the imaginative thrust of the "longed-for lands" is to render them properties for imperialistic design. One absence provokes another. The hungry self grows hungrier. The other it ate is now no longer available for sustenance. Psychological and imaginative experience flesh out in actual countries to form a circle in which "real and unreal" are condensed in the workings of desire:

> it follows that
> Real and unreal are two in one: New Haven
> Before and after one arrives or, say,
>
> Bergamo on a postcard, Rome after dark,
> Sweden described, Salzburg with shaded eyes
> Or Paris in conversation at a café. (pp. 485–486)

In the first example, "New Haven before and after one arrives," the sense of anticipation—"New Haven before"—is built on prior imaginative experience. Even if we have never physically been there, the city exists in our mind. Conversely, the actual city persists without us. In terms of the imagination, our being there is immaterial. In terms of the real, our being there is irrelevant. The imagined and the real New Haven are the same. The "before" anticipates the "behind," as chronological sequence closes off geographical distance. Inwardness is all. The unreal New Haven, the reality in the mind, is a symbol whose existence depends on imagination. Our sense of "the thing" is governed by "said words of the world" (p. 474). The actual encounter (after one arrives) merely projects out again the previously swallowed (or read) experience. City after city becomes both still-life (reality captured) and moving-life (transposition incorporated) in the way that silhouette postcard packets foreshadowed the motion-picture. The newsreel is the old real that returns to the already said. The stillness of the image as impression records a previous absorption into the self as a primal introjection. The flickering between images becomes the force that propels the next one as a secondary projection. The motion picture projector eats and then spits out again the photographed impression, as the impression in turn shapes our anticipation. The real city in geographical space and the unreal city in psychological time occupy the same territory: "reality exists in the mind." The city is an imagined construction: "Paris in conversation at a café." Does all of Paris fit—by compression—into its conversational image? Or—by expansion—do we project Paris across the ocean through a café culture that homogenizes everything so that the actual city fits our expectation? If "reality exists in the mind" as a recorded impression, then reality comes to exist *through* the mind as a self-fulfilling prophecy. All "things" are conveyed by the same filtering mechanism. "The theory of poetry" becomes, in the end, the "theory of life" because the real is the belated reflection of an already shaped image: "New Haven before and after one arrives." David anticipates Christ as forgiveness is factored into the psalms. Laura generates her avatars as the form crystallizes and then projects its cultural expectations forward.

If the twelfth canto moves into the visual oxymoron of statues and newspapers, the twenty-eighth canto turns from the visual to the verbal, evolving a double oxymoron that reparses the "solid space" of "So-and-So" with the "intricate evasions of as." The "intricate evasions" turn the already introjected other into the belatedly desired other. The doubling spatializes the mind image, rendering the constant reversion to poetic form equal to the expansionist "longings" for geographic space. Poem for land as religious expression. Solids emerge guilty in the "intrication"; guilt evaporates in the space of the evasions. Picasso disappoints Raphael in retrospect but Raphael also spoils Picasso in anticipation. Poem for woman, as sexual acquisitiveness. Heavens and hells are the geographic extensions of Rome and Bergamo, just as Laura and Mary are the female extensions of poet and priest. Reality becomes what we read of it.

The oxymoronic condition of the twelfth canto heightens the connection between art and politics, statues and newspapers. In the twenty-eighth canto, the oxymorons hover in the juncture between art and religion, as Mary is reincarnated in the drive for empire behind dynastic desire. Narcissus confronts Medusa in this canto in the way that, in "Three Academic Pieces," Stevens embeds her in the "glassy stream." In the essay, he counters anticipation with a surprise which is, nevertheless, also anticipated by a previous violation. The reflection includes the repressed image even in the very moment that we cancel the expectation. Deniability follows from repression. Simultaneously as Stevens annuls the serpent in the text, he insinuates it into the denial. The "intricate evasion" takes the shape of the serpent as "intimate invader," the slippery outward sign of a demonic inward desire. At the end, the serpent represents the invasive acquisitiveness repressed at the origin: "[Narcissus] did not expect, when he looked in the stream, to find in his hair a serpent coiled to strike" ("Three Academic Pieces," p. 79). The expectation breaks through the denial, is part of the coil.

The central oxymoron of the twenty-eighth canto is partly the effect of a mirroring that reveals the unexpected serpent. "The intricate evasions of as" contains two sets of opposites that return the image to the history of image making. The sign is all, but is inevitably human. Escaping confinement in the evasion, the "I" returns to the constrictions of intricacy. The evasive simile, "as," is rooted in the implicated origin, "of." The history of escape is the history of return. Life "as it is" cannot be seen as separate from poetry as it was. New Haven in the mind is partly the old havens of Europe, just as the new art of Picasso is partly the old art of Raphael. The origins of resemblance in poems and family revert to the ancestry and herding instinct of "common flocks and herds and shoals of things alike." If "the theory / of poetry [is] the theory of life," then the family and its legacies and the poem and its origins absorb the individual and his sightings. Describing his escape route in the "intricate evasions of as," Stevens visualizes the metaphorical device in terms of a spatial prolongation, substitution as extension. The sexual desire of the twelfth canto with its temporal and generational prolongation becomes in the twenty-eighth canto, the imperial thrust of geographical and expansionist dominion: "the heavens, the hells, the longed-for lands."

With the double oxymoron in "the intricate evasions of as," Stevens arrives at what Harry Berger, Jr. (quoted by Charles Altieri) calls "as-kissing raised to the level of a humanistic ideal."[16] Altieri dismisses Berger's quip as "the disdain for ideals that only a deconstructive historicist can muster" (*Painterly Abstraction in Modernist American Poetry*, p. 344), arguing that "the abstract *as* refers directly to the way poetry crosses life, because it names the state of equivalence basic to all acts of valuing" (p. 346). Stevens actually anticipates both Altieri's positive and Berger's negative, with a positive that instantly (through the oxymoron) reverts to a negative and an evasion that is complicated by its being too closely connected to an historical origin. The intricacy unravels in the evasion. The evasion is weighted down by the intricacy. "Of" refers to origins; "as" refers to analogy. Altieri reasons that "identity depends not on substances but on relationships" (p. 346). However, reading "the intricate evasions of as" oxymoronically heightens the connection between the virtual and the actual. The impulse to sever—with the evasions—returns to the impulse to connect—with the intricacy. The two are inseparable. "The intricate evasions of as" details not just an "equivalent as value," but the full weight and inevitability of historical connection as determinant. The shift of analogy is inevitably backward. With Stevens's oxymoron, "as-kissing" reverts to "was kissing": Adam and Eve caught in the act. In Genesis 2, man's origin in the dust of the earth—his *of-ness*—erases man's likeness to God in Genesis 1—his *as-ness*. The serpent of Genesis 3 (who joins sex to insight) promises Adam and Eve that they can deny their dependency and move straight back to Genesis 1 where they shall be "as God" again. But the deterrence to such intricacy is the very impulse of intimacy. Analogy is sexuality unfulfilled. Realized sexuality disappoints the desire in analogy, yielding a generational dullness. Petrarchism or the excitement of the unreachable reverts to the routine of the family plot or the boredom of the accessible. The virtual equivalence of metaphor in *as* is an inevitability derived from the actual human heritage in *of*. The habit of "asing" comes too close to "kissing" and kissing leads inevitably to the doomed family story of Genesis 4 and its derivative inheritance in "of-ing." "As-kissing" helps when life fails. Conversely, the family story only comes into play when Petrarchan desire is answered. Families are the fallback solution. "Ordinary Evening" returns to "Auroras": "[Intricacy] is where the serpent [still] lives." The theory of life is the theory of poetry because the *asness* of metaphor cannot be separated from the *ofness* of dependency. In poetic terms, *as* is routed back through *of* in XXVIII by a fusionary cycle identical to the one in XII where, in "burnishing," Apollo implants himself in Daphne and, in "reverberation," Narcissus introjects Echo. In XXVIII, Picasso returns to Raphael as the religious impulse results in imperialistic designs.

Recovering the Less Legible in Canto XXXI

Like the others, canto XXXI has two parts. The second half follows through on the thesis of the first. Canto XII first situates the poem as the "cry of its occasion" and then merges all occasions in the second; canto XXVIII attempts to evade the pull of history in the first half and resorts to an imperial intricacy in the second. Reversing the pattern, canto XXXI begins by acknowledging the past, locating the poet in the context not of this occasion but as the inheritor of past occasions. Accepting his intrication as a given, the speaker imagines other connectors at the end, agents who might change the configuration to propose an ultimately different telling. Occupying an ambivalent position from the start, Stevens acts as reader (deciphering the "less legible meanings" of others) and as writer (expressing the "less legible meanings" of self). In fact, writing becomes reading and "legibility" turns the world of the poem into the word of the text. "Legible" in his text are previous texts. Folded over, they surface again in his. In the "intricate evasions of as," the world is "created from nothingness" (p. 486), an emptiness that produces "longed-for lands." But the escape is short-lived. With the "intricacy," the poet returns to a repression at the origin. While XXVIII begins with a vacancy and ends in the expanded territoriality of longed-for lands, XXXI assumes something is there at the start—Constantine as holy Roman empire-builder. But it ends with an American "Blank." The president looks back to imperial history, as America merges with Europe.

In XXXI, the poet uncovers an *a priori* world. Mr. Blank fills in for Constantine. "Flicking" through historical layers, the poet moves (with the surge of a zoom lens) backward to emperors and forward to "photographs" of the late president. In XXVIII, the image moves. Postcards are sent across the ocean. Here the picture shifts historically and geographically with the speaker's eye. Like all the other "fidgetings," the personal and the political coalesce:

> The less legible meanings of sounds, the little reds
> Not often realized, the lighter words
> In the heavy drum of speech, the inner men
>
> Behind the outer shields, the sheets of music
> In the strokes of thunder, dead candles at the window
> When day comes, fire-foams in the motions of the sea,
>
> Flickings from finikin to fine finikin
> And the general fidget from busts of Constantine
> To photographs of the late president, Mr. Blank. (p. 488)

The chronological "flicking" reduces events of seeming consequence to "fidgets," tiny bubbles on the cosmic calendar. The motion picture of XXVIII produces the "flicking" in XXXI, but the images shrink as the notion of imperial power loses its significance The mighty emperor is a midget. The many Constantines merge with each other; all the U.S. presidents converge in the nameless Blank. The most recent in *belated* becomes the previously deceased in *late*. The direction changes, just as the late president yields to the populist flow of anonymity, "Mr. Blank," and pulls the imperial thrust of Constantine into oblivion as well. In XII, when "statues are like newspapers blown by the wind," they emerge solid: lethal weapons. In XXXI, when Constantine dissolves into Mr. Blank, imperial power seems vacant, spacey. All Constantines are one emperor and all Presidents are Blank. The turning point in "Auroras"—when "this named thing nameless is / And is destroyed" (p. 416)—evolves naturally in the second part of "Ordinary Evening." Namelessness leads not to a destruction but to a leavening and a vision of a political power that abandons the empire-building imperatives of XXVIII—"the heavens, the hells, the worlds, the longed-for lands" (p. 486)—and acknowledges the flatness of emperors and presidents. The nameless late president also suggests the possibility for a new script. Since he leaves no impression behind, the political future remains in the undecidability of blank. The ties between the political and the poetic in XII and XXVIII are "solid": newspapers merge with statues so that they have the potential "to hit someone in the back of the head"; desired dominions become real territories.

In XXXI, the "spaces" loom larger as, in the political sphere, blankness opens things up. In the artistic realm as well, the monolithic form appears to contain other "meanings," less legible ones. And it is to these meanings that Stevens turns in the last part of the canto, as he simultaneously drowns and recharges himself in the "fire-foam" at the center. The oxymorons in the first half of the canto are nouns that epitomize the chronological fidgets. Both "fire" and "foam" are the result of dynamic bursts, explosions of light and sound that imply the resources of a larger and more influential agency. The oxymorons in the second half reflect movements that are similarly self-canceling, producing a proliferation of impelling sources—evening, philosopher, woman—themselves containing and restraining the explosive possibility. In XXVIII, "real and unreal" are "two in one," as the mind sucks in "things" and spews out its ideas. In XXXI, reality occupies *spaces*. Shades "traverse," move between and through each other, emphasizing the permeable and the admissable, just as Blank is simultaneously an erasure of memory and an opening to something new. As ghosts, the shades dissolve into the present. As outlines, the shades anticipate the future. In the "*realized*" of the "little reds" of the opening ("not often realized meanings") and in the re-realized "*reality*" of the new premise at the end, vague spaces solidify and firm solids decompose in a process of construction and deconstruction repeated throughout the last canto. When space opens up, the real becomes less and less determined:

It is not in the premise that reality
Is a solid. It may be a shade that traverses
A dust, a force that traverses a shade. (p. 489)

Realization is fourfold: first, an act of perception, situating the writer as reader who works toward understanding the missing element in the other; second, an act of liberation, situating the writer as expresser, who works toward untying the missing element in the self; third, an act of restoration, a making palpable the missing energy absorbed in the introspective-projective cycle of literary appropriation; finally it is a source of revelation, through the materialization of "the unnamable in the secret of names."[17] As reading, the "realization" involves a perception of the repressed in the original text; as writing, it demands a presentation of the repressed in the current text.

In "Three Academic Pieces," Stevens projects the woman missing from yesterday's discourse as the retaliative bomb that explodes in the face of the song. In "An Ordinary Evening in New Haven," Stevens sets up a different beginning as he puts the woman missing from the original back into the opening moment of representation. The inner men behind the outer shields are the Kleinian introjected women who, in the "fire-foam," force themselves on to the present scene. As Stevens reverts to other mythologies, the "foam" spews out Echo's voice in the boom and Aphrodite's body in the wave. When he moves from "candle" to the oxymoronic "fire-foam," Stevens first acknowledges the explosions that previous discourses made inevitable.

Fire-foam is the splitting of the atom in the fusionary moment. But fire-foam is also the metamorphic *impossibilia* grounded in the metaphoric possible and working two ways. The fire-foam is the mirror image of the sky in the water and of the water in the sky. Specks of foams are stars, shining in water. Stars are foam crystallized and etherealized. But when he speaks of the "*motions*" of the sea, Stevens expands the metaphor into the metamorphic, as Florizel does in his injunction to Perdita in *The Winter's Tale:*

When you do dance, I wish you
A wave o' the sea, that you might ever do
Nothing but that, move still, still so. (*The Winter's Tale*, 4.1. 140–142)[18]

In Florizel's oxymoron, the "still" of "move still" suggests both an image held in perfection (still as a marble statue) and an image that is self-perpetuating, "still" in the Elizabethan sense of always. The moving stillness of Perdita's art anticipates the "statuas moving" so central to Shakespeare's play and to the imagery in Stevens's poem. In Stevens, as in Shakespeare, the stillness is rendered mobile through the wave of the sea which, in its repetition, remains constant. The shift from the stillness of art to the motion of the waves replaces creativity and the statue, as mirrors of imagined life, with reproductivity and the womb, as sources of actual life. The Shakespearean wave ties Perdita's maternal potential to the reproductive life of the ocean as fecund origin of all things.

Stevens's "fire-foam" similarly connects to the oceanic womb. It brings the sky down into the ocean, as the sun is mirrored in the sea. It also refers to the diurnal cycle, as the "fire" turns us back to the candle in the window, the image of the day in night. It therefore intersects art—words, music, artificial light—with the larger motion of thunder and the heavenly stars. The small light is unkillable. With the "fire-foam," Stevens renders sun and water equal. Nothing vanishes. The inside is brought out and the upper is brought lower. Fire-foams are: (1) the remainders of the candle reflected in the window; (2) the heavenly sun contracted in the earthly water; (3) dynamic motions that eviscerate in explosive contact, fire canceling water, foam sparking fire. In the fire, the motion mirrors the process of the solar sky by day as, by night, it follows the tidal pool of the moon. When he moves out finally to "fire-foams in the motions of the sea," Stevens draws the sun into the water and then adds the moon, since, as causer of the tides, the moon works on the sea and includes both the illumination of the sun and the shadow of the earth. The poles of the Petrarchan love poem— moon and sun—are part of the "swarming activities of statement," as "said words" and art (music and candles) bow before the strokes of thunder and day. Finally, as he does in canto XII, Stevens pulls Apollo into the story of Narcissus with the reflective mirror and connects Echo to Daphne with the circular motion of the wave chase and the repetitious cadence of the wave sound.

But he also suggests another myth in the "fire-foam," a myth that goes against the law of the father and that returns generative power to the woman. Stevens's "fire-foam" rebirth parallels the birth of Aphrodite in Hesiod's *Theogeny*. The full body of Stevens's analogy coheres its scattered parts, as Aphrodite in *The Theogeny* incorporated the "immortal flesh of her father and grew a lovely maiden":

> And vast earth rejoiced greatly in spirit, and set and hid [Cronos] in an ambush, and put in his hands a jagged sickle, and revealed to him the whole plot.
> And Heaven came, bringing on night and longing for love, and he lay

about Earth spreading himself full upon her. Then the son from his ambush stretched forth his left hand and in his right took the great long sickle with jagged teeth, and swiftly lopped off his own father's members and cast them away to fall behind him. And so soon as he had cut off the members with flint and cast them from the land into the surging sea, they were swept away over the main a long time: and a white foam spread around them from the immortal flesh, and in it there grew a maiden. Her gods and men call Aphrodite, and the foam-born goddess and rich-crowned Cytherea, because she grew amid the foam . . . And with her went Eros, and comely Desire followed her at her birth at the first and as she went into the assembly of the gods.[19]

In Hesiod, the myth of Aphrodite centralizes the woman's initiative. Female Earth launches the story with her plot to turn the sons against the father and feminized Desire, gathering herself into shape, ends it, as she leads her followers "into the assembly of the gods." The fires are not extinguished from the poetic; after reading differently, they can be regendered as inspirational spark. Desire and its train are female, as, in the next line, philosophy and its abstractions are realized through the practice of departure and return that mimics the ebb and flow of tides, seasons, and day.

The "littler reds" of the candle are simultaneously the sources that don't usually come to light (the repressed) and the inspirations that are not often recognized (the forgotten). They are precisely what never made it into the representational process. But, like the "lighter words . . . the sheets of music . . . [and] the dead candles," they can be brought to a realization (both an initially experienced life and a subsequently understood life). They can be made to have their full potential as themselves and made to bear their full weight in the narrative formula. There is another beginning and Stevens finds it in the female, lifebearing, womb of the sea, as in "Auroras," he had named it both the "hall harridan" and the "summer straw in winter's nick."

But when Stevens returns to other beginnings that the world yields to him as reader of the legible, he opens up to other writers as they represent the pluralizing possibilities of multiple agencies. Forms proliferate into formulae when the "swarming activity" is seen as a release from the patriarchal dominion of a single "language [that the poet] must [speak]" (p. 507):

These are the edgings and inchings of final form,
The swarming activities of the formulae
Of statement, directly and indirectly getting at,

Like an evening evoking the spectrum of violet,
A philosopher practicing scales on his piano,
A woman writing a note and tearing it up.

It is not in the premise that reality
Is a solid. It may be a shade that traverses
A dust, a force that traverses a shade. (pp. 488–89)

"Final form" is itself provisional, both an "edging"—a cutting—and an inching—a mending. When deliberately used, the separating device and the returning instrument offer, first, an understanding and, second, an alternative. Without facing the responsibility inherent to the connection between "fire-foam" and mushroom cloud and between the individual and the larger selves, there is no possibility for an alternative to the old forms. The birdsong anticipates the bomb. To bring back the repressed female force is to open the discourse to other realities and the reality of the other.

In the most remarkable section of the canto, Stevens moves toward and away from the dreaded complex. With the "swarming activities of the formulae," Stevens suggests that the form itself is not static, that the gathering in a "compact cluster," which the form represents, also provides the element for escape with the mass exit from the parent of all those permutations and imitations in the "swarm." The formula changes from the univocal forum of a culture and its "automata" to a multiplication of terms. The "formulae of statement" lose their imperatives as they exponentially increase in the swarming. Weighed on the philosopher's "scale" are both the possibilities of ascent and reversibility. The three active agents (evening, philosopher, woman) are positioned at the crucial center of sight, sound, and text so critical to this last canto. The lines work both in and around each other, in a forward-backward arch that includes the desire to expand, and the need to relinquish, power.

In the first of the similes ("like an evening evoking the spectrum of violet"), Stevens once again returns to Shakespeare's sonnet 73 and "twilight of such day / As after sunset fadeth in the west, / Which by and by black night doth take away, / Death's second self that seals up all in rest" (*Shakepeare's Sonnets*, p. 257). But, while Shakespeare's "twilight" is victimized by the light-snatching Night, Stevens's "evening" is the active agent of its own overtaking. Hence, the "spectrum of violet" is both the haunting specter of darkness and the entire range of violet, with its intense mix of red and blue, fire and water. The "spectrum" looks back to the "fire-foam," inward to Apollo and Narcissus, and away again to the birth of Aphrodite. When "evening evok[es] the spectrum of violet," it summons up, rather than runs from, the darkness and, in its fragility, takes on both the oceanic coldness of night and the scorching flames of the sun. The red and blue of "fire-foam" coalesce in the violet.

If, at the beginning of the canto, the "little reds not often realized" are recognized by the alert reader, here the "littler evening" itself summons forth the enveloping element. The dual meaning of spectrum suggests the ghost of the past and the complete coverage of the darkness to come. Day becomes part of night, reversing divisions, and anticipates the next day, fostering the separation that makes identity possible. Great theories are reduced to routine and constantly repeating occurrences, as negotiable as day and night. The philosopher practices his diurnal scales.

With the last image, Stevens gives to the woman both the generative force of the pen and the demonic instincts of Cronos. She writes the note and tears it up, evoking power and scattering it to pieces. In the "tearing up," Stevens suggests all the scattered parts of the leaves of XII and the bloody drops of Hesiod's ocean bearing foam: the little reds in the larger whole. The substance of the note—torn up—is "less legible" but still contains the initially conceived meaning. Like the scattered leaves in the "casual litter" of XII and the "intricate evasions" of XXVIII, the separating device is also reminiscent of the gathering force. As writing agent of the note, the woman might also be uttering her own complaint or, alternatively, silencing it, stopping the cycle before it is read and exercising her freedom to opt out of the system altogether. The image of the woman writing sets her clearly at the central axis of the discourse of love and at the pivotal meaning of correspondence.

Finally, with the possibility that "tearing it up" with the hands might also suggest "weeping down on" with the eyes, an alternative appears, one that recasts the *Rime sparse*. In 265, Petrarch implores Laura to be more "natural":

> I live only on hope, remembering that I have seen a little water by always trying finally wear away marble and solid rock:

> There is no heart so hard that by weeping, praying, loving, it may not sometime be moved, no will so cold that it cannot be warmed. (*Petrarch's Lyric Poems*, p.434)

When he sets up the contraries, Petrarch posits a process that lends him hope. If nature can change art (rain soften marble) then art (weeping, praying, loving) can soften nature (move hard hearts, warm cold wills). Like the steady stream of rain, the steady flow of the Petrarchan arsenal (weeping, praying, loving) subdues the recalcitrant other as rain renders marble permeable. But, while Petrarch puts himself in the subject position of the rain and thereby names the woman he invents as the hard-hearted stone, Stevens's "tearing" woman is slightly different. Since she weeps all over her own production, rendering her own meaning "less legible," she takes responsibility for cause and effect, thereby controlling the divisions—of empires of love and war—that are constrained by—and explode in—the realization project. With the emphasis on the "less realizable reds," the region of the not-yet-expressed opens to counter the dominions of the already "said words of the world."

Imagining other agents, Stevens admits to alternative discourses, and perhaps even to the disruption of discourse altogether. Those shifts render the culturally "knowable" other not quite fixed and the culturally transmitted system less determined. The notion that reality might be many solids, rather than a solid, allows for readings that might produce other texts and other writers. Evening, philosopher, and woman, the usually passive victims so easily overtaken by the more aggressive night, politics, and men, are here seen as shapers of their own destinies, fostering small "rebellions" against the automata of time, ideology, and gender. In all three instances, there is the contrition of remorse, as "evoking" spreads out into the full expression of the "spectrum," as practicing implies that all expression is provisional, and as "tearing it up" suggests both that words might wound and that perhaps some things are better left unsaid. One way of rebelling is to refuse the temptation entirely. In all three instances, the rebellion involves a revelation of a creator who is not "concealed."

But those double readings can only occur if the duplicities of history—the outer shields, the strokes of thunder—are acknowledged as enunciations of a construct that maximizes difference and that thereby produces the "shadowy contentless figure[s]" ("How Bodies Come to Matter," 281) it marginalizes. In reading, Stevens "realizes" and so comes to understand those figures. In observing the woman writing, he imagines the different tellings her note might prompt. Through the repentance of tears blurring the note in smudges and the restraint of tears cutting the note in pieces, the historical form is rendered less definitive. If the text is flawed (in pieces by her ripping it up, in smudges by her blurring it up), then the fixed "shields" emerge permeable. Both the torn and tear-strewn letter "rework" the circulation of the note so that its "usual" and determining form is called into question. If the writer can no longer depend on the univocal because reality proliferates, then solids might suggest the alternative spaces of "less legible meaning."

The oxymoronic habit (in "evoking," "practicing," and "tearing") returns (in its repetitions of assent and denial) the exhilarating likenesses of "as" to their beginnings in the bodily groundings of "of":

> It is not in the premise that reality
> Is a solid. It may be a shade that traverses
> A dust, a force that traverses a shade. (pp. 488–89)

Stevens's force resonates with the remembrance of the past (the "shade" as ghost, haunting back) and the premonition of the future (the shade as out-line, stretching forward). But it also includes the representationally "forgot-ten"—the tiny dust and the vague shade—which, gathering strength as they pierce through the "outer shield," recast the "inner men" in the image of the repressed woman. Her flowing tears suggest another pool for Nar-cissus in the womb of his watery origin. Her cutting tears dismantle the discourse altogether, shattering the form. In the process of traversing each other, "dust" and "shade" undo the order of first and last and so revise the history of Genesis 2. What if the woman writing came first?[20] Would her sadness encourage her to blur the differences textuality promotes? Would her change of heart transform the text altogether, scattering the signs so that the original form is too diffused to cast its imperialist shadow on the future? Such "traversings" of chronological order suggest that "said words" (p. 474) may no longer be "the life of the world" (p. 474). They can be con-founded: first, by the conscious decision to retract them, evidenced by the torn, scattered, and finally discarded shards; or, second, by the overflowing remorse of hindsight, represented by the smudged, and tear-stained, anamorphic blur.

Beyond "An Ordinary Evening" and into a New Dawn Song

At the very end of "An Ordinary Evening in New Haven," Stevens imag-ines the possibilities of revising the forms of desire, positing scenarios in which a woman cancels the circulatory trajectory or, alternatively, blurs the words so that the "said" appears less definitive. In a still later poem, "The World as Meditation," Stevens follows the implicit command of canto XXXI to read for the "less legible meanings" (p. 488) of a woman's mind and to look for meanings repressed behind the "outer shields" (p. 488) of the forms and formulae of his poetic. There he evokes the aftermath of a war fought over a woman's body and celebrates the possibility that a woman might reverse her objectification in the Petrarchan poem to imagine a man into being.[21] The sub-genre he revises is the *aubade*, dating from the troubadour *aube*, where the desire for desire, usually expressed by a male poet through a woman's voice, adds a nostalgic dimension to the Petrarchan lyric, rendering the wooing stage before consummation more appealing than the ruing stage of the morning after. As Gale Sigal puts it, "the lady complains that she has literally been turned from prized to despised."[22] What the lady misses in a dawn song, like John Donne's "Breake of Day," is what she had before she yielded.

The nostalgia of the sub-genre is for the main Petrarchan genre: a form of "déjà-woo" all over again. But since, in its usual incarnations, it is a male poet who invents the woman who vents her spleen over her lost desirability, she turns out to want what the male poet wanted all along: his words. When male poets ventriloquize the woman's complaint, they voice their own desire for an earlier vocabulary.[23] But when Stevens writes a different *aubade* in "The World as Meditation," he quietly unsettles what Judith Butler calls "the articulated norms that govern the sphere of cultural intelligibility."[24] In this poem, he leaves behind the Lacanian void of "So-and-So," where the woman mirrors the poet's desire to retreat into his own "idea" and the Kleinian debilitations of "Auroras," where the poet projects his destructive impulses onto the woman who avenges him. Rewriting the Petrarchan poetic by allowing it to "founder on its own founding laws" (*Antigone's Claim*, p. 82), he turns the vague "space" of Petrarchan "ideas" into the "solidity" of natural "things," as he evokes "the little reds / Not often realized" (*Collected Poems*, p. 488).

In this dawn song, he portrays a woman who wants "nothing [her lover] could not bring her by coming alone" (p. 521). Expecting "no fetchings"— no come-hither words or things to corroborate his desire—the Penelope of "The World as Meditation" needs only Ulysses's presence to validate the past. Symbolic rememberment is achieved in this poem by a belief in what D. W. Winnicott calls "the interplay between the personal psychic reality and the experience of control of actual objects."[25] Penelope recreates the potential space activated by her union with Ulysses in the past into the actual space of her current realistic position. She is able to achieve such a return because her meditation binds her to natural occurrences and "actual objects" outside her private domain. That connection allows her to extend her observation of the day's return in the sun and spring's return in the leaves into a confidence that Ulysses will come home. The poem describes how Penelope's anticipation of recovery stems from her memory of an originary union. When Stevens writes a different dawn song in "The World as Meditation," he alludes to the past of secure ties, abandoning the signature psychological imago of Petrarchan loss and opting for, what I will suggest is, a Winnicottian stability over the "bottomless sight" (*Collected Poems*, p. 488) of his earlier work.[26] Penelope's firmness is matched by material commitment, a repetition that (like the body of Echo) is elemented by sound.

The pattern of renewal determines the rhythm of the poem as Penelope's circle is mirrored in the recurrences of day and of year:

> The trees had been mended, as an essential exercise
> In an inhuman meditation larger than her own.
> No winds like dogs watched over her at night. (p. 521)

Penelope's meditation is met by the "inhuman meditation" that presides over the ebb and flow of the universe but that fits outside her like a glove to her hand. Her weaving or "mending" parallels seasonal renewal in terms of artistic enterprise. Like the philosopher's practicing scales on a piano in "An Ordinary Evening in New Haven," Penelope's ravelling and unravelling, mounting and surmounting preserves the essential footage. In Stevens's "Meditation," temporal expansion includes growth: "the trees had been mended as an inhuman meditation larger than her own." Mind beat is recorded in heart beat, image merges with sound, and Narcissus reverts to Echo:

> She wanted nothing he could not bring her by coming alone.
> She wanted no fetchings. His arms would be her necklace
> And her belt, the final fortune of their desire.
>
> But was it Ulysses? Or was it only the warmth of the sun
> On her pillow? The thought kept beating in her like her heart.
> The two kept beating together. It was only day. (p. 521)

In her rejection of "fetchings," Penelope recasts art in bodily terms even as she turns Petrarchan sublimation into material form. As art (necklace), the arms adorn the self. As body, the arms double the self, providing an upper torso mirror (she inside, he outside) to a lower body union (he inside, she outside). The chiasmus of arms as necklace and belt as body cements the union here, as, in the next stanzas, mind and heart follow the same configuration, inverting and so supporting each other. The Winicottian holding space is doubled in Penelope's anticipation and preparation. When Ulysses returns, "his arms would be her necklace." When Penelope waits, her jeweled waist signals the luminescence of her bodily receptivity and comfort: "her belt, the final fortune of their desire." The putting on of the necklace is reversed in the predicted taking off of the belt, the "final fortune" of fate simultaneously the absence of materiality in desire and the presence of physicality in the bodily necklace.

The visual pattern of repetition in the mirrors precedes the vocal pattern of repetition in the naming:

> She would talk a little to herself as she combed her hair,
> Repeating his name with its patient syllables,
> Never forgetting him that kept coming constantly so near. (p. 521)

By naming him, Penelope evokes Ulysses. Her constancy transfers epithets that describe *her* ("Patient Penelope") to *him* ("patient syllables"). Her repetition both reincarnates the past and refigures its personae. "Never forgetting him that kept coming constantly so near" situates the faith of constancy as the origin of consistency. Memory itself conjures up the future.

The act of combing is an imaginative representation, as the hair takes shape, and an act of unravelling, as the hair is detangled. Combing implies its own undoing, as day precedes its own un-daying. In combing and uncombing her hair, Penelope follows the pattern of construction and reconstruction that is established in the poem. Penelope imagines the sun and envisions it, as she renders Ulysses both the *doppelganger* of Apollo and the self she names. As namer, she in turn emerges the Apollonian source of her world. The circles within circles of this poem operate not as a means of assimilation or absorption of like by like. Instead they form a shelter in order maternally to protect rather than poetically to usurp or assimilate the other. Ulysses's duplication does not erase either the sun or Penelope. He is, instead, strengthened by the mutual rhythms of both. In her meditation, Penelope integrates the "déjà-woo" of Petrarchan imagination with the déjà-vu of elegiac memory. But instead of becoming the source of a cynical repetition (how boring, we have been there before), her meditation uses the past as a sign that recovery is possible (how exciting, we can be there again). For the disembodied pleasure of poetic sublimation, the past emerges the source of erotic stimulation.

Like day and night, spring and winter, Ulysses "keeps coming constantly so near." If the worldly instruments of return (the woof, the comb, the planet) enable reincarnation, so the mental instrument of meditation becomes the tool that turns the immaterial into the material. Mind and heart beat together. In "So-and-So," all "things" similarly revert to "ideas," as the poet renders the real woman "forgotten" in her material reality and then "forgets that forgetting" when he conceals the violative nature of his introjected generativity. He retains her as his "idea." Penelope's familiarity suggests excitement, a diachronic expectation that connects the heart beat of experience to the mind beat of thought and thereby links memory to anticipation.

The poem's question at the opening—"Is it Ulysses?"—is both answered and rephrased in the process of the poem—"It was Ulysses and it was not." Since the time passing in the poem follows the time passing in the day, imminence emerges a felt experience that anticipates its own re-experientiality. If, like the sun, Ulysses keeps coming, then, like the sun, he will keep coming again: "so near." Nearness is at once a temporal and spatial indicator, denoting an almost completed act and an almost congruent space, *near upon* as a particular time, and *near upon*, as a reasonable likeness. Simultaneously metaphor and metonomy, Stevens's "nearness" is close in approximate resemblance and incomplete as missed connection. Since it never suggests absolute occupation, it is never fully over and never totally embodied. Its memory includes expectation, the excitement of heart beat. Its emptiness prepares for a fullness still to come, the constancy of heart beat. The poem therefore reopens its orbit, encircling its potential within its own experience, coming and going at once. In noting that Penelope "talks a little," the narrator records her traffic in the voice lane without speaking for her. In her circular repetitions, Penelope rewrites—by living again—the past so that it she can project the imagined possibility.

The name itself encircles desire, as naming becomes both the word that abides—"patient syllables"—and the sound it approximates. ULYSSES (YOU LIS[T] SEES) is what "you *want* [to] see," if "list" retains its medieval sense of desire. Her repetitions embody leaning, listening, and cataloguing as she chronicles her desire and dedicates the desired as the image of her longing. In naming Ulysses, with its "patient syllables," Penelope composes him in terms of the "constancy" she wants to believe. That naming, in turn, positions her as what he wants to see. Ulysses "keeps coming constantly so near." The act of calling, like the act of combing, becomes a repetition that both unravels and reconstructs, a pulling apart and a putting together that assumes a stable center. Her repetition names the object of her desire and thereby brings the object inward, into meditative reality.[27] In naming Ulysses, Penelope situates desire (and its absent presence) as part of a larger framework that centralizes renewal. Like her, the world both knows what it wants to see—spring and day—and acts to produce the objects—leaves and the sun—that will incarnate that desire. In doubling rhythm, Stevens opens the "spaces" to make room for a reconfiguration of "solids." With word and image synchronized, such materializations suggest that the woman's thought might substantiate and so herald the rearticulation Stevens sought to entertain in the "hall harridan" of "Auroras" and to reconfigure in the "tearing up" of "An Ordinary Evening."

In "The World as Meditation," Penelope revives what she has stored in memory. Like the winter leaves that are mended in the course of the poem, that vivification makes possible the restoration at the end. "Repeating his name," Penelope renders Ulysses her only narrative, as she makes sure she "never forget[s]." When Stevens reshapes the *aubade* and chooses as his story a myth based not on the denial of desire but on the return home (from war) of the remembered, he writes a postwar poem that implicitly challenges the narrative exclusions of his own work as well as that of his European predecessors. Reshaping the poetic, he renders "never forget" as a watch word and so counters the inexorability of foreclosure. In "never forgetting him that kept coming constantly so near," Penelope imagines an alternative to the limit of the inaccessible Lacanian object that involves the deferral of never realizing. In Penelope's "never forgetting," the "never" does not refer forward to an impossible future but backward to something already experienced and corroborated by memory. Through the approximations of "nearness," Penelope undoes the self-justifying circles of lyric desire, proffering the affirmations of "constant" coming for the eternalizing stillness of Petrarchan denial.[28]

Like Stevens, Lowell and Rich also rewrite the *aubade* by animating the stabilizing function of the other. In "The Downlook" of *Day by Day*, Lowell imagines a woman who sustains male sexuality and in the "Epilogue" of that book, he renders the generative woman the source from whom the poet "steals" in order to break down the rigid boundaries of Petrarchan forms. In "For a Friend in Travail" of *An Atlas of the Difficult World*, Rich stands at the cusp of day to soften the break of the dawn song with an air of expectancy. In her revision, she departs both from the ventriloquism of the traditional aubade and the mind-reading of Stevens's variation. She simply asks a question that presupposes an other who will answer. In the futurity of that expectation, she enters the other into what Butler calls "the discourse of intelligibility" (*Antigone's Claim*, p. 82) that augurs an "aberrant, unprecedented future" (*Antigone's Claim*, p. 82). All three poets ground their Petrarchan re-formations in the beginnings heralded by the dawn song, returning to the Petrarchan landscape and the infinite future of a responsive Laura-Eve. But that future can be envisioned only after they work through, as Stevens does in "Auroras of Autumn" and "An Ordinary Evening in New Haven," the difficult terrain of their own desire for the language of desire.

Chapter 4 ∽

"INFINITE MISCHIEF":
ROBERT LOWELL'S FICTION OF
DESIRE IN *THE DOLPHIN*

"You can say anything in a poem—if you place it properly."
　　　　　　　　—Robert Lowell, as remembered by Frank Bidart[1]

Like Wallace Stevens in stanza XII of "An Ordinary Evening in New Haven"—with his flying statues and newspapers—Robert Lowell resorts to a surrealistic anti-logic to characterize the inexorability of poetic love. In the 1972 *The Dolphin*, Lowell strategically "places" himself as a poet devoured by his own appetite: "the insatiable fiction of desire" (p. 35). He is overwhelmed by an historically laden form (the culturally predetermined and deindividualizing fantasy of Petrarchism) and victimized by a never satisfied and self-consuming sexuality (what Shakespeare calls the "perjured . . . extreme[s]"[2] of carnality). In the sonnet series at the middle of the book, "*Winter and London*," and one at the end of the book, "*Flight to New York*," Lowell puts into practice the strange emanations of lyric desire he defined in the "Afterthought" of his 1970 *Notebook*.

First, he crams everything into one image through the contortions of "unrealism" (a word he substituted for the "surrealism"[3] of the 1969 *Notebook*). The 1970 version, with its detractive impulse—an "un"doing rather than the "sur"feit of the earlier edition—sets the stage for his immediate contradiction as he spreads everything thin and lets the whole picture fizzle out into the vagueness of anamorphism:

> I lean heavily to the rational, but am devoted to unrealism. An unrealist must not say, "The man entered a house," but, "The man entered a police-whistle," or "Seasick with marital happiness, the wife plunges her eyes in her husband swimming like vagueness on the grass."[4]

Unrealism suggests a Volkswagon-clown compactness, as if, playing a game with himself, Lowell speculated: "Let's see how many selves can be stuffed into a single vehicle and how much history—both cultural and personal—can be condensed in one allusion." Anamorphism pulls apart the tightly woven structure, as Lowell turns around yet again, to play still another game: "Let's turn the compressions of unrealism into the spaciness that points to a Lacanian 'lesion, a locus of pain.'"[5]

In its "themes and gigantism" (*Notebook*, 1970, p. 263), the sonnet provides a form for Lowell to incorporate both the diffusions of anamorphism and the density of unrealism. "A poet can be intelligent and on to what he does," Lowell writes in the "Afterthought" (p. 263), casting himself as an aerialist on the tightrope of the oxymoron. But he immediately contradicts the sense of control by juxtaposing forgetfulness with learning: "and yet he walks, half-balmy and over-armored—caught by his amnesia, ignorance and education" (1970, p. 263).[6] Lowell's definitions are themselves oxymoronic, revealing the self as simultaneously pathetically vulnerable and menacingly protective. "Over-armored," he is both too defensive and too much in love (excessively amorous). Confessing an essential irresponsibility and detachment—a "balminess"—at the core, Lowell finds himself at home in Petrarchan impasse.

Lowell's unrealism plays itself out through enclosures that jettison the repressed past onto the present scene, its distortions calling attention to surrealistic and "balmy" expressiveness, its compressions betraying a narrow and fixated desire. The compressions work oxymoronically in the spatial dimension, fusing covert feeling with blatant expression, ocean and land, man and woman. Any man literally can enter a house but what man can fit in a police-whistle? On the temporal level, his images spell out the disaster that was there from the start, pulling down the houses of Lowell's own marriages. His definition of unrealism intertwines the bizarre—the man in the police-whistle—and the psychological—the wife's directedness, the husband's vagueness. The wife not only controls the husband by fixing him in her gaze; she also turns the tables on poetic objectification and forces him to see what she feels, rendering him (like her) seasick. If what she sees initially is he and he makes her sick, then the infection will spread backward as, plunging her eyes in his head, she will both transfer her malaise to him and will no longer have to see him at all. Inside him, she can look elsewhere or anywhere. The gaze is hers, as she both eliminates him from the scene and becomes the source of his vision. Does the sharpness of the wife's eyes precipitate her husband's contrasting haziness? Or is he hovering—in apprehension—waiting for her to plunge into him—in overwhelming waveness—and so give him her sense of direction? Christ can walk on water but can man swim on grass? The only way such repositioning can occur is to cast the temporal result of an experience as a spatial preamble to it. In the first example (substituting the man's entrance into a police-whistle for his entrance into a house) the literally imaginable dissolves into its consequence and takes into account the repressed internal conflict, placing it at the representational forefront, out in the open for the whole reading neighborhood to see.

With such reversals, initiating acts immediately become incendiary. By entering a house, the symbol of domesticity, the man splits the cultural nucleus. Marriage and the homing instinct won't work. The police will have to be called. Violence is the end result of familial constructs. In the second image, the human psychological interior superimposes itself on the visible natural exterior. Lowell's English *marital* suggests *maritime* in the way that the amniotic fluid of *la mère* (mother) fuses with the watery origins of *la mer* (ocean) in French. Wife becomes mother as husband floats in vagueness (waveness) and thereby retreats to his prenatal origins. Sea-sick, the wife anticipates the nausea of pregnancy. She is "sick" of her generativity and sickened by the husband who would turn her into the mother of his child. Lowell's image of marriage in unrealism is regressive, as the overbearing wife becomes her husband's possessive mother and, in a switch of Kleinian introspection, enters him. Her fluids render him helpless—back to a gestational amorphousness—and subject to her dominating vision. He sees through her eyes as she pushes him back to a primal dependency even as she hesitates to mother yet another child.

In the second series of images, Lowell turns from the compressions of unrealism to the deconstructions of anamorphism, as Lyotard defines it:

> The play of two imbricated spaces forms the principle of the anamorphic picture: what is recognizable in one space is not recognizable in the other. The good form of representation is deconstructed by bad forms: the skull in Holbein's picture.[7]

The anamorphic picture destabilizes what we think we see. One image unsettles another, causing us to reimagine everything we have just thought or read. If self-consciousness means a certain objectification, then the anomorphism of *The Dolphin* lies in Lowell's repeated presentation of his self as the "bad form," the self who breeds death. As the skull does in Holbein's "The Ambassadors" (the most famous anamorphic painting), the demonic in Lowell's work starts unravelling what seems to be a solidified image even before its representation takes hold. The anamorphic shadow picture loosens the Petrarchan construct, breaking down the very boundaries (between self and other, past and present) on which the poetic builds. In *The Dolphin,* Lowell sets two families against each other, eroding all impulses toward comedy. In turn, he distorts the love poem sequence out of which his poetics evolve. The comic marriage plot falls apart in unrealism. Nothing remains stable. The mother is empty. The Petrarchan story is blown up in the anamorphic image. Nothing was there from the start. The other remains inaccessible.

The two visual constructs (one image enlarging itself in the zaniness of unrealism, the other image effacing itself in the haziness of anamorphism) prove dangerous to culture and family. While Lowell confesses that "perhaps [he] plotted too freely with [his] life" (p. 78), his friends did not exonerate him. They urged him not to publish the book. Elizabeth Bishop, for example, tells Lowell in a letter that she has no doubts that *The Dolphin* is "wonderful poetry." But, she warns, its "abuse" is its "mixing of [what Thomas Hardy called] fact and fiction in unknown proportions. Infinite mischief [Hardy wrote] would lie in that."[8] *Dolphin*'s "infinite mischief" extends beyond Lowell's mixing of Lizzie's words and Caroline's situation with his own; it applies to the way Lowell fuses his personal love story with the most troubling events of his time.[9] Posing as a World War II victim (Holocaust Jew) in the London poems, and Cold War victim (about to be exploded by a [metaphoric] nuclear submarine) in the New York poems, Lowell includes Petrarchism as part of the cultural machinery implicated in the twentieth-century horrors he cites. Lowell's "mischief" is double edged. The biographies chronicle how—in his manic phases—his grandiose ravings were often Hitlerian or Napoleanic.[10] But in *The Dolphin,* his self-aggrandizement turns him into the *victim* of those forces, even as his "self-incrimination" (p. 76) identifies him as the mechanism that instinctively presses those forces into play.[11]

His gender mischief—becoming the woman by speaking in her voice—creates the abyss of a social mischief that reveals itself as murderous. In the London poems, Lowell suggests that a poetic that objectifies women is part of a culture that excises Jews and similarly a part of a nature that annihilates what seems out of place or excessive. Lowell's gender crossings are not just examples of playful transvestitism; they're aimed at upsetting the cultural constructs he inherits. In the New York poems, Lowell plays the innocent woman and her abductor until—in the last sonnet—he claims to be the device that will blow up woman, city, and poem. The "gaping jaws" (p. 77) of the shark perpetrator in the New York poems absorb the little fish

Lowell becomes when he casts himself as victim in the London poems. ("Wash me white as the sole I ate last night," p. 45.) Lowell's name for those displaced outsiders changes in the course of the London poems: from fish, to woman; to mastodon; to Jew. In the New York poems, the outsiders are respectively: Lowell's third wife (Caroline Blackwell); the mythical Pluto; and all of Europe. In both series, all "*others*" are randomly fed into the same voracious abyss. And Lowell seems to find no reason not to play all those excessed others. *Dolphin* doesn't just expose his second wife, Elizabeth Hardwick and daughter, Harriet Lowell. It takes on the entire question of poetry after Auschwitz and in the nuclear age:

London	*New York*
Woman=Jew=Mastadon	Lowell=Pluto[nium]=Kore
poetry=fascism=nature	**poetry=nuclear fission=self**

When Lowell turns Petrarchism inside out and undoes its gender assumptions, he recovers something already present in the original that anticipates the horrifying variant (or anamorphic counter) he himself supplies.

In *The Dolphin*, Lowell records "flashbacks to what [he] remember[s] and fables inspired by impulse" (*Notebook*, p. 263). Taken together, history and fiction produce the curiously "insatiable" circle. The flashbacks work off cultural memory to make all of the past Lowell's own story and the fables impinge on the contemporary situation to render real people subject to Lowell's fantastic invention.[12] The political and poetic image-maker descend from the same sources. The random impulse turns into the historically demonic tool. If Lowell is an unreliable narrator, it is partly because life itself is so changeable, his "flashbacks" subject to the instability of memory, his "impulses," to the momentariness of whim. In the "Afterthought" of *Notebook*, Lowell argues that his metaphors feed off of lived experience. "The true unreal is about something and eats from the abundance of reality" (*Notebook*, 1970, p. 262). In the oxymoron of "the true unreal," the fable fattens itself on the cornucopia of history simultaneously as it nibbles away at the truth to make reality less certain. Its virtual insatiability grabs up everything, rendering reality itself virtual. Its spinning weaves the flashback into the fabric of the present where history seems fabulous again. Culminating in the "nuclear and protective" (p. 77) mother at the end of the book, the oxymoronic habit connects the historically repressed failures (of mothers and lovers) to real and potential deaths, in the genocide of the London series, and the impending explosions of nuclear buildup in the New York poems.

When Lowell gets fed up with the phantasmagoria he creates, he introduces the anamorphic image that demolishes the edifice he has just constructed and changes the players he has just introduced. Lowell's unrealism is encyclopedic in its allusiveness. Lowell's anamorphism is deadening in its cynicism. Unrealism is savage in what it consumes. Anamorphism starves the consuming self. Functioning through unrealism, the New York and London series present mythical, cultural, and theoretical images that emerge at once dazzling and destructive. Functioning through anamorphism, each series projects the alternative Lauras Petrarch wrote into the *Rime sparse* to deconstruct that mythos as well. "Unrealism" appropriates the past to apply it to Lowell's situation. His images find new uses for old texts. Anamorphism retrieves the past postmodernly to recover what was abjected from the very beginning.

As part of the mythic vortex of unrealism, all Lowell's wives and lovers in *The Dolphin* intersect with three over-lapping stories: Orpheus and Eurydice; Medusa and Perseus; and Diana and Actaeon. The snake that bites Eurydice ("will the worm turn and sting her victor heel," p. 39) reflects both female associations—"the gorgon arousing the serpents in her hair" (p. 42)—and male ties. The poet refers to his serpentine presence: "my tan and green backscales were cool to the touch" (p. 18) and later calls Caroline a "Rough Slitherer in your grotto of haphazard" (p. 37). Finally, he retracts his snake: "I lack manhood to finish the fishing trip" (p. 37) as if he were the beheaded Medusa, the castrated victim of a Freudian Perseus. Lowell begins as a version of Actaeon—"a green hunter . . . / groping for trout in the private river" (p. 18)—and ends up the violated Diana to Caroline's instrusive Actaeon—"her witness bugles to my dubious shade" (p. 39). The Actaeon-hunter-Lowell sports a "new brass bugle slung on his invisible baldric" (p. 18). When Caroline plays Actaeon, the orally intrusive bugle is recast as an ocularly exaggerated projection: Caroline's "bulge eyes" (p. 35). The play continues until bulge and bugle merge in her *globular* (p. 60), pregnant, belly. Caroline's stomach protruberance is phallic in its excess. The expectant woman—carrying the boy child—equals the impregnating male and his bulging parts. "The wife plunges her eyes in her husband" (*Notebook*, 1970, p. 262). By contrast, Caroline's "*bel occhi grandi*" (p. 36) diminish to "just eyes" (p. 36) and expand to excessive "ball-eyes" (p. 55): Giacometti's wedge and ball. As the gazing Actaeon, Caroline undoes her own beauty, exposing it to a critique it cannot outface. Petrarchan compliments melt into Lowellian grotesqueries, linking surrealistic extravagance to its opposite, anamorphic abstraction. Too much becomes too little. In Lowell's work, Narcissus melts into Echo.

As part of the cultural vortex of unrealism, Lowell follows and often overturns three Shakespearean tragedies and a dark comedy. Safe inside Caroline's London flat, he reverses the charitable Lear on the heath ("the crude and homeless wet is windowed out," p. 16); for the victimized king offering to protect the windowless destitute, Lowell substitutes a self who is satisfied to keep Lear's houseless at bay. Hamlet in familial agony becomes a cursing child: "I feel how Hamlet, stuck with the Revenge Play / his father wrote him, went scatological / under this clotted London sky" (p. 49). The whole London series short circuits the circulating blood ties (of families and race) into an end-stopped disaster. Nothing flows. The ghost of the past haunts the streets, jamming the arteries in traffic, stopping the forward impulse with anterior—and primal—sin. Macbeth fighting vacillation signals Lowell's procrastination. *"If it were done, twere well it were done quickly"* (p. 53). Turning himself into a trammeling Macbeth spurring on his own Hamlet, Lowell's reaction to his tragic exaggeration is to describe his entrance as an exit: "I come on walking off-stage backwards" (p. 53). Like Lear in the fool's quip, he ends up, in *"Winter and London,"* making his daughter his mother. But the Shakespearean play that centralizes Lowell's anxieties in the London series is *The Merchant of Venice*. Identifying with the avenging Shylock, Lowell raises the specter of anti-semitism in the European context and aligns himself with its cultural victims.

As part of the theoretical vortex of unrealism, the London poems refer to Sigmund Freud's *Moses and Monotheism*, the New York poems, to Ford Maddox Ford's *The Good Soldier*. Each book has at its base a necessary extinction and a ritual murder. And, from each book, Lowell acquires his position as victim of political and social forces. In the London sequence, Lowell ends up the detritus of life's hard seas and a cruel family ("a body washed up lifeless on the shore," p. 46). Harriet renders him a donkey and pins him in her tale. How can the racial cleansing of the Holocaust not be seen as the poet's desire to wipe out his family, to trade in New York (with Lizzie and Harriet) for London (and Caroline's children)? In the New York sequence, Lizzie's scathing question, "why don't you lose yourself / and write a play about the fall of Japan?" (p. 79) does him in again. How can the fall of Japan not be seen as the Hiroshima of the poet's confessed destructive devices? In both cases, he is defeated by the annihilating familial critic who demands that he find an altogether different poetic.

Both inspiring books similarly play with established myths. *Moses and*

Monotheism posits two Moseses, one who was Egyptian and another who was not, to argue, finally, for an arrogant Jewry who killed the father and then denied their role in the conspiracy. If the Moses story doubles the plot of the Bible, *The Good Soldier* reverses and doubles the plot of the Petrarchan poem. With Freud, Lowell casts himself in the good form, as victim of a Jew-hating culture, and then presents a worse form, the admission that the Jew and the self retaliate against the culture that frames them. In the New York poems, Lowell spins out an abyss with Lizzie as active artist, Lowell as passive artifact, in a scenario whose anamorphic image threatens the cozy family. Both series of poems underscore Lowell's strategic indeterminacy.

The Good Soldier doubles Petrarch by multiplying loves and stories. Lowell extends into his own life the "triangle" of Ford's *Saddest Story* (p. 74), where the hero, Edward, is chased by two women and the chase is doubled as one woman (Florence) dies and is replaced by another (Nancy). All the characters become interchangeable "shuttlecocks":

> And she repeated the word "shuttle cocks" three times. I know what was passing in her mind, for Leonora has told me that, once, the poor girl said that she felt like a shuttlecock being tossed backward and forward between the violent personality of Edward and his wife. Leonora, she said, was always trying to deliver her over to Edward and Edward tacitly considered that those two women used *him* like a shuttlecock. Or rather, he said that they sent him backward and forward like a blooming parcel that someone didn't want to pay the postage on. And Leonora also imagined that Edward and Nancy picked her up and threw her down as suited their purely vagrant moods. And there you have the pretty picture . . . and to think it all means nothing—that it is a picture without a meaning.[13]

Lowell's unrealism settles in the self-canceling image that wipes out what Ford calls the "pretty picture." Each wife becomes part of a circular game and the image dwindles into "a picture without a meaning." Lowell whimsically plays favorites, as he includes himself in the circulating game: "tossed back and forth." In the New York poems, Lowell takes on the woman's part, shuttling, via airplane, between wives and cities, pushed around by all of them, until, near the end, Lizzie suggests a different script altogether. But, finally, Lowell comes first.[14]

In the London poems, Lowell becomes the "Jew" (p. 46). Like Freud in exile and Moses in the desert, he is the useless relic, eaten by the children he fathers. Central to *Moses and Monotheism* is a cannibalism that indicts the Hebrew nation:

The brothers who had been driven out and lived together in a community clubbed together, overcame the father and—according to the custom of those times—all partook of his body. This cannibalism need not shock us, it survived into far later times. . . . That is to say, they not merely hated and feared their father, but also honoured him as an example to follow; in fact, each son wanted to place himself in his father's position. The cannibalistic act thus becomes comprehensible as an attempt to assume one's identification with the father by incorporating part of him.[15]

Moses and Monotheism is Freud at his most Kleinian. Cannibalism is introjection taken literally. And, in his London poems, Lowell follows the practice of Freud's book. Child-eaten father, Lowell invents a serial innocence for himself in London, first linking himself to Freud, the Jew in exile, then (in the end) contrasting himself as futile effigy to Freud's surviving statue (p. 46). Readying him for the devouring flames, Harriet places herself "in [her] father's position," rendering him Isaac to her Abraham, Lear to his daughter. In the first five poems, Lowell devours Father Freud and then becomes, with him, the exiled Jew. He is reduced, liquidated, and prepared for sacrifice. Freud's book is a narrowing down in the face of Holocaust extinction, to say that the world is killing its kings. Lowell's London sequence is a narrowing down in self-mockery to say that the world is killing its poets. If Freud actually says the unspeakable (that, by denying their cannibalism, the Jews set themselves up to be eaten), Lowell implies that his victimization is similarly self-imposed: he is the intrusive Actaeon to his daughter's avenging Diana; he is the raped Medusa to the culture's Perseus.

As poems that function through anamorphism, the London and New York series undo Petrarchism by following Petrarch's own deconstructions of the primary *Rime sparse* pairing where Laura is Daphne, the object of poetic pursuit, and Petrarch is Apollo, the poet who turns his loss into an excuse for a poem. In *The Dolphin*, Daphne is played by Caroline Blackwell. But in a book presumably written at the height of his relationship with Caroline, Lowell insists on giving both former and present *inamoratae* a chance to play some version of Laura. Even Lowell's first wife, Jean Stafford, makes a cameo appearance. *The Dolphin* introduces two alternative Lauras found in the *Rime sparse*: (1) Laura as Mercury or woman who puts down Petrarch (as she does in *Rime sparse* 23) by defining her own configuration. In the London poems, the role of Laura-Mercury is played by Lowell's daughter, Harriet. In the New York poems, Lizzie gets that part; (2) Laura-Medusa who, avenging her violation (as she does in *Rime sparse*

179, 197, and 366) becomes a violator herself. Reversing genders, Lowell gives the Medusa role to himself. No one is left out of Lowell's Perarchan gaming. Lowell finds a part in the play for all of his women, and even masquerades as one himself.

The Times of London: *Child-Changed Father*

The images in poems 1–5 of the London series follow a pattern of unrealism that is expansionary. The poet fattens himself by nibbling away at all excesses. Those in poem 6 create instead a pattern of anamorphism that dissolves the encyclopedic self. First, Lowell parallels the cannibalism of *Moses and Monotheism*. When Freud reiterates the Christian argument about Jewish pride contributing to, and fanning the flames of, anti-semitism ("they will not admit that they killed god," p. 216), he condemns accuser and accused and betrays his own racial ambivalence. As *Moses and Monotheism* reflects doubts about Freud's Jewish forebears, so *Dolphin* seems uncomfortable with Lowell's poetic ancestors. Freud revives the image of the Jew as father-murderer; Lowell recovers the image of the poet as silencer of female voice. In his textual revisionism, Freud reassesses the biblical tradition; Lowell disowns his Petrarchan inheritance. Both writers probe something in the canon that was there from the very inception. *What was there* in Judaism for Freud is a Jewish self-aggrandizer. The sons eat the father in "an attempt to assume [their] identification with [him] by incorporating part of him" (*Moses and Monotheism*, p. 216). Read through unrealism, the god-devourer in Freud undermines the Jewish ascendancy. Read through unrealism, Lowell's Medusa appears as the rival of Athena. *What was there* in Petrarchism for Lowell is a female avenger. Redefining victimization, Lowell plays the Medusa that Petrarch describes in *Rime sparse* 366. First he is a female fish. Then he is a Shylock whose own words place him in the subject position of the helpless woman. Finally, he is an animal species excessed out of life. As fish and Jew, he is an unwilling partner to male aggression; as mastodon, he plays a male who isn't male enough.

If Shakespeare renders the two merchants (Antonio and Shylock) mirrors of each other, so Lowell becomes the mirroring subject of his poems. In play and poem, those equations are dynamized through what Hélène Cixous calls "an incessant process of [Medusan] exchange," where one image crosses over into the "living boundaries of the other."[16] The myths wrap around each other as each side rushes to preempt (and so defuse) the monster it mirrors. Through the same process, in the hall of mirrors that allows Lowell to become fish, woman, Jew, and Medusa, the London poems reiterate the mythic crossings Shylock projects in *The Merchant of Venice*. To contend with the Venetians, Shylock must become them, just as, to defeat Medusa, Perseus must mirror her. He kills the monster with her own image, and then (in subsequent battles) uses the image (again by wearing it) to kill other alleged monsters. In presenting Athena with the decapitated monster for her aegis, he forces her to acknowledge her resemblance to Medusa, thus recapitulating an earlier likeness which, in some versions of the myth, causes Athena to cast the spell that rendered Medusa snaky in the first place.[17] Lowell's unrealism echoes Shakespeare who, in turn, reflects Greek and Roman mythography.

And he begins the first five poems by representing himself first as fish to be eaten and then as woman to be objectified in the male trap. Even in those guises, he resembles Shylock who, in the "hath not a Jew eyes" speech of 3.1.46–66, places himself in the female subject position: "if you prick us do we not bleed?"[18] By poem 3, Lowell is fish and fisherman. First, comparing himself to the fish, he reclaims his victimization and innocence: "white as the sole I ate last night." Then, as fisherman, he inveighs against the pesty sole who gets what he asked for. Poem 3 moves into poem 4 through two parenthetical clauses that bespeak opposite world views. Retreating backward from the present tense of an affirmative God who "sees all" to the unavailing God who hears nothing ("the heavens were very short of hearing then"), Lowell shifts from a notion that purity is possible in the sole's whiteness to a feeling that nothing can be washed clean once it has been "splashed red," labeled for extermination. Like Shylock, he links victimization to retaliation:

> God sees—
> wash me as white as the sole I ate last night,
> acre of whiteness, back of Folkestone sand,
> cooked and skinned and white—the heart appeased.
> Soles live in depth, see not, spend not . . . eat;
> their souls are camouflaged to die in dishes,
> flat on their backs, the posture of forgiveness—
> squinch-eyes, bubbles of bloodshot worldliness,
> unable ever to turn the other cheek—
> at sea, they bite like fleas whatever we toss.
>
> *Mastodon*
>
> They splashed red on the Jews about to be killed,
> then ploughed them back and forth in captured tanks;

the wood was stacked, the chainsaw went on buzzing.
In the best of worlds, the jailors follow the jailed.
In some final bog, the mastodon,
curled tusks raised like trumpets to the sky,
sunk to their hips and armpits in red mud,
splashed red for irreversible liquidation—
the heavens were very short of hearing then.
The price of freedom is displacing facts:
Gnashed tusk, bulk-bruised bulk and a red splash.
Good narrative is cutting down description;
nature sacrifices heightening
for the inevitable closing line. (p. 45)

The prayer for innocence in poem 3 includes what Freud, in *Moses and Monotheism,* calls the "return of the repressed" (p. 125). Lowell is first the white sole he ate "last night" and then the bait-tosser waiting for the biting fish: "the jailors follow the jailed" (p. 45). Finally, however, he moves into another story: that of irreversible liquidation. Reduced to a "red splash," the Jew of the third poem and the mastodon Lowell introduces in the fourth are doomed—trapped (like soles) by their own appetites: "At sea [the soles] bite like fleas whatever we toss."

But when he retaliates, Lowell picks up something from the Medusa myth that is even more devastating than the fact that she avenges Perseus. In some versions of the myth, Medusa is also a double for Athena. The resemblance prepares for the retaliation. Lowell turns the victim into the avenger. Emerging from an initial wound is not just an innocent child but a monster. The poet-victim sets himself up as the poet-destroyer. Springing from his invention is the child, who, in turn, reinvents him. In the London poems, Lowell's audacious displays of unrealism emerge through a process of similar compressions. First he molds himself in the image of the Jew and then turns on the culture that declared the Jew the enemy. "Good narrative is cutting down description." If description heightens difference, Lowell's so-called "good narrative" eliminates the other he first defines: fish=mastodon=Jew. In the hall of mirrors Shylock creates in *The Merchant of Venice,* the other becomes the self. "Better[ing] the instruction" (3.1.66), Shylock raises the stakes. Bettering Shylock, Lowell moves from fish to Jew to mastodon, casting Nazi and nature as the same other-destroying force. Like Shylock, Lowell is "unable ever to turn the other cheek" (p. 45), bound on the cycle of revenge that leads him to assert that the Jew is both god murderer and avenger. Naked and passive, he is also the woman whose "soul is camouflaged" (p. 45), hidden by the male cook who presents her as a dish to be consumed by the male reader in the circulation of the text. Like Shylock, Lowell conflates Jew and woman. Lowell's condensed version of the Shylock revenge speech ("to bait fish withal," 3.1.46) places him in the position of Jewish avenger. He is the sole that "bites." Victimized, he becomes, like Shylock, the Medusa. As sole, Lowell is "bait[ed]" so that, even though he bites, he is nevertheless trapped, caught at the mouth, leaving blood on the waters and identified by his own "red splash."

The lines of Jews "splashed red" in their ploughed graves merge with the mastodons stuck in the mud. Who is up to "their arms"—four legged mastodons or Jews turned into animals by their Nazi victimizers? Liquidation—the word for economic bankruptcy—is also the symptom of the bodily confusion in the mass graves of the Second World War, as "nature sacrifices heightening / for the inevitable closing line" (p. 45). All victims are similarly animalized just as, in the end, Lowell's daughter turns him into the four-legged donkey. In poems 3 and 4, Lowell surfaces: as fish (passive victim of a womanizing male cook); as Jew (female victim of the imperious male Nazi); and third, as male animal (target of a cruel and castrating nature). His logic therefore renders cook, Nazis, and nature equal victimizers. The systematic annihilation of the Jews by the Nazis is equated with nature's Darwinian elimination of a species. The fittest survive. Nazis emerge, like the cook, part of a natural and rapacious cycle. The white purity of the ocean sole yields to incarnadined seas. Woman victim in poem 3, Jewish victim in poem 4, Lowell takes his place "in line." Finally, however, Lowell acknowledges his complicity with the "killing machine."

"In the best of worlds, the jailors follow the jailed." The mastodons bugle their own downfall as their "raised trumpets" conflate Actaeon with Diana to herald the extinction of an entire mythology. The Jews "splashed red" and the mastodon "splashed red" are singled out and whittled down. Identified by their signifying marker, the victims are reduced to that marker. The "red splash" is the last remaining sign before total erasure:

> gnashed tusk, bulk-bruised bulk and a red splash.
> Good narrative is cutting down description;
> nature sacrifices heightening
> for the inevitable closing line. (p. 45)

The resolution and reversal of the twice repeated verb and adverb—"splashed red"—into the noun and adjective—"red splash"—typifies unrealism as it intensifies the conflation. Lowell looks at soles, Jews, and mastodons, and finds himself in their trap. The "red splash" is the only trace of the "bruised hulk." Jew and mastodon are equalized by their fate. Fish becomes Jew; Jew becomes mastodon. Liquifying punishment produces the liquidated victim who, in turn, is signified by his punishment. Like Diana's splashing in the Actaeon myth, that victimization becomes the signal that initiates cannibalizing. The flesh-eating dogs follow. If the mastodon analogy connects the Jews' extinction to a natural design, the reversal of the "red splash" links art to nature. As equalizing marker, the "red splash" is also the emblem of dehumanization. Holocaust Jews lose their individual identities as they become the same target for the firing squad. "Splash[ing them] red," the Nazis reduce them to their punishment: "the red splash." Remembered by their death, they seem to have had no life. Lost in the massification of their slaughter, they vanish in the minimalism of the executioner's economy. The "red splash" is the sensational story the mass murders make. What is left is only art at the end of poem 4, as nature's stop-at-nothing plan edges toward art's "inevitable closing line." Lowell mirrors Freud who—in turn—admits that he descends from god-eating cannibals. Lowell eats Freud, but—in the end—joins him in the executioner's line. As writer whose "inevitable closing line" works toward the elimination of anything extra, Lowell's own desire to clean out his poem, to condense the "gigantism" ("Afterthought," *Notebook*, 1970, p. 263) of his themes in the minimalism of the sonnet, mimics ethnic cleansing and natural evolution: "Good narrative is cutting down description." The true story of what happened in the War is equated with the fictional story in the "splash" of "good narrative." Harriet, finally, confirms Lowell's victimization, as he becomes Battus to her Mercury. The story teller is bested by another tale: "*M. de Maupassant va s'animaliser*" (p. 46).

Lowell's implied riddle—"what's black and white and red/read all over?"—becomes in the sixth poem his daughter's newspaper cartoon. In the last poem of the series, anamorphism takes over and unpacks the condensations of unrealism. The first five poems cast the poet, along with nature, as the line maker who draws women into the posture of forgiveness; in the sixth poem, the unforgiving child "doodles," both pens and spawns, the father into mocked being. In the picture drawn by his daughter, Lowell's mastodon punishment is already muddied. No longer the red splash, he is drier and returned to the sepia dust of caricature. The remaindered mastodon is remanded to foolish donkey in his child's party game. Her anamorphic image displaces his lines:

> On this blank page no worse, not yet defiled
> by my inspiration running black in type,

I see your sepia donkey laugh at me,
Harriet's doodle, me in effigy,
my passport photo to America
that enflames the soul and irritates the eye—
M. de Maupassant va s'animaliser. (p. 46)

In the mockery of Harriet's donkey, all writers are *defilers.* They reduce everything to a black line or a blank nothing. Turning people into lines, they
render them into objects. When Lowell runs black in type, he overruns and
hence liquidates everything. Form erases content. Newsprint preempts
good narrative as image replaces word. When Jews become mastodons and
when men become animals (*"M. de Maupassant va s'animaliser"*), animals
turn "to things" (as Lowell writes in "Plotted," p. 49).

Objectified by his daughter, Lowell is her "play-thing." Turning Lowell
into her image, Harriet becomes yet another woman Petrarch imagined,
the Laura-Mercury of *Rime-sparse* 23. Harriet pins the tell-tale tail on the
donkey of her father. In the Battus story of 23, the anamorphic image of
a creative Laura is a retaliation for the physical decreation Petrarch first
enacts on her, just as Harriet turns poetry into parody in her drawing. The
lines of buried Jews waiting for the grass to grow over the mass graves, like
the lines of Lowell's poetry not yet written, merge in the sepia image of
the effigy that is a cartoon version of the stony monument in the Battus
story. In the London poems, Harriet arises as Laura-Mercury to her father's
Petrarch.

Harriet's doodle, simultaneously a spontaneous scrawl and a cock's crow,
calls attention to her figure writing over his. The female design produces a
silly male voice: doodle inverts the rooster's cock-a-doodle. The white page
becomes a palimpset, as Lowell "walks on stage backwards" (p. 53) and
allows his daughter to emerge his artistic father. She brings him into being
as effigy: a body washed up lifeless (like Shylock's dead fish) on shore. In
the end, however, the palimpset makes way for the palindrome as Lowell
rewrites and doubles the experience. The anamorphic image of Harriet's
doodle heralds the woman artist and a totally different story. Harriet's effigy
finally separates Lowell from Freud. Freud got his statue; Lowell is written
out as cartoon figure. Nothing survives the new script. As Laura-Medusa,
Lowell turns the mirror on himself. As Laura-Mercury, Harriet suggests a
totally different art. Remanded to blank page, Lowell is excluded from the
rank and file of his daughter's new order. Anamorphism replaces unrealism
and so wipes out the poet.

"Flight to New York": *Mothering the Self*

In the New York poems, anamorphism similarly annuls Lowell when Lizzie turns on him and discounts the entire Petrarchan edifice with her suggestion that Lowell find a totally different poetic: "why don't you lose yourself / and write a play about the fall of Japan?" (p. 77). When she urges Lowell to abandon Western culture with its burden of lyric sentimentalism, Lizzie plays Laura-Mercury to Lowell's Battus, urging him to write a history totally divorced from his divorcing. But, since Lowell is the exploding nuclear device ("like a submarine," p. 77), Japan's fall becomes Lowell's responsibility. In the logic of Lowell's confession, the end of Western culture is brought about by the mechanisms of that culture and Lowell is the mechanic who brings down the world. With its twelve poems for London's six, the New York sequence doubles the number of mythological characters. The poems introduce Persephone and her Pluto as well as Medusa and Perseus. This time the mirroring even pulls in Narcissus. Lowell turns against Caroline and sex in the first eleven poems and against himself and poetry in the last one. While Lowell's method in the series is to pull back to an earlier time in his life, Lowell also reverts (in the last poem) to an earlier generation, naming himself the maternal originator of the disruptive "shadow of departure" (p. 77).

The concluding lines bring on a second anamorphic image, one that undoes even Lizzie. It's as if the last sonnet does everything twice. In that doubling, Lowell insists that he is the demonic mother who comes before, and so discounts, everyone. Finally Lowell turns against all the families and all the marriages he celebrates in New York. Threatening the Christmas warmth is a wintry discontent:

> We are at home and warm,
> as if we had escaped the gaping jaws—
> underneath us like a submarine,
> nuclear and protective like a mother,
> swims the true shark, the shadow of departure. (p. 77)

Submerged in the contented family lies its original deconstructor. Lowell comes back uncannily to emerge the child-eating mother. The "shadow of departure" turns the water into a reflective mirror simultaneously as it raises questions about its own origin. If Departure is the shadow, who is the original? Is the body Departure personified, something in the present self that exists as the image of destruction? Or, is the body—Departure—something external—like Pluto—waiting to snatch Persephone? Is the shadow reflective of Caroline Blackwell at the other side of the ocean casting a long-tentacled menace? Or is it the narcissistic Lowell, standing at the brink and doubled in his restlessness?

At the very moment that the domestic triad seems most comfortable in Christmas tranquility, Lowell suggests that the interior spatial position is an anterior temporal one. Athena is Medusa. Inside us, the submarine is part of the self. Before us, the submarine is mother to the self. As shadow, the other is inward: nuclear-genetic-origin. As shadow, the other is death: nuclear-explosive-fission. The future has a prior being, a mother. And that prior being returns to a time early enough to eliminate both Caroline and Lizzie as Lowell feeds the shark with his own wives. Lowell emerges Pluto to the Persephone he has been playing all along. In the London poems, Lowell is a belated victim: woman, Jew, Mastodon. As line maker, he takes his place in line: the jailor follows the jailed. In the New York poems, Lowell emerges the first victimizer, steadily replacing Caroline in the triad and then swallowing Lizzie and Harriet as well. Lowell's habit in the New York poems is to revert to a previous epoch. He avenges Caroline by returning to New York and his former family. He superannuates Lizzie by trading her in for his own mother. Finally, his mother, too, gets locked out, as Lowell mothers himself.

Lowell's "gaping jaws" are an underwater equivalent to Andrew Marvell's "slow-chapt" bird at the end of "To his Coy Mistress":

And now, like am'rous birds of prey,
Rather at once our time devour,
Then languish in his slow-chapt pow'r.[19]

But the concluding lines of Lowell's New York poems turn Marvell's airborne carnivores to an underwater predator:

We are at home and warm,
as if we had escaped the gaping jaws—
underneath us like a submarine. (p. 77)

The internal rhyme of "escaped" and "gaping" links Petrarchan gossip, with its sexual obsessions, to visual objectification and its appropriative habits. Marvell's "slow-chapt" mouth becomes Lowell's sharp-eyed revelation, "gaping" a visual act that renders the physical "escape" a mere illusion. Lowell's mouth widens to tell, violating the family's privacy by exposing its secrets and allowing the reading world to "gape" in open-mouth wonder at what Lowell reveals. But, while Marvell's birds are diachronically pitched against the lovers so that the poet can impel their rescue, Lowell's underwater menace ticks away, like Captain Hook's crocodile, in a world where neither Peter Pan nor sex is of any avail. A cross between Narcissus as spy and Neptune as predator, the lurking shark in the water renders the self-loving poet and violating monster identical. In returning to the originating myths behind the poetic, Lowell acknowledges that the danger he depicts in the shadow of departure pre-existed his arrival. Nostalgia for earlier inconsolability is pointless because the impending rupture contradicts the eternalizing impulse of the poem. Why does the poet compare the smasher of all forms—the nuclear submarine—to the bearer of all forms—the mother? Is "nuclear and protective" an oxymoron that categorizes all mothers as Medeas, all protection a sham? Or, in his desire to usurp maternal generativity, and (in Melanie Klein's terms) claim all origination as his own, is the poet the "true shark" as the phallic, determining, and flesh devouring "I" of the poem?

Speaking to issues of global annihilation, not just the death of the poet but the end of the world, the two similes that refine Lowell's oxymoron— "nuclear and protective"—still further— *"like a mother, like a submarine"*— simultaneously suggest an insular and self-nurturing family and the lurking umbrella of the mushroom cloud. The maternal impulse to fold in at the center with the nuclear family is split open by the patriarchal intrusiveness of a disruptive desire. In connecting departing mother to restless lover, Lowell's oxymorons point to the psychological basis of Petrarchan poetics and its fixation on absence. Infantile separation anxiety merges with romantic loss. His sonnet therefore turns the usual subject of the *aubade,* a vanishing recent past—here today, gone tomorrow—into a psychological quest for an unretrieveable earlier closeness—going today, gone yesterday. The lover who turns away *now* is the mother who was unavailing *then.* Worse still is the thought that behind the castrating mother ("underneath us") is, finally, a self who might take down the whole world. In their anteriority and resemblance to Marvell's slow-chapped birds, the gaping jaws "underneath" also suggest an underwater version of the "sharp-shinned" hawk in Lowell's 1962 essay on William Carlos Williams.

The essay, which starts off as a tribute to Williams, ends up by demonstrating how Lowell devours Williams, just as he threatens to engulf all the women—Lizzie, Jean, and Harriet—who populate the New York poems. Lowell's anteriority in the New York poems systematically eliminates all present competitors as he emerges, in the penultimate poem, the mother who eats all his creations. In the Williams essay, his habit of erasing the near past destroys the rival poet. As predatory bird, the hawk remains:

> When I think about writing on Dr. Williams, I feel a chaos of thoughts and images, images cracking open to admit a thought, thoughts dragging their roots for the soil of an image. . . . An image held my mind during these moments and kept returning—an old-fashioned New England cottage freshly painted white. The house . . . came from the time when I was a child, still unable to read, and living in the small town of Barnstable on Cape Cod. Inside the house was a bird book with an old stiff and steely engraving of a sharp-shinned hawk. The hawk's legs had a reddish brown buffalo fuzz on them; behind was the blue sky, bare and abstracted from the world. In the present, pinpricks of rain were falling on everything I could see, and even on the white house in my mind, but the hawk's picture, being indoors I suppose, was more or less spared. Since I saw the picture of the hawk, the pinpricks of rain have gone on, half the people I once knew are dead, half the people I now know were then unborn, and I have learned to read.
>
> An image of a white house with a blotch on it—this is perhaps the start of a Williams poem.[20]

The "stabbing detail" of the hawk intensifies the penetrating impact, as the initial image widens to a flood and then narrows into a condensation, the pointed reminder of death. Deep inside, the extinct hawk comes alive as the center of the abyss to which new life eventually yields. The older image absorbs the newer one, thereby annihilating it. In the last poem of the New York series, Lowell reverts to a nuclear past, as the core of life reveals its explosive potential. In the beginning is the bomb. In the Williams essay, Lowell's central image is a bird-beast-buffalo, a predator already (like the mastodon of the London poems) extinct. Safe inside the early house, it remains protected from the waters of change. Gray sky becomes blue and thereby crystallizes the hawk in triumphant Apollonian sun. In the beginning sits Lowell. Like the shark in *The Dolphin*, the hawk hovers, waiting to strike.

In the Williams essay, Lowell gives way to writing about himself, making his own past so present that Williams himself fades, and we are left with a book in which Williams never could have existed, one that refers back to a time when Lowell was a child "still unable to read" (*Collected Prose*, p. 37). In the child's imagistic world, Williams never was. Lowell seems to have preceded him. The soil and roots of the Williams poem were already planted in Lowell's head. Following the logic of that abyss, Williams is in a sense unnecessary. The child Lowell preempts him and writes the potential Williams poem before Williams even wrote it. The circle of enclosures that begins with Lowell's memory moves steadily inward—inside the house, inside the past, inside the book. But the center of all those inwardnesses is Lowell's self. In the same way, the shark at the end of the New York poems suggests that Caroline and the shadow of departure were implicated in all Lowell's marriages: inside the very inside is the image-making mother who devours what she spawns. Like Williams, neither Caroline nor Lizzie need exist. Lowell is mother to his wives and mother to other poets. Like Stevens's "thing as idea," all "others" revert to Lowell's generative mind. The word is preceded by the image as—in *The Dolphin*—the poet's gaze precedes his lines. The "shadow of Departure" reflects his own menacing instability.

If Lowell returns at the end of the New York poems to a time so early in chronology that he eliminates Lizzie and Harriet by naming Departure his own mother, he begins the series by calling the more recent past into question. He first excludes Caroline. In poem 8, the New York poems suggest that, like Ford Maddox Ford, Lowell turns the Petrarchan dyad into a triad. The thrice repeated "threes"—wives, space, writers—refer to another past, crowding Caroline out. The New York poems are clubby, homey, cozy. There's no room for the newest wife when Lowell takes her place in the circle:

> complaisantly on the phone with
> my three wives, as if three-dimensional space were my breath—
> three writers, none New Yorkers, had their great years there. (p. 76).

Crossing gender boundaries, he becomes the gossipy woman shunning the newcomer from the group. First there are "three wives," Jean, Lizzie, Caroline. Then there are three writers, Jean, Lizzie, Bobby. The "three writers" close out the third wife as Lowell brings in Jean Stafford to make the triad literary rather than libidinal. Writers replace wives as the imagining body stands in for the desiring body and "three-dimensional space" is reduced to Lowell's "breathy" word. The New York poems flesh out an artistic abyss. Lowell pulls his first wife into the group of "three writers" and then takes Caroline's place in the triad.

The triangle does away with the London vision altogether, moving back to an anteriority where Caroline never was. In the London poems, the currency of the newspaper lines wipes out the past, replacing it with the anamorphic opposite: Harriet's donkey, a cartoon effigy for commemorative statue. In the New York poems, the poetic past moves still further backward as Lowell recovers an earlier past: "through the thirty years / to the New York of Jean Stafford, Pearl Harbor, the Church" (p. 76). The European war of the London poems is replaced by the American war, as former "onslaughts" (p. 76) are remembered. Pearl Harbor outlasts Belsen in the poet's consciousness. There is no Caroline. There were no Jews. Three-dimensional space allows only for the "brea[d]th" and depth of Lowell's pre-Caroline past.

In poem 11, Lowell constructs yet another triangle with himself in the middle: "We have no choice—we, I, they? . . ." (p. 77). This last triangle can only be understood by following Lowell's habit of becoming the woman in the preceding poems. If all the parts of a triangle are equal, then the "geometrical romance" (p. 73) implies that the "we" of the pair, the "I" of the self and the "they" of the other are all the same. By poem 6, the reborn Lowell of the first poem acquires the gender position of the woman eager to be unwrapped:

> I come like someone naked in my raincoat,
> but only a girl is naked in a raincoat. (p. 74)

Poem 7 begins with the question that ties the girl in *Death and the Maiden* to death as her abductor. She seeks Pluto and darkness instead of an earthly husband and life: "Did the girl in *Death and the Maiden* fear marriage?" (p. 75) But the image is complicated as male and female images merge to fuse Persephone's narcissus with the Kore herself. Addressing Lizzie and remembering Maine, Lowell writes:

> One morning we saw something, half weed, half wildflower,
> rise from the only thruhole in the barn floor—
> It had this chance in a hundred to survive.
> We knew that it was someone in disguise,
> a silly good person . . . thin, pealnosed, intruding
> the green girl who doesn't know how to leave a room. (p. 75)

The intruder in the barn is not Pluto reaching beyond but the green girl who becomes the narcissus Persephone sought. The voyeuristic scene— Lowell and Lizzie watching the green girl, and the green girl intruding on them—merges Persephone with Pluto. If she doesn't know how to leave a room, neither does he. She is he, the protruder, as he is she—the intruder watching him watching her. It's Lowell who can't leave the room, backing away from London to New York, and, from New York, reverting to London, in a series of regressions that leave him trapped. Outside him is the place where Lowell can see, and not see, himself. Thus the green girl appears like a green boy "rising [phallically] from the . . . thruhole." Walking on stage backward, her function is disruptive.

If the intruder is Lowell, then it's he who fears marriage. But which marriage? If he is the Kore, then he is guilty, as he says in poem 9, of narcissism or "self seeking tenderness" (p. 76). The reflective mirror turns him into pupil of his own history lesson. He watches himself watching himself. Roberto Calasso describes the way in which the Persephone myth and the Narcissus myth meet:

> Kore looked at the yellow "prodigy" of the narcissus. . . . Narcissus is also the name of a young man who lost himself looking at himself.
>
> Kore, the pupil, was thus on a threshold. She was on the brink of meeting a gaze in which she would have seen herself. She was stretching out her hand to pluck that gaze. But Hades burst upon the scene. And Kore was plucked away by Hades. For a moment, Kore's eye had to turn away from the narcissus and meet Hades' eye. The pupil of the Pupil was met by another pupil, in which it saw itself. And that pupil belonged to the world of the invisible.[21]

When, in poem 8, Lowell looks at it all with a "yellow eye" (p. 75), he speaks through the image of Narcissus, remembering his own greenness ("when I came here ten or twenty years ago," p.75). The green water boy becomes the yellow flower. Jaundice is close to green, yellow touching on green in sickness, just as the live Christmas tree sinks into its "acrid" (sick-yellow, p. 77) rind in poem 11. In the Calasso passage, Persephone sees herself as Pluto. He is what she wants. When everything is a signifier, "the world of the invisible" becomes interchangeable with our own. The victim self yields to the victimizer in the self. And, when Lowell plays the woman's part, he emerges Persephone, green girl reflected in yellow flower. His Narcissus fuses with Persephone's Echo, as everything is sucked back into the vortex where Lowell plays Pluto.

In poem 12, the colors are primary but move toward the blackness and sepias of the London series. The poem begins with yet another scene, a reviewing of what was already observed: déjà-vu. But the second sight is projected, not recollected. Lowell merges the anticipated brightness of the sky (bluer days will come) with an expected darkness of mood. The blues of depression will inevitably arrive. Lowell has seen all this before:

> The tedium and déjà-vu of home
> make me love it; bluer days will come

and acclimatize the Christmas gifts:
redwood bear, lemon-egg shampoo, home-movie-
projector, a fat book, sunrise-red, inscribed
to me by Lizzie, "Why don't you lose yourself
and write a play about the fall of Japan?"
Slight spirits of birds, light burdens, no grave duty
to seem universally sociable
and polite. . . . (p. 77)

The certainty that bluer days will follow turns the haziness of déjà-vu into the sharpened edge of predicted unhappiness. Manic depression takes its expected course. When "the bluer days to come" will "acclimatize the Christmas gifts," they will make them part of the self and similarly tedious. As *defilers* (p. 46), the inky lines in the last London poem parallel the lines of Jews and mastodons even as they threaten to desecrate everything and undo the line maker as well as the line. Similarly here, the anticipated *acclimatization* suggests both a perpetuation of the family group and the artificiality of the scene. The acclimatizing is natural—a way of getting used to something. It simply suggests another triangle—the bear, the shampoo, the projector—to put into the abyss machine. The acclimatizing is also unnnatural—Lizzie imposes an Eastern theme as Harriet had suggested the donkey effigy. Lizzie's message about seeking a new mythology in the East speaks to her role as author of a new self and Lowell emerges Petrarch-Battus to her inscription. The red sun of Japanese mythologies replaces the yellow sun of Apollonian song. Lizzie initiates a different cycle as inscriber of Lowell's self. In fact, it is Lizzie who suggests the image that prompts Lowell's representation of himself as nuclear monster. But Lowell retaliates this time with a totally other mother—the shadow of departure—as he brings in, once more, another fish story. Unrealism returns to anamorphism in this poem. Lowell mothers his own restlessness and therefore renders himself as the undoer of Lizzie and Caroline.

The London poems center on World War II; the New York poems move on to the Cold War period. But, like the London poems, the New York poems return to the same cultural history. Because of the association with Narcissus, Kore, Demeter, Pluto, Medusa, and Perseus, the shadow keeps moving inward. Mother is self, giving birth to its own reflection. As in the London poems, metaphor is doubled (*like* a mother, *like* a submarine) but then gives way to metamorphosis. The mother merges with the Plutonian abductor. As internal mother, the true shark suggests that the "shadow of departure" is not the seductive other, but the demon in the self, *fore*shadowing what, in the London poems, Lowell calls "the inevitable closing line" (p. 45). Through such closure, the London poems merge a Jew-hating culture with a cannibalistic nature and a woman-destroying poetry. In the New York poems, the inevitability of the shark—as shadow self duplicating the "I," as shadow self ejecting the "I"—implies that the origin of the anamorphic image is the poet himself. Lowell emerges as Stevens's "child of a mother fierce / in his own body" (*Collected Poems,* p. 321). If Caroline is Lowell's shadow self, and if the Kore is Pluto in the same way that Medusa is Perseus and Shylock is Antonio, then the anamorphic image is part of the design that reveals the designing self. The poet carves the other in his own self-seeking image only to name her the maternal source of his being.

With the mirror of Narcissus in the New York poems and the mirror of Medusa in the London poems, the signifying culture is at once indicted by, and emblazoned in, the poem. In *The Dolphin*, Lowell's unrealism projects dizzying reversals that allow his poems to "say anything." His anamorphism similarly invites him to *be* anything, as he eats away at the comfortable picture of "abundant" reality to reveal the devouring shark underneath. Lowell's over-armored self counters his overly loving self. In his self protection, he is also dangerous, his armor a weapon, his habit of doubling—wives, family homes—covering over the half-balmy self at the core. In the end, he is nuclear mother to his own deformations, as he realizes his desire to detach, in balminess, from the very ties he most wants. His "overarmoring" and "ignorance" ("Afterthought," *Notebook,* 1970, p. 262) are triggered by the same oxymoronic pressures. In *The Dolphin,* "the insatiable fiction of desire" renders him ultimately defenseless against the "over-amorous" appeal of the Petrarchan plot.

Chapter 5 ∽

"SOLID WITH YEARNING": LOWELLING AND LAURELING IN *DAY BY DAY*

"The man who keeps the Gorgon becomes the Gorgon."
—Peter Shaffer, *The Gift of the Gorgon.*[1]

Uncrowning the Family Petrarch

Robert Lowell's last book of poems, *Day by Day*, parallels the anamorphism of Sidney Nolan's cover portrait for the July 2, 1967, issue of *Time* magazine. Around Lowell's disembodied head in that portrait is a zig-zagging laurel wreath that looks at any moment as if it might turn into a gauntlet of snakes. At first glance, Lowell appears to be wearing the crown of the American poet laureate. But, from another angle, the disembodied snaky head seems to be that of the Gorgon. It's the look that's disturbing. The portrait bears little resemblance to the kindly, benign Lowell we see in the photographs accompanying the cover story. Inside the magazine, he appears quizzically tenuous, puzzled by all the fuss about him or philosophically gentle, wondering about the nature of existence. The cover uncovers a poet barely suppressing his rage, not just dreamily out of things but potentially a subway bomber, as if he were waiting merely to lift his eyes and turn a nation of *Time* readers to stone. Eyed awry, Nolan's image of *Time*'s anointed Petrarch conflates the poet with Medusa.[2]

The dual possibility of the portrait—Petrarchan laurel or Medusan snake—anticipates the alternatives Lowell fluctuates between in *Day by Day*. Should Lowell accept unchallenged the good form of Petrarchan lyricism he inherits from his European poetic forebears and preserve untarnished the good name of the family pedigree he acquires from his distinguished American ancestors?[3] Or should he be the Medusa to both

FIFTY CENTS   JUNE 2, 1967

TIME

Poetry in an Age of Prose

ROBERT
LOWELL

VOL. 89 NO. 22

Lowells and laurels and expose poetry and family to their own horrors? In the ambivalence toward his poetic and familial inheritance, Lowell picks up something buried in the original laurel story on which *Day by Day* is modeled: Petrarch's *Rime sparse*. In *Rime sparse* 366, Petrarch blames his own wandering eye as much as Medusa's gaze for his stoniness: "Medusa and my error have made me a stone dripping vain moisture" (*Petrarch's Lyric Poems*, p. 582). If the "I" is capable of acting in conjunction with Medusa and if the punishment is petrification, then the "I," like Perseus reflecting the Gorgon image on his shield, is indistinguishable from the monster he deceives. Lowell, the poet laureate, similarly keeps the gift of the Gorgon and becomes her in *Day by Day*.

In *The Dolphin*, Lowell shifts between Medusa, the victim, and Medusa, the avenger, ultimately to argue that one Medusa leads inevitably to the other. History yields to the primal Lowell as he becomes the nuclear mother. In *Day by Day*, Lowell shifts not so much between two selves as between two strongly established predecessors: the family of Lowells and the family of poets. With those moves, he attacks his biological mother by turning her into a poet and his poetical father—Petrarch—by deprivileging the discourse and opening it up to women and realized love. He therefore challenges both Lowells and laurels, playing stone throwing Medusa to his family[4] and deconstructive critic to Petrarchism. Like Stevens and Giacometti, Lowell sees the connection between his amorous adventurism and his familial dependency. His disloyalty to family and poetic works against his future biographers and critics to unhinge their certainty that *Day by Day* chronicles Lowell's farewell to Caroline Blackwell in a final flourish of masculine sexuality. It also represents a prime example of Lowell's Petrarchan revision, a regendering brought to full fruition in the last section.

If the *Rime sparse* are Petrarch's daily transcript of his love (one poem for each day of the year, plus leap year), Lowell's *Day by Day* is a miniature version of the poetic record, one that offers both homage and challenge to the tradition. In part III of *Day by Day*, Lowell's "antics" (p. 125)[5] allow him to play the woman's part as he emerges Daphne in the Petrarchan complex, articulates the female *aubade*, abandons the Petrarchan sun, and appends the female moon as his symbol. In turn, Lowell's women correspondingly play Petrarch to his Laura in "Unwanted," Eve to his Adam in "The Downlook" and "The Day," and origin of his poem in "Epilogue." In "Unwanted," Lowell fuses the Oedipal plot with the Petrarchan plot in terms of a generational split. His mother is denying Laura to his pursuing Petrarch. But then, in the same poem, he turns his biological mother into his objectifying Petrarchan father. She invents him (the way Petrarch did Laura) as a corollary to her narcissistic desire. In "The Day" and "The Downlook," Lowell writes against the grain of Petrarchan poetry—in which the woman is Daphne—denying the poet—and the poet is Apollo—pursuing the woman—to convert the tradition, as Petrarch himself occasionally does in the *Rime sparse*, into a poetic celebrating successful love. In "The Day," he represents the beloved as Eve to his Adam, just as Petrarch does in *Rime sparse* 181 and 188. In "The Downlook," Lowell doubles for the Petrarch of *Rime sparse* 237. Like Petrarch in that poem, he outdoes Adam and turns to the Endymion-Selene myth, reversing the tradition yet again with his configurations of a woman who actively initiates love and a self who passively accepts it. Finally, in "Epilogue," he contracts both myths and reverses their order, as the "girl" in the unnamed Vermeer painting[6] emerges Apollo and Adam, pulling the sun into her centralizing lap and drawing the poet into her originating self. Lowell's split with conventional Petrarchism works both through his portrayal of the woman as desiring other and his suggestion that the self-cancellations of the oxymoron might be transformed into self-stabilizing additions.

When he changes the presumed formula of the love poem and assumes the female subject position, Lowell unhinges the order of the family poem. Dredging up the past, and using material from prose he had written during his Payne Whitney confinement in 1954, the Lowell of "Unwanted" superimposes several histories over his present situation, rendering his images anamorphic. In back of the life story he presents in "Unwanted" is an earlier text, that of his mother's history. Lowell works in much the same way as Judith Butler does when she connects the interpretation of texts to the interpellation of gender by fusing family and its inherited pressures with language and its determining powers:

> Consider the medical interpellation which (the recent emergence of the sonogram notwithstanding) shifts an infant from an "it" to a "she" or a "he," and in that naming the girl is "girled," brought into the domain of language and kinship through the interpellation of gender. But that "girling" of the girl does not end there. On the contrary, the founding interpellation is reiterated by various authorities and throughout various intervals of time to reenforce or contest this naturalized effect. The naming is at once the setting of a boundary and also the repeated inculcation of a norm.[7]

What Butler says about "girling" can be also said about Lowelling. In his poetry, Lowell "contests the naturalized effect" of "it's a Lowell," both on the expectations of poem and family. In "Unwanted," he imagines himself as his mother and then allows his mother to play him. He thereby loosens the boundaries and opens the "norm" of family and poem, producing a counter-cultural "unnnatural" effect. He causes a parallel havoc in the love poems by imagining (in "The Downlook," "The Day," and "Epilogue") the desired woman of the Petrarchan complex as the desiring self.

Lowell's *Day by Day* anamorphism expands the technique of unrealism he defines in the "Afterthought" of the second edition of *Notebook* and plays out in *The Dolphin*. In *Notebook,* Lowell reverses images so that results and preliminaries merge. In *The Dolphin*, unrealism casts all the players as Lowell, artists of some sort or another. In *Day by Day*, he reverses players, so that the same game, the same genre, acquires still another perspective. "Contesting [a] naturalized effect" of the self in the anamorphism of *Day by Day*, Lowell similarly "contests" preconceptions of the image as he reworks "unrealism" with yet another twist, turning the sexual dynamics of "Afterthought" into a generational split, a habit he had already evidenced in *The Notebook*'s "Five Dreams" sequence. There, he introduces in poetic form the prose images he will extend and turn upside down in "Afterthought." In the "unrealism" of "Afterthought," the sexual battle begins with the sad end of the love plot: "a man enters a police whistle." In "Five Dreams," it reverts to a family story (pp. 41–43), as Lowell becomes Orestes to his father's Agamemnon and his mother's Clytemnestra. In "Agamemnon," he blows the whistle on his parents: "Can I call the police against my own family?" Lowell plays "Afterthought" and "The House of Argos" against each other as slight linguistic shifts change the meaning entirely. A prefix here, or a noun there, precipitate cataclysmic alterations of perspective.[8] In "The House in Argos," *unhappiness* substitutes for the *happiness* of "Afterthought":

"Afterthought," *Notebook,* 1970[9]

"The man entered a police-whistle," or "Seasick with marital happiness, the wife plunges her eyes in her husband swimming like vagueness on the grass." (p. 262)

"The House of Argos," *Notebook,* 1970

      his mother,
seasick with marital *un*happiness—
she has become the eye of heaven, she hates
her husband swimming like vagueness, like a porpoise,
on the imperial scarlet of the rug . . .
His corpse in the candles is a red gold lion. (p. 42, italics mine)

In "Afterthought," the husband swims outside the house, on the grass. In "The House of Argos," he is totally housebound, trapped by his wife's housekeeping, a bind Lowell reworks with still another turn in the "Unwanted" of *Day by Day*. In the subtle shifts from "Five Dreams" to "Afterthought," Lowell changes places with his father. In the poem, he is the child who watches his mother kill his father. In "Afterthought," he is the husband dominated by his wife. In the "Unwanted" of *Day by Day*, Lowell goes one step further, playing both child and husband to his own mother. In all cases, content and context overflow each other's boundaries. The plot is circular. The source of Clytemnestra's psychic immersion (seasickness) is the inverse of her husband's sexual plunge into her. "Swimming . . . on the imperial scarlet of [her] rug," he is caught in his wife's dominion. She is with him at sea as he retreats back to the embryonic liquidity of his beginnings in his mother who, it turns out, is his wife. She dives into and therefore validates his oceanic regression, emerging the maternal origin of his wishy-washy self. Vagueness—desultory lack of being—becomes waveness—amniotic precursor to being.

In both *Notebook* examples, the unrealism erases the sense of future and past: the after-life of death sounded by the police whistle and its inevitable criminalization of the family; the pre-life unravelling signaled by the immersion and consequential infantalization of the husband. In the unrealism of "Five Dreams," Lowell avenges his mother by stripping away the gold-plated veneer of marriage and by accusing his mother of killing his father, a process he had already begun in *Life Studies*. In "Five Dreams," Lowell's mother is the controlling Apollo to his father's Daphne. She is the sun, "the eye of heaven." As the hapless Daphne running, his father swims vaguely away, a frightened porpoise on the "imperial" scarlet of her rug. Alive, he is a trained fish, a porpoise. Only in death is he lionized. His "corpse in the candles is a red gold lion" (*Notebook*, p. 42). In *Notebook*, Lowell works out the opposition in the interval between poem and commentary. In the "Unwanted" of *Day by Day*, reversals occur *inside* the poem. Playing husband, son, grandfather, and lover, Lowell finally wipes his father out of the picture entirely. Moving across genders and generations, he becomes his mother, doing to her what she did to his father. In "Five Dreams," the generations are stable. In "Unwanted," they are completely overturned, as Mother wants not to be wanted by her husband or her child. Clytemnestra to her husband's Agamemnon, she plays Petrarch to Lowell's Laura, inventing a dynamic in which Lowell replaces his father by mirroring *her* father. In retaliation, Lowell reveals the secrets of his mother's sexual and generational machinations as he switches roles yet again, rendering her unyielding and playing Petrarch to *her* Laura.

Human as I am: Lowelling with Mama

As Medusa, Lowell avenges his mother by turning the mirror around and doubling his victimization. In that configuration, Mother emerges, first, as the violating Pluto in the Ovidian story and, then, the cruelly abandoning parent in the novel plot. If the eternally unavailable becomes the mother, then the eternally unwanted becomes the child. Lowell turns the Lacanian denying lover of the Petrarchan plot into the Kleinian cruel or often missing mother of the Dickensian novel tradition. "Unwanted," he is the abused child of the novel. "Unwanted," he is the scorned lover of the poem. Poor *perdu*, poor lover. The poet "loved what he missed" (p. 121). A Petrarchan chase is thereby initiated. In this poem, Lowell cites "recollections of things [he] did not [literally] see"[10] from his Mother's history as if they were his own. Returning to scenes from "Antebellum Boston," written in 1957, Lowell describes life before he was born: "More and more I began to try to imagine Mother when she was happier, when she had been merely her father's favorite daughter, when she was engaged and unmarried. Perhaps I had been happiest then, too, because I hadn't existed and lived only as an imagined future" (*Collected Prose*, p. 293). In "Antebellum Boston," Lowell works himself back into his mother's past. As "imagined future," he is repressed before he comes into life, ghosted before he was born. His mother's suicidal desires kill him prenatally. In "Unwanted," Lowell similarly pushes "the ever retreating borderlines of being" (*Day by Day*, p. 39) backward to the time of his mother's pregnancy, rendering his biological future the source of his mother's psychic depression. His coming into being fuels his mother's desire not to be.

Fusing the unwanted child with the unwanted lover, Lowell initially stresses his isolation and abandonment. How did Lowell arrive "alone here tonight" in England on an anti-alcoholic drug—Antabuse? To get at his status as lover, Lowell has to go back to his origin as child. His quest is both a search for comfort and a suicide wish:

> surrounded only by iced wine and beer,
> like a sailor dying of thirst on the Atlantic—
> one sip of alcohol might be death,
> death for joy. (p. 121)

The Byronic "death for joy" is also a Byronic desire for excess and risk. One sip will tip the balance and make him sick. To be the thirsty sailor on the Atlantic is also to be the child at the breast, dying of thirst, and the child in the womb, returning to his oceanic origins. As recovered beginning, the amniotic ocean becomes "this tempting leisure" (p. 121). A place where he feels both at ease and at rest, *this* hour reverts spatially to an Eden whose identifying marker is its temporal end, the temptation. It is both regrettably too late for the traditional remedy for loss, and too early for the traditional first cause. By using time as a place, Lowell both recovers his innocence (leisure) and eats the apple (temptation). The world lies ahead as other causes "come jumbling out." His mother never had anything to give: "Mains tenant le vide." The alternative choices renegotiate the issues of mother and child to produce two stories: first, the story of the child abandoned by the mother; then the story of the lover pursuing the mother: "maintenant le vide." Both stories are doubled, as Lowell's vindication renders him Perseus's mirror to his petrifying mother. In turn, she becomes the scorned lover and the abandoned child he initially was. Using her art to get well, he becomes she. Keeping the gift of the Gorgon, Lowell's Perseus switches places with his Medusa-mother. The alternative choices also yield one end: Antabuse, the drug whose use counters abuse but whose cause is a misuse. For sustenance, the poet turns to a false mother who therefore becomes, for her child, the displaced object. She remains not what he regrets having lost but what he never had. Antabuse offers both an anterior use (an ante), providing a totally different past—preceding real beginnings—and an antidote for the past (an anti), countering the burden of abuse with forgetfulness. Soothing pacifier, the drug numbs desire: death for joy or forgetting. Truth serum, the drug allows the autobiography to spill out. Hence, the past is purged.

The poet opens up another history. The end-product of the truth serum is the poor orphan story—the helpless child cast out to sea. The end-product of the lethe story is the poor lover—Petrarch chasing the unavailing Laura. The poem wavers between the desire for art and its forgetfulness, in the evasions that avoid the self, and the insistence on truth in the question that stops the poem: "unwanted before I am?" The temporal unrealism inspiring *Notebook* is present here as Lowell turns the dread of his anticipated birth (writing "unwanted before I am") into the history of his unhappy past (implying "unwanted after I was"). If Antabuse cancels alcoholic forgetting, it also heightens sober remembering. First it brings back the mother as unavailing to the child; then, shifting deferrals, it brings back the child as maternal love object. In both cases, the poem turns to Lowell's mother: in the first, forging a poetics that annuls her power by denying she had anything to give; in the second, with a poetics that meets her power by mirroring her evasiveness.

The central pursuit of the poem is circular: the nurture-seeking child chases the unavailing mother and the narcissistic mother seeks the unmoldable child. In both cases, the love is consuming. The child is absorbed by his desire for what he missed, absented *in* pursuit. Pursued by his mother for what she missed, he is absent *as* pursuit. The telling of self is the story of the undoing of self. The child seeks the mother it cannot get. The mother denies the child she would rather not beget. As lover, he is unwanted, hence evaded. As child, he is unwanted, hence absorbed, taken back to the time when he was only an imagined future. To be loved consumingly as desired object is to be eaten up. To love consumingly as pursuing subject is to be burned out by the fire of desire. When Lowell regenders and contemporizes the Petrarchan quest, he demonstrates how its imagined hierarchies turn back to the failed mother.

The Antabuse opens up the same subject, only this time it goes to the source, returning to a place and time before Lowell was born:

> In 1916
> father on sea-duty, mother with child
> in one house with her affectionate mother-in-law,
> unconsuming, already consumptive . . .
> bromidic to mother . . . Mother,
> I must not blame you for carrying me in you
> on your brisk winter lunges across
> the desperate, refusey Staten Island beaches,
> their good view skyscrapers on Wall Street . . .
> for yearning seaward, far from any home, and saying,
> "I wish I were dead, I wish I were dead." (p. 123)

In the chronology of the poem, Mother's desire to be homeless and lost at sea in the middle of the poem follows Lowell's poetic pleasure "on the Atlantic" at the beginning. But in the retrospect of chronological causes, her desire comes first. Like Lowell plunging through metaphor into the mid-Atlantic, Mother "yearns seaward." Her legacy to her child is the death wish, a desire that separates her from the weaklings, consumptive mother-in-law and ineffectual husband:

> Unforgivable for a mother to tell her child—
> but you wanted me to share your good fortune,

> perhaps by recapturing the disgust of those walks;
> your credulity assumed we survived,
> while weaklings fell with the dead and dying. (p. 123)

On the one hand, Mother creates her child by parthenogenesis as a counter image to the paternal family. On the other hand, Mother passes on to her child—in the telling—her consuming cry. If it is unforgivable for a mother to tell her child of her desire not to be, so is it unforgivable for a child to tell on his mother and expose her as would-be child murderer. In the first half of the poem, Lowell is erased. As unwanted child, he should never have been. In his life, he is his grandfather, returning uncannily as a being he never was. Thus, his mother's desire to remake him is her poem. His mother's desire to undo him is the story Lowell tells. Poor lover, he will never have her. Poor child, she never wanted him.

In the second half of the poem, Lowell widens the anamorphic frame and accepts his dowry. He becomes his mother's mirror image—what she wanted him to be: her and hers. But in that becoming, he exposes her and that is his revenge. The second half of the poem portrays the child as image of the mother. Her lack of confidence is corroborated by his lack of love. Excluded from the circle of desire are the husband and his family:

> That consuming love,
> woman's everlasting *cri de coeur,*
> "When you have a child of your own, you'll know."
> Her dowry for her children . . . (p. 123)

Mother's desire to disappear as material object—"I wish I were dead"—is expressed as a desire to make her image disappear—"I wish my child would never come into the world." The anti-narcissism of the death-wish necessitates the elimination of the reflecting child. But the death-wish is resolved when Mother remakes the child into the image of her father. Mother can cancel her own life if Lowell reflects and so becomes Grandpa Winslow. The dowry, which should be a present for a husband, becomes the gift to her child.

Lowell's revenge in turn is to take away his mother's uniqueness and subjectivity: to make her over into a love object as quest rather than maternal being as source. In the next section, the comparison of mothers to wives classifies all in the same category. Mother is the same as all the others, just not as bright. The twice repeated statement diminishes her importance. She is less than the wives. The way to get even with the mother is to get back at her in kind, to be truth teller and reflector. Equal to the wives, she is yet another in a string of love objects he can, in time, replace. Lowell erases his mother in the same way as the woman is objectified in the conventional Petrarchan poem. As part of the convention, she is measured only in comparison to other women. Of the same co-opted *genus*, she loses her generative genius. Lowell gets back at his mother in two ways: first, he objectifies her as one of his wives and therefore no longer special. Mother is someone he invents; second, he mirrors her, by matching her *cri de coeur* with his screeching. She is simply he:

> She was stupider than my wife . . .
> When I was three months,
> I rocked back and forth howling
> for weeks, for weeks each hour . . .
> Then I found the thing I loved most
> was the anorexia Christ
> swinging on Nellie's gaudy rosary.
> It disapeared, I said nothing,
> but mother saw me poking strips of paper
> down a floor-grate to the central heating.
> "Oh Bobby, do you want to set us on fire?"
> "Yes . . . that's where Jesus is." I smiled. (p. 124)

Echoing mother, the infant rocks back and forth in a continual repetition of the primal sound, going nowhere but to an impossibility that drowns the self: consumption by watery tears, suicide on the Atlantic.

For the toddler, to love the anorexia Christ most is to love self-denial. But it is also to love the fetishistic object of his desire. Like Giacometti's "mains tenant le vide," the thin god mirrors the denying mother. Ungrateful, the child drops her down the grate with the rosary and then renders her what she is to him: the blazing object of desire. Burning for her, he sets her on fire. In this context, the son is both unwanted alive and consumed by his desire to die: self-immolated and, if the house is "on fire," immolating. As the agent provocateur, "poking strips of paper / down a floor grate to the central heating," Lowell is also anti-Christ. He is the cunning snake in the garden, the Iago who masters the mother by projecting his emptiness onto her. Whittling away from little to less, Christ is the apostle of self-consumption. The child repeats the mother. With the second image, the child exceeds the mother. In the last stanza, however, Lowell links himself to her. The one unpardonable sin is "our fear of not being wanted." Why is being the victim—not being wanted—a sin? The answer is decidedly

Kleinian. Out of "*fear* of not being wanted," mother and child invent themselves as Petrarchan lovers, pursuing the unattainable. Out of fear of *being*, mother and son invent themselves as pursued, escaping as unavailing. "Getting well" is thus a form of created victimization: Petrarchism as Kleinian persecutory anxiety. Mother and son live out their lives in compensation for the question that ends the poem:

> Is getting well ever an art,
> or art a way to get well? (p. 124)

Mother's penance for wanting out of the house is to "go on cleaning house," a sublimation that, in turn, renders the house unlivable, that passes on the lack—of a really affectionate nature—by excessively pretending to be *mater familias*. Her art, cleaning house, is a form of revenge. Wanting to get out of the houses of families, she makes them unlivable for her family. She cleans *out* the house, stripping away at the veneer of familial protection. Like Stevens's "it is an illusion that we ever were alive . . . lived in the houses of mothers" ("The Rock," *Collected Poems*, p. 525), Mother Lowell's "unlivable house" demolishes the homing instinct. If art is the recovery instrument, then Lowell's art exposes an absence, a black hole, at the core. Nothing in herself, Mother becomes an image of the poet.

"Near the Unbalanced Aquarium," Lowell's memoir of his 1954 confinement in Payne Whitney hospital, begins with a similar equation between mother and son:

> In my distraction, the walls of the hospital seemed to change shape, like limp white clouds. I thought I saw a hard enameled wedding cake and beside it, holding the blunt silver knife of the ritual, stood the tall white stone bride— my mother. Her wedding appeared now less as a day in the real past than as a photograph. (*Collected Prose*, p. 346)

Unrealism and anamorphism combine in this passage. The hard stone walls of the hospital melt into "limp white clouds" and mother and child first merge with each other in the flesh and then calcify apart from each other. Each remains fixed in isolation. As stone bride, Mother is poised, knife in hand, ready to kill the not-yet-made child, but locked herself in the patriarchal ritual that demands she be an icon of womanhood. In her stoniness, she becomes the traditional statue on the cake but she is clearly next to it, ready to pass bits of herself to the guests who will swallow her: Lowell has the cake and eats it, too. Mother acquiesces to her prison in the ritual, but she wields the knife against the collops who mirrors her. As object of art—stone mother—she anticipates her avenging—stone throwing—son, striking out against the patriarchal institutions that marry her to death. As subject of myth, she is converted by her Medusa-son to the stone bride. His "seeing" demands her petrification even if what he sees is a version of his self. Like Petrarch's error and Medusa, Mother and son are interchangeable. Locked in by reciprocation (Lowell's mother is his self) and opposition (Lowell's mother wields the weapon and so becomes his imprisoner), Mother and son reflect each other, as one is victimized by the other's trap: the alliance that determined Lowell's being. Mother's imprisoning marriage becomes Lowell's strait jacket. Why is *her* wedding not her real past? Why does it become, instead, Lowell's story? Introjected, Mother is merely the signifier of the son who has swallowed her with the cake. Projected, she is knife bearing Medea to her child, eternally locked in her role as Kleinian threat.

In Love with Our Nature: Laureling the Other

The poems of the family result in the simulacrum: child mimics mother in Medusan petrification. The love poems retreat to another beginning—Genesis 2 and the immaculate birth of Eve. In these poems, Lowell is the mother of his lover—Adam to her Eve. With that new role, he recovers the initial joy of Adam's discovery in Eden and rids himself, finally, of the biological trap. Finding "another breathing body in my bed," Lowell repeats the feeling Petrarch evokes in the *Rime sparse* poems where, as Adam waking, he undermines his own poetic with an Eve whose look returns his desire. In "Unwanted," Mother is Laura-Daphne to Lowell's Petrarch-Apollo. There, Lowell places himself in the role of conventional Petrarchan lover and rebels against an unyielding mother either by treating her as his *inamorata* or by eluding her as lover. In "The Downlook," "The Day," and "Epilogue," Lowell strikes out at a dominant poetic by speaking of a reciprocal love. But in that becoming, he subverts the dead-end Petrarchism that fuels "Unwanted" and reiterates Petrarch's subversion of his own poetic in *Rime sparse* 181, 188, 237, and 354. In these poems, Petrarch, at least temporarily, gets Laura. She becomes Eve to his Adam. In the family poems, Lowell strikes out at his biological mother by turning her reluctance to be and to bear him into his own death wish. In "The Downlook" and "The Day," he cuts himself free from his poetic father by picking up on Petrarch's poetic self-doubt, creating an Eve who responds.

The cyclical nature of "The Downlook" parallels that of Petrarch's sestina in 237, the poem where Petrarch bypasses even Adam and Eve and chooses as his mythical counterpart Selene and Endymion. In "The Down-look," Lowell does Petrarch one better. He reverses genders, plays Selene to the beloved's Endymion, and opens by linking himself not to the Apollonian sun but to the retiring monarchy of the full moon who, like Selene in the myth, "looks down" as if to still the sparrows who herald the dawn. That down-look allows the moon to precede the sun both in terms of hierarchical ascendancy and chronological sequence. It reverses the order of sun and moon as well as the male and female parts in the *aubade*. In Lowell's poem, the retirement of sleepiness comes before and so seems to herald the advancement of the waking day just as the woman in the poem stimulates the poet's belief in return. As instrument of waxing and waning, the usually feminized moon anticipates the rebirth of love. In the same way, Lowell's awakening to "find another body breathing in my bed" recalls Adam's initial excitement at discovering Eve. The circularity fuses the fading night with the oncoming day:

> For the last two minutes, the retiring monarchy
> of the full moon looks down on the first chirping sparrows—
> nothing lovelier than waking to find
> another breathing body in my bed . . .
> glowshadow halfcovered with dayclothes like my own,
> caught in my arms. (p. 125)

When the moon "looks down," it looks backward to the future.[11] Retiring as monarchy, it seems to be recalling exactly what the speaker currently enacts. A glimpse of what is past becomes a prologue to what lies ahead, a halfway mark on the border between day and night: "glowshadow halfcovered with dayclothes." The remnants of passion spent are also oxymoronic anticipations of passion renewed. The doubled man and woman of the poem pull toward each other in fused idealization and away from each other in corroborated reality. They are one and separate: Adam dreaming of Eve and Eve confirming Adam. Lowell's recalibrated oxymorons turn the dejection of downlook into the snobbery of disdain. As the lovers outsmart the day, they anticipate the return of reciprocated love. When the moon re-tires, it also puts on the clothes of the next night and anticipates the return of fatigue (in the re-tiring of the next day). Thus dawn heralds its reverse, the love-in-night. It dresses (at-tires) and undresses to redress (retire once more) the passionate self. "Halfcovered with dayclothes," both lovers hover between the preceding night and the coming day, somewhere in the interspace between the original light (glow, as lingering luminosity) and the still unformed image (shadow as glimmer of illumination still to come). Half-covered, they are also half-opened, prepared for the return of an earlier night's closeness. The other is both "another breathing body" and a "glowshadow," the outer light of an inner self: the moon as solar double. Half covering is a prelude to uncovering and the recovery of sexuality. "Caught in [his] arms," the beloved cannot leave because she hasn't yet been born. "Caught in his arms," she returns as Eve to the nascent Adam, recapitulating an original union. She remains still un[re]covered, returning to an earlier earliness, when nothing has yet happened. Yet she exists, as "another breathing body," objectively to corroborate her imagined being. Everything awaits the future as glowshadow emerges the merest hint of a life before life. "Caught," her distilled past suggests that dreams can be realized.

The gender crossings foster Lowell's faith in renewal. The moonlit image precedes the sun and already anticipates the dissipation of borders between light and darkness, exposure and revelation, night and day. In "Unwanted," Mother contracts into son. The mirror image consumes the original as Medusa turns her enemies to stone and Perseus becomes her to undo her. In "The Downlook, doubling replaces the mirror:

> another breathing body in my bed . . .
> caught in my arms. (p. 125)

The other is both second (an-other) and self (the first). "Caught in my arms," she emerges "like my own," a reverse Eve, having crawled back the way the retreating moon does. Suspended in his body, she is also an inverse Adam, still dreaming of love. Casting her own light in the glow and mimicking him in the shadow, she is other and self.

The doubling returns as a counter to consumption in the penultimate stanza to speak of something in the self simultaneously corroborated by the other. If the other is Eve, she meets the self who dreams of her:

> Ah loved perhaps before I knew you,
> others have been lost like this,
> yet found foothold
> by winning the dolphin from the humming water. (p. 125)

The dolphin provides a foothold, a way out of the humming waters of death and inundation. As dual natured, the dolphin breathes in air and water, providing a sign of the land where the "I" can find a bottom and a sign of the sea where the "I" can be newly baptised. Winning the dolphin, the "I" is successful, having caught it (like the arms of the beloved) as a response, having ridden it (like Arion) to safety. Finally, like Cleopatra's Antony ("his delights / were dolphin-like," *Antony and Cleopatra*, 5.2.88–89),[12] the dolphin straddles borders and allows the "I" to cross over into the other. But it also kindles something in the self that counters the familial pressure merely to mirror. Eve responds to Adam because she once was he: "loved before I knew you." In "Unwanted," the "I" goes back to the time before he even was born to claim that he was never wanted. In "The Downlook," he is already loved, since he feels himself capable of inventing a reciprocal—rather than a denying—other. By returning his love *now*, she makes him feel loved *then*. Lowell invents an antecedent mother to match his present love and to replace the mother of "Unwanted." This Eve is "like my own" and "another." The wished for alikeness of metaphor is corroborated by the actual "closeness" of metonymy. The present union retrospectively denies past alienation. The poet rewrites his past. Maintenant le plein. Mains tenant le plein. (Fullness now and from now on. Nurturing earlier and until now.)

The mother in "Unwanted" consumes the body; the dolphin in "The Downlook" carries it to safety and so restores another set of memories:

> There's no greater happiness in the days of the downlook
> Than to turn back to recapture former joy. (p. 125)

Helen Vendler speculates that this is a poem about impotence and the memory of easy flow last summer.[13] But it is also a poem of sustained belief in independent female desire. The vague humming solidifies into formed word as the poet rides the dolphin to solid ground. The rivulets of welcome signify her desire as amniotic origin of his being. The amorphous fluid of the water becomes, in the "winning," the articulated sound of the Muse. Caught in his arms, the dolphin nurtures a musical foot to meet the poetic hand. Humming water is transformed into lyric rhythm. Like Petrarch in *Rime sparse* 237, Lowell sings the female aubade, identifies with Selene in her wish to still the moon and is cured by her, in her wish to instill desire. The poem expresses confidence in the woman's capacity to return love and in the poet's capacity to invent love. She is loved before he knew her. In the before-time of *The Dolphin*, everything vanishes as the poet-shark eats others and returns them to his mind. In the restored-time of *Day by Day*, the past is shared. The mutual memory ensures consequent materialization. This year *is* because last year *was*. Retrospect applies to all years preceding. Lowell is "loved before." In "The Downlook," Lowell renders the present part of the process by which it is signified. He thereby rewrites Petrarchan hierarchies and realigns the world outside the poem, finding a way to solidify the past. The air of poetic music—like the air through which the moon travels in its cycle of departure and return—closes the gap between water and sky and parallels the ebb and flow of the tide. It carries self and other back to a primal union.

The "former joy" as original event is celebrated in the opening poem of *Day by Day*'s third section. "The Day" recovers the initial moment of discovery. Unlike the self-destructive "flashes" (p. 121) in "Unwanted," the "lightning in an open field" of "The Day" results in a full blown flowering:

> the day is still here
> like lightning on an open field,
> terra firma and transient
> swimming in variation,
> fresh as when man first broke
> like the crocus all over the earth. (p. 53)

If "The Downlook" recovers the past, "The Day" celebrates a present discovery that is reproductive, "like the crocus all over the earth" or like Eve's materialization of Adam's dream. Man's first break becomes, then, not the Miltonic tasting of the apple and sin but the Edenic separation from Eve that leads conversely to plenitude and fullness. If "Unwanted" insists on replication, this poem offers duplication instead: a difference that needs a break, like Adam's first split, to be born. In "Unwanted," the mirroring leads to the disgust of self-hate. Here, the doubling yields the pleasure of self-fulfillment: "in love with our nature." Adam and Eve come from the same flesh ("our nature") and are immersed in the same spirit ("in love"). Lowell's lines—"when we lived momently / together forever"—echo Petrarch's sense of a perfection vanquished by time.

In *Rime sparse* 181, 188, and 354, Petrarch evokes the memory of the momentary possibility of union and (in the same line) the actual impossibility of return. Eve is both unequaled in her perfection and unrealizable ever again:

> the birdcall was never so soft and quiet since the day when Adam opened his eyes; (p. 326)

> unique in her sweet dwelling, she flourishes, without an equal since Adam first saw his and our lovely bane. (p. 334)

there has never been a form equal to hers, not since the day when Adam first
opened his eyes; (p. 550)

In both Petrarch and Lowell, there is a sense of perfection (Petrarch: "without an equal"; Lowell: "together forever") and a sense of the fleeting
(Petrarch: "never again"; Lowell: "momently"). In Lowell's line, however,
the lovers are compound in their response to each other—our nature—and
in their union—together. In Petrarch, the "never" and the "unequaled" render the initial moment ultimately disappointing because, in its uniqueness,
it can neither be held still nor returned. In Lowell, "momently" is both
temporary, a singular spectacular event, and plural as a series of cumulative
events, moment *by* moment additions. Unlike Petrarch's "never" or "without an equal since," Lowell's "momently" opens to the lovers' lasting union,
"together forever." The "momently" softens the marble perfection of
poetic distillation as, through the accumulation of moment by moment,
the stillness of "together forever" accrues to the possibility of flux.

The process of undoing inherent to the oxymoron prepares for a redo-
ing that loosens forms. And, like the cows strung on a hill, the days form a
necklace of equality:

> From a train, we saw cows
> strung out on a hill
> at differing heights,
> one sex, one herd,
> replicas in hierarchy—
> the sun had turned
> them noonday bright. (p. 53)

If the initial discovery of Caroline-Eve reflects a male procreative self, it also
reawakens an earlier creative self. Seen from the train window, the cows repeat
a childhood memory, a residue left over from the past. The image of the
pre-lapsarian time that forms the basis of "The Downlook's" "loved before
I knew you" becomes here a faint sign of an art before Petrarchism, image
before word. In "The Downlook," Lowell's before-time expectation annuls
the biological mother. In "The Day," it comes before the poetical father:

> They were child's daubs in a book
> I read before I could read. (p. 53)

In the Williams essay,[14] the pre-school reading results in the voracious hawk
talons. In "The Day," the cows, as one-sexed nurturing source, confer mater-

nal generativity and paternal authority on the calves. As they fuse together, the real cows are one herd, "replicas in hierarchy." Like the "loved before I knew you" of "The Downlook," they are remnants from an innocent age when—part of the self, unmixed by teaching or knowledge—the images existed "noonday bright," unobscured by shadow or darkness, simple in their primary whiteness, unambiguous in their clearly delineated outlines.

The cows objectify something in the self that stands apart from the frightening mirrors of the Lowell family legacy and the inescapable confines of poetry's inherited forms. "One sex, one herd / replicas in hierarchy," the cows bypass the ordinary mothers and fathers of traditional families. As "daubs," they exist outside the rigid forms of traditional poems. Drawn from the self, they are the child's own. "Daubs" are what letters on the page look like to a child. When he reverts from linguistic sign to painterly smudge, Lowell validates a prelapsarian impression of his own, generating image as a language. The sign becomes the object. The black and white cows on the hill repeat the child's version of print. They are unformed by culture or family. Unlike the mirrored mother and child of "Unwanted" who compete for mastery to create one all consuming self, these replicas are multiple, equal, selves. And, unlike the typical Petrarchan formula that demands that each new poem repeat its predecessor, these "child's daubs" exist apart from the imperialism of the already formed. Lowell's infinite regression in "The Day" promotes the self's prior subjectivity as a counter to the hierarchical order of already determined meanings. Like the crocus that "breaks out [from nowhere] all over the earth," the cows seem to have no paternal "stem" in language and no maternal attachments in need. "One sex," they reproduce themselves. "One herd," they nurture themselves. The idyllic world Lowell creates is without knowledge of prior beings or prior texts. "Read before I could read," the text is totally original as, in "The Downlook," the self is totally loved. "Reading before" and "loved before," the poet is undetermined by Petrarchan plot, undeterred by Petrarchan loss.

If "The Downlook" and "The Day" end with a passing reference to the instinct in the self to destroy the family through the "trespassing tongue" (p. 125) and the instinct in the family to consume the child through the "marriage with nothingness" (p. 53), the last poem in the book begins with yet other instincts in the self—to disparage both the family portrait and the love poem; to move into abstraction, something beyond the poem:

> Those blessèd structures, plot and rhyme—
> Why are they no help to me now

I want to make
something imagined, not recalled?
I hear the noise of my own voice:
The painter's vision is not a lens
it trembles to caress the light. (p. 127)

The desire to experience light unmediated (to caress the light) renders the painter a narcissist. As artist, Apollo is the light. Therefore, the painter "trembles to caress" something in the self—a reflection of innerness—that is art, specifically Petrarchan art, the art that invents the other. In this vision, "something imagined" comes from the self, heard as echo (the noise of my own voice) and seen as shadow (the desire for one's own selfhood in the mirror of the caressed light). But, in the end, Lowell arrives at an origin he never expected. The "blessèd structures" of Petrarchan form lead him to a still older story. In "Unwanted," the "recalled" surrenders to the dead end of Mother. In "The Downlook" and "The Day," it yields to the anticipatory beginning of the poet. But, in "Epilogue," Lowell returns to something that exists *apart* from the poet and arrives at something totally different:

Pray for the grace of accuracy
Vermeer gave to the sun's illumination
stealing like the tide across a map
to his girl solid with yearning. (p. 127)

With the "grace of accuracy," he rests neither with the self—and its private probings—nor with the form—and its imposed feelings—but with the other and *her* imaginings. When he turns to "what happened," Lowell bypasses both the already said of the predetermined Petrarchan mythos and the already dead of the murderous family plot. In the end when he prays for the "grace of accuracy," he moves away from the "blessèd structures" meant to feed the inventive self, to an unstructuring that changes the Petrarchan plot and imitates a giving that involves reciprocation. With the oxymoron—"solid with yearning"—Lowell turns to the woman's desire. Petrarchism yields to the vaporousness of misty deferral: "something imagined." In "Epilogue" desire returns from the air to the earth.

In the first part of the poem, photograph becomes snapshot, a lethal blow to independence. Replication is all. In the second part, the photograph records movement as an homage to lived experience. When the tide overtakes the map, it breaks boundaries, conflating the man's plastic lines with the woman's liquid desire and recalling Endymion and Selene. To compare the sun's illumination with the tide is to bring back—as Lowell does in "The Downlook"—the moon. But it is also to enter the woman's space: to begin with the tide as the woman's initiation of desire. There is another reason for "accuracy" and that is the commanding subjectivity of Vermeer's "girl." Like Eve confronting Adam, she returns, "solid with yearning," as other clearly defined but wanting something of her own from the sun. The tide reflects a reflection: first, the sun illumines the moon; then the moon shines in water. The circle completes the pattern of return suggested by "The Downlook," from rivulets of earthly welcome to circles of heavenly return. In "The Downlook," the movement is upward in the retiring monarchy of the moon. Here the moon lowers itself, stealing across the map, to turn the flat earth globular, referring back to the sun which, in its turn, imitates it. In "The Downlook," lunar shadow merges with solar glow. Here the solar glow shadows the moon by mimicking it. Slipping away, like Pistol in Shakespeare's *Henry V* ("To England I will steal and there I'll steal, 5.1.90),[15] the Apollo of Lowell's poem "steals" *to* the woman as he crosses the map and "steals" *from* the woman as he imitates the tide. Shifting the order of poetry, the solar god follows the moon. Shifting the order of generativity, the "grace of accuracy" is an oxymoron that gives the giving back to a truth of biological reproduction. The source of the poem (the grace of musing) is the woman's life giving capacity (the grace of maternity). In the conventional Petrarchan poem, the sun is the originator of representation. Grace is usually thought of as a broad talent inherited—a genetic endowment—from someone else, accuracy as a concentrated attention—specific to a circumstance—in the self. Grace is divine; accuracy is human. When Lowell combines texts and switches Adam for Apollo, he offers a partner for Eve. And when it steals—"like the tide across the map"—Lowell's sun wipes out the flimsy signifier of the map and returns to the solidity of the earth. Seen now as the lunar tide, the sun erases natural boundaries, loosening the demarcators between land and sea. As flood, it smudges ink marks, rendering the constructed borders—the maps of prescribed representational terms—indeterminate and the text for his poetic flexible enough to incorporate divine grace and poetic accuracy. The metaphors work; the love poem is re-mapped.

To imagine the other "solid with yearning" is to annul the image of the stone mother and bride, solid in denial. It is to flow into a poetic of mutual desire and liquid space. In "The Downlook," the woman is "caught" in the poet's arms. Returning love, she enters him as nascent Eve and frees both poet and lover from the rigid hierarchies of the Petrarchan tradition. As dolphin in the same poem, she transports him to a safety only she can give.

Stealing across the map in "Epilogue," the sun enters the girl and suffuses her with warmth. In turn, she reflects it in permanence, matching its abstraction with her *terra firma*. To be "solid with yearning" is to oppose the narcissist's self-consuming desire for attenuation. It is to be met by the other, as the male sun in the Vermeer painting returns the girl's desire and then "caress[es] [her inner] light," finding in her an already existent self. The oxymoron "solid with yearning," turns the petrified statues of the Medusan image to the melting forms of poetic yielding. But the analogy is based ("stealing like the tide across the map") on the female lunar cycle. In that scenario, the girl in the painting joins the artist in desire. Her inside (liquid) is his outside (fire); his outside (sun) is her inside (moon). If she is, like the Petrarchan poet, "solid with yearning," he is, like the liquid woman, the "tide across a map." Sole subject of the painting, Vermeer's girl offers an alternative to the family group, as she pulls the viewer—with the sun— into her lap. As "girl," she offers everything as potential. She has yet to be lover and still to be parent. Answering the death-dealing Mother in "Unwanted," her desire starts the process of rebirth that the poet completes in the poem. "Solid with yearning" opens to a newly conceived oxymoron. The "girl's" solidity is based on the constancy of dependable return. She invents herself, rendering her own desire the source of her physical being. Desire sustains her as she feeds herself with it. Instead of fading into the "empty space" of Petrarchan attenuation, this desire strengthens the self. The Apollonian sun mimics the moon, stealing from it and so losing itself in the liquid that washes over differences, between sea and shore, man and woman.

Lowell's love poems subvert a poetic tradition that annihilates the other and a familial tradition that annihilates the self by celebrating—as Petrarch does in those rare *Rime sparse* moments in 181, 188, 354, and 237—a doubling that records an other whose subjectivity meets the sun and whose Eve matches his Adam. He thereby superannuates the impulse to revenge and the impulse to dissolve that spurs the family poem into being. In "Unwanted," Lowell follows a pattern of dissolution: day eats day, each new one swallowing (in its repetition) the one gone by, each generation becoming the other. *Medusan revenge as inspiration.* But, in the love poems, the "poor passing fact" serves as a concrete sign that turns the diurnal into a repetition that lasts. The sun "steals" across the map to fill the girl's emptiness as the tide replenishes the shore, taking into account with that *overlap*, the woman's space. "Stealing" across the map, the lunar tide acquiesces to the prior existence of a solid earth, as the sun reverses the order of things and mimics the moon, blurring boundaries in the way the wave overlaps the shore. The girl's days accumulate one by one. Each return to the painting brings on yet another sun. *Sexual realization as inspiration,* a substitute for Petrarch's futile pursuit and Mother Lowell's consuming love. Like the dolphin, the "girl" gives form to the abstract light, offering a foothold, something from the other, that solidifies the self, something in the other that reflects a desire independent of the poet's and so opposes what Lowell calls the narcissism of the self-consuming "tapeworm minute" (*Day by Day*, p. 116).

Such a return is met by a poet who, having exhausted the poetics of conventional Petrarchan form by linking it to the poetics of the unconventional death-dealing family myth in "Unwanted," discovers (in Petrarch's own subversion) an other to fuel his art: "fresh as when man first broke / like the crocus all over the earth." In "The Day," the first break of male parturition—in the genesis of Eve from Adam's rib—parallels the first break of a natural flowering—"like the crocus all over earth"—that survives the narcissi of Petrarchan self-imagining. Lowell's faith in sexual love outdoes the oxymoronic "[breaking] out all over" to dispel the worn-out solid with the bud of the ephemeral, "terra firma and transient." In "[breaking out] all over," the beginning (breaking out) immediately conjures up an end (all over). But "terra firma and transient" (p. 53) incorporates flux into the premise. Reveling in the solid and the fleeting, the idea of the other merges with the fact of the other. Solid yields to idea, and idea solidifies in the other who welcomes the self.

With the oxymorons "grace of accuracy" and "solid with yearning," Lowell opens the tradition to lived experience (in the precision of accuracy and the stability of solid) even as he revitalizes it in the excitement of awe-inspiring desire (grace and yearning). The slight shift renders the poetic imaginatively fertile in its heightened possibility and creatively reciprocal in its realizations. Observing the "girl" in "Epilogue," Lowell discovers a desire that supports the self and recalls the initiation of love. In the "momently together forever" of "The Day," he similarly suggests an accumulation—bit by bit—that replaces the stillness of a deadening perfection ("together forever") with the commitment of fluid return. In the overlap of "Epilogue's" "stealing like the tide across the map," he suggests the union of land and sea, self and other that, as in "The Downlook," puts the moon and the feminine before the sun and its masculinist order. When he finds alternatives to the self-consuming forms of Petrarchism in "terra firma and transient . . . momently together forever . . . and solid with yearning," he opts for flux and renders desire the source of stability. The image of the woman in these poems (Laura-Selene who revives love in "The Downlook," Laura-Eve who returns love in "The Day," and the originative "girl" of "Epilogue") answers the Laura-Daphne mother in "Unwanted." When the crocus "breaks" out all over the earth and the tide steals across the map, their subversions undo the maternity of familial origins and the paternity of poetic authority. If the Petrarchan Apollo runs *after* Daphne, this sun runs *to* the girl who returns, in her yearning, the gift of light, as inner talent and as exterior luminescence. Replacing the black hole of Petrarchan absence with a replenishable resource like the tide, Lowell challenges his poetic forebears with a woman whose solidity fills in for the "anorexia" (p. 124) of unavailing mothers and denying *inamoratae*—all the Petrarchan fetishes—poets traditionally "love . . . most" (p. 124).

In the oxymoron of *Notebook*'s "Afterthought," the "true unreal" becomes "something" whose "abundance" the artist diminishes as he eats at it in unappeasable Kleinian introjection. Poetic imaging becomes larger than life. "Abundance" shrinks as the indefatigable poet nibbles away at hunger-inspiring life. In *The Dolphin*, the oxymorons threaten to devour "abundance" in an all-consuming flash, as the poet reveals himself to be "nuclear and protective" of his own self-engendered annihilations. In the "Epilogue" of *Day by Day,* the artist continues to gnaw away at reality as, in stanza XII of Stevens's "Ordinary Evening," the sun's burnishings shrivel the leaves. But in the "stealing" of the "tide across the map," Lowell admits to the creative reciprocity of nature's constantly yielding bounty. With the simile, "stealing" becomes an imitation of an existent reality whose inheritance Lowell's *Dolphin* "antics" sought, through the spiral of his "infinite mischief," to annul. The oxymorons of "Epilogue" suggest an "abundance," a largesse copious enough—in its infinite "grace" and reciprocal "yearning"—to keep giving back what the poet subtracts. That "solid" appeases, for a moment at least, the "half-balmy" spaciness of "the insatiable fiction of desire."

Chapter 6 ~

RE-VERSING THE PAST:
ADRIENNE RICH'S OUTRAGE
AGAINST ORDER

> The past is betrayed by the simple fact that the present it was is made absent.
> It lacks a certain mode, the tone of the quick, the lively, even as it is recalled.
> —J. F. Lyotard, "The Survivor"[1]

Citing the consistent failure of any symbolic system to represent women, Judith Butler asks: "If the representations that do exist are normative phantasms, then how are we to reverse or contest the force of those representations?"[2] As a woman and as a writer in *An Atlas of the Difficult World,* Adrienne Rich anticipates Butler's unease and performs precisely the contestation Butler seeks. More self-consciously than Stevens or Lowell, Rich is cognizant of her ambivalent position as representer. In her most recent work, she challenges that position by contesting her own representations, widening the Petrarchan revisionism she began in the 1978 "Twenty-One Love Poems" of *The Dream of a Common Language* to voice both the questions the imagined other, replaced in the poem, might raise and the answers the repressed self, silenced by the poem, might give. Rich enacts the revisionist linguistics Butler proposes by "considering the limits of representation and representability as open to signficant rearticulations and transformations" ("Against Proper Objects," 20). It is the openings Rich seeks even as she recognizes that, "like the dyer's hand," [she] is suffused by what [she] works in."[3] To forge such openings, Rich begins by admitting that poetry is part of the problem. She follows though by recognizing her responsibility not only to identify the expropriations as they occur but to restrategize the forms so that they might flesh out the traditionally muted other.

Rich's subject in *Atlas* is the theory of representation itself. Form appears in the book both as seductive and dangerous, the only means Rich can use and the only prospect she has for articulating her resignifying project. Those revisions involve entering into a previously unthinkable dialogue with the writing self, the poetic form, and even the dead. First Rich imagines the unimaginable and then she gives the unimagined a body, voice, and forum. Unhinging the very signifying structures to which, as poet, she is so powerfully drawn, Rich moves into a country she had never before penetrated so deeply. And it is a risky territory.

While she has received much critical praise for "re-engendering the love poetry sequence" with the 1978 "Twenty-One Love Poems,"[4] in the 1991 *An Atlas of the Difficult World,* Rich confesses how much her own desire for words threatens to make her part of the problem she seeks to solve. In the acknowledgment, Rich takes her poetry into a theoretical domain chronicled neither by those who see her as a militant feminist whose art isn't worth taking seriously nor by those who see her as a formalist poet whose ideology can be theoretically discounted.[5] In *Atlas,* Rich returns once more, as she did in *The Dream of a Common Language,* to Petrarchan poetics. This time, however, she questions whether her earlier deconstructions went far enough. "Twenty-One Love Poems" ends defensively on a note of self-determination: "I choose to walk here. And to draw this circle."[6] In her retrospective reading—and in ours—it remains clear that, in 1978, Rich was still establishing herself as the shaping force of the Petrarchan construct: the poet chooses self, other, and words.[7]

Atlas begins with the assumption that "choice is a very loaded word,"[8] that poetry involves what Butler calls "the melancholic reiteration of a language that one never chose."[9] In *Atlas,* Rich returns to the old forms of representation with a postmodern impulse and exposes the moments of entrapment in the works of her predecessors in order to release the forgotten other. She thereby renegotiates the poetic heritage she had already challenged in "Twenty-One Love Poems." No longer content in 1991 to diagnose suffering "as personal, individual, maybe familial, and at most to be 'shared' with a group specific to the suffering," Rich struggles toward "a vocabulary for pain as communal."[10] The poems in *Atlas* go beyond identity politics into the much more difficult terrain of both imagining again—returning to the original form—and reimagining—superimposing the voice of the repressed on the image of the previously imagined. Dealing with the incommensurable by risking the unspeakable, Rich gives the "other," displaced by the form, a forum in her poems despite the fact that the "other" who speaks will turn around and indict her as a complicitor in the displacement process.

In "Final Notations," "Through Corralitos Under Rolls of Cloud," and "For a Friend in Travail" of *Atlas*, Rich works through the various forms of containment she poetically inherits from generic Petrarchism—of the sonnet, the serial poem, and the *aubade* respectively—to emerge with a vision that includes her own contributions to the process she questions. If it is language that culturally traps us, then what needs to be changed is the language itself. Not only does Rich take issue with her own Petrarchism; she also takes on that of the predecessors whose forms originally seduced her into the other-confining turns of their repressive techniques. When she transforms the Petrarchan poetic in "Final Notations," "Through Corralitos," and "For a Friend," Rich often speaks in the voice of the other who remains repressed in the early, and late, modern male poems her work parallels: Marvell's "Mower's Song"; Stevens's "The Idea of Order at Key West"[11]; and Donne's "Breake of Day." In alluding to those poets who were already reflecting on the power of the desired other (Marvell), the brutality of mere survival (Stevens), and the terror of physical separation (Donne), Rich takes their deconstructions one step further and brings her own work to a deeper exploration of Petrarchism than she had ventured in "Twenty-One Love Poems."

Rich's sense of form as irresistible and claustrophobic is summarized by "Magic Glasses," Edwin Romanzo Elmer's anamorphic cover painting of *Atlas*. There the landscape and the sky are refracted and illuminated again and again, through the forgrounded window pane and magnifying glass, the ciborium-vase at the center, the leafy pattern on the vase and in the blue and brown motif of the marble table. The circles become eggs and the phallic lines at the edge move from square to rectangular, rendering the images both female and male. The distorted images in the magnifying glass and doubled mirrorings in the ciborium neutralize and hence undercut the sexual engenderings they seem to suggest.

The mirrors subtract what the fall landscape completes: the cycle of the seasons that would, by implication, bring on renewal. Since there seems to be no relief, the mirrors also imply that the only thing to be reproduced is the barren landscape that already exists. The clearly defined windows, marking the separation of inner from outer, instead bring the outer inside. The landscape fills the cup and so takes it over. But the ciborium is actually empty, mirroring and revealing the empty self who placed it there. If the inside is the outside, then the self has nothing to offer. If the outside is the inside, then there is no other to satisfy the self. The process of doubling reorganizes the landscape into an empty signifier that the magnifying glass bends out of shape once again. The magical glasses are black magical

Edwin R. Elmer, "Magic Glasses," oil on canvas, Courtesy of Shelburne Museum, Shelburne, Vermont.

glasses, threatening to render all things merely signs, proliferating in an endless process of dissatisfaction. Brittle glass becomes vaporous air as the many containers drift from the blackness of the window panes to the gray of the horizon into which everything fades. The blackness seems to creep up and absorb the colors just as the reversed earth and sky eliminate each other. The painting becomes anamorphic, as one image struggles against, and then obviates, the other and both merge into non-differentiated and figure-absorbing space.

The unresolved doubling in the cover painting expresses in visual terms the poetic of the book where Rich turns the forms she inherits into vehicles through which she can articulate her own overarching questions. In the process, Rich revives the other overcome by her predecessor's repressions and her own repressive self. As her poetic magnifying glass mirrors its earlier mirrorings, she threatens to double the exposure. The repressed self appears uncannily, hauntingly, compellingly, to challenge the sign by which it is identified. Through her magnifications, the other "forgotten" in earlier texts comes to the surface; the visual presence in turn renders audible "the less legible meanings of sound" (*Collected Poems*, p. 488). Rich's reading of Marvell, Stevens, and Donne overturns their reading of Petrarch, as the current text "enters a field of reading as partial provocation, requiring a set of prior texts in order to gain legibility and initiating a set of appropriations and criticisms that call into question their fundamental premises" (*Bodies that Matter*, p. 19). The imbricated "prior text" in all three poems is Petrarchan. When Rich alludes to Marvell, Stevens, and Donne, she follows their habit of recasting Petrarch and Petrarch's habit of recasting himself.

Rich's use of prior texts in *Atlas* is a way of getting at prior beings, both those the poem represents and those it represses. At the center of *Atlas* is the question that stops the book: "What does it mean to say *I have survived?*" (p.48). With Lyotard, Rich may be saying that "the survivor always survives a death, but the death of what life" ("The Survivor," p. 144)? In "Final Notations," it is the life of the self overcome by the deadening form Rich personifies; in "Through Corralitos," it is the life of the buried earlier self and the indifference of the survivor-murderer to the self who dies. Admitting her vulnerability to the deadening force in "Final Notations" and culpability for some of the deaths in "Through Corralitos," Rich negotiates for change in "For a Friend" and thereby loosens the bind of the forms through which she realizes herself.

First and Last Testament:
"It will become your will" in *"Final Notations"*

"Final Notations" chronicles the imposition of a form so seductive and so totalizing that its mere existence makes both a return to self or an attachment to the other impossible. Representation destroys the representer because the signifier usurps everything. The compulsions of "Final Notations" echo those of the Marvellian text of "The Mower's Song," which in turn reflect those of the Petrarchan text, specifically of *Rime sparse* 23, where, disguised as Mercury, Laura turns Petrarch to stone and declares herself inviolate and unobjectifiable. Marvell invents a Juliana who takes over his profession and mows him down. In 23, Petrarch invents a Laura who is similarly his inventor and similarly his undoer. And that is precisely what the "it" is for the speaker in "Final Notations" where form immobilizes the self in the way that the stone-casting Laura does Petrarch in *Rime sparse* 23.

If Petrarch imagines the woman as imaginer who retaliates by rendering him an object and subsequently by rendering herself unknowable, Rich goes one step further, imagining the "its" desire to permeate everything, not just to privilege dark secrets in an irretrievable locale. While Petrarch's Laura-Mercury indicates the extent to which male forms and their rationales fail to accommodate the woman, Rich's "it" probes even deeper in its destruction of the poet, emerging more compelling than Petrarch's woman. And, while Petrarch instantly turned to stone at Laura-Mercury's command, the victim of "it" experiences a much more drawn out form of torture. For the Laura who actively cuts and speaks and escapes, this "it" "takes," "touches," and "occupies" like a magnetic force that expands with what it extracts. Laura leaves Petrarch cast in stone. Rich's "it" turns the self into "it." As infectious disease, "it" reduces everything, including its discoverer, into a symptom. The moment of contagious takeover is always imminent. That's the poison. The speaker can never get over her vulnerability because she keeps reinfecting herself with what can only be described as a desire for the diseased forms of her repression.

Petrarch invents a Laura-Mercury who challenges his invention; Rich invents an invention, a simulacrum that behaves like Petrarch's evasive Laura-Mercury. In this mechanized world, the deadening impact of the seductive form is indistinguishable from the denying presence of the desired woman who, in turn, bespeaks the "ineluctable absence" of the original self. Slavoj Žižek writes that "the ultimate lesson of virtual reality is the virtualization of the very true reality. By the mirage of 'virtual reality,' the true reality itself is posited as a semblance of itself, as a pure symbolic edifice."[12] In the same way, Rich's "it" behaves like the woman in the poem who is an image of the woman in the poet's head. Rich's devouring form equals Marvell's man-eating Juliana, who is another version of Petrarch's poetry-corrupting Laura-Mercury. Rich's unnamed "it" reflects both the poet's desire to control the other it invents and the poet's admission that the invention undoes the inventor, as Laura-Mercury turns Petrarch-Battus to stone, and Juliana threatens Damon when she merely "comes." In naming the other "it," Rich enacts the revenge of the other who, responding to its objectification, refuses to yield. Like the laurel tree, the "it," as a thing not a person, is absolutely unavailable in a form to which the speaker has access.

Nowhere does Rich play with pronouns so unrelentingly as in "Final Notations," where the absorbable "it" is never fully defined and never fully evaded. What is missing from the sonnet is the poetic "I":

it will not be simple, it will not be long
it will take little time, it will take all your thought
it will take all your heart, it will take all your breath
it will be short, it will not be simple

it will touch through your ribs, it will take all your heart
it will not be long, it will occupy your thought
as a city is occupied, as a bed is occupied
it will take all your flesh, it will not be simple

You are coming into us who cannot withstand you
you are coming into us who never wanted to withstand you
You are taking parts of us into places never planned
You are going far away with pieces of our lives

it will be short, it will take all your breath
it will not be simple, it will become your will (p. 57)

In "Final Notations" the form engulfs the self in the way that Juliana mows Damon in "The Mower's Song," a poem whose inexorability "Final Notations" follows. Deforming the self, the form ensures that no original being remains. Damon's allusions to Juliana progress chronologically from a history that has already been lived to a malignancy that is about to erupt, a narrative thread that becomes an emotional threat:

When Juliana came and She
What I do to the Grass, does to my Thoughts and Me.[13]

Damon's past is replaced by Juliana's presence: she takes over his being. His beginning lies with the fatal "when" of Juliana's initiation into his life just as his end will result from the imminent danger of her being about-to-arrive. The past is never over for Damon. It keeps happening again. The fatal moment (when Juliana came) is the cause of his present dissolution (because Juliana never goes away). She becomes his Mower, doing to him what he did to the grass and what Laura-Mercury did to Petrarch-Battus. In her presence, he is objectified as grass to her will. She walks all over him.

When Rich adopts Marvell's menacing tone and renames the fatally attractive woman as the fatally compelling form, she too splits the poem to link the memory of desire to the anticipation of death. And, if death climaxes with a war simile, love begins with a sex symbol, the bed as the place for birth (accouchement) and conception (engendering):

> It will occupy your thought
> as a city is occupied, as a bed is occupied

As Petrarchan other, Juliana emerges indistinguishable from Damon's self. But if Damon demonizes Juliana in a rather simple exchange of Petrarchan other for Petrarchan self, Rich's demon is much more complex. In the overlap of "it will not be simple" as occupier of the poem's beginning, middle, and end, Rich indicates that becoming the other (as Damon does) embattles sexuality and leaves the battle of the sexes unresolved. War (as a city is occupied by an invading army) and sex (as a bed is occupied by a beloved partner) are totalizing and equal. Like Stevens's couch, Rich's bed is both the place of the sexually desired other and the seat of the creatively fecund mother. But, in vacillating between a military zone and an erotic site, her similes not only heighten the connections between infantile and sexual desire. They make the connection between love and war clear.

With the thrice repeated, "it will not be simple," Rich outlines the threefold nature of the takeover that dissolves the collective memory of historical experience ("as a city is occupied"), involves the present feeling of collective loss ("you are taking parts of us"), and commands the future occupation of a new task ("it will become your will"). "It" is consuming (like love) and fragmenting (like death). In the end, the complexity devastates: as desire (will), it is an all-inclusive obsession; as legacy (will), it remains all that is left behind for future generations: "It will become your will." With the doubled "will," Rich bequeathes her compulsions to her successors. If Marvell speaks to the heraldry of death in the familiar meadow, Rich anticipates new forms ("you are taking parts of us into places never planned"). Those new places lie beyond the limits of conventional representation.

In the octet, the "I" preaches to an implied "you" as a teacher preparing a child for a difficult lesson but, in the crucial third stanza, the "I," joining with her fellow pupils, speaks directly to the intruder, describing the invasion as it occurs: "you are coming into us . . . you are taking parts of us . . . you are going far away." As current actions that signify a debilitating and destabilizing process, "entering, taking, and leaving" contemporize the devastation. The anticipated threat comes now. Like a television reporter caught in a media event as it unfolds, the narrator incredulously witnesses the imminent takeover. Only the reporter is also the victim in the narrative she relates. The vulnerability she describes is her own: it is, as the "we" indicates, "ours." The "I" is trapped by the picture she describes. The scenario demands total surrender—"we cannot withstand you"—and represents a desired end—"we never wanted to withstand you." Unable to defend the self, "we" are broken from the start. Unable to perpetuate the self, "we" are retrospectively phrased in terms of a negative desire. Thus, the "you" effaces the past—"you are going far away with pieces of our lives"— and changes the future—"you are taking parts of us into places never planned." In this case, the self is overridden by the fragmentation, as the desired other becomes the invading army and the love poem is overcome by the war poem. As other, the "will" threatens the self even though, as self, the "will" expresses its desire. That sense of unauthorized ownership (as a city is occupied) violates the assurance of reproductive enterprise (as a bed is occupied) to make the assumed form of renewal the actual source of annihilation. The speaker is *pre-occupied*. "Final Notations" suggests that sublimation not only requites the desiring body; it replaces it: "it will become your will."

In "Final Notations," form dominates everything. Caught in the signifying web, the self is immobilized by a desire which, in its capacity to take over the self, replaces the woman Petrarch and Marvell demonize. The form is all. "Final Notations" also chronicles the connection between poetry and politics. Love poems may lead to bed-time stories. But the mechanism is the same as that of war-time stories. The totalizing form of their trap is interchangeable: "as a city is occupied . . . as a bed is occupied." Rich argues that the impulse behind the love poem is a death drive, a preoccupation present in the poetic from the start. But she also incriminates the self as occupant of the form that is so compelling. "Through Corralitos" speaks on behalf of the self forgotten by the compulsions Rich indicts in "Final Notations." There, the self replaced by the sublimating poem continues uncannily to exist. That spectral other gathers strength as "Through Corralitos" progresses and the deformed self is imagined in all its ghastly emanations.

Outraging the "I":
"Through Corralitos Under Rolls of Cloud"

In "Through Corralitos," Rich revives yet another Laura implicated in the *Rime sparse*: the Laura-Medusa of 366 who rises to utter her revenge against the surviving Perseus. The series opens, however, on the traditional terrain of Petrarchism and the laurelized landscape of trees and fruits. Rich prepares for her devastating attack on the poet-Perseus-self by first writing about the typical victim in the poetic construct, Laura-Daphne:

> Through Corralitos under rolls of cloud
> between winter-stiff, ranged apple-trees
> each netted in transparent air,
> thin sinking light, heartsick within and filmed
> in heartsickness around you, gelatin cocoon
> invisible yet impervious—to the hawk
> steering against the cloudbank, to the clear
> oranges burning at the rancher's gate
> rosetree, agave, stiff beauties holding fast
> with or without your passion,
> the pruners freeing up the boughs
> in the unsearched faith these strange stiff shapes will bear. (p. 46)

The "ranged apple trees . . . oranges burning at the ranchers gate . . . rose tree . . . agave" are, like Petrarch's laurels in the *Rime sparse*, former Daphnes "holding fast." They are arranged by pruning man whose mutilating purpose is paradoxically to propagate. He lays the trees bare so that they will in turn "bear" fruit as testimony to the patriarchy. If the denied sexuality of the poetic Daphne annuls female reproductivity, these Daphnes have already given in to the demands of their pursuers. As previously mutilated Daphnes, the "stiff beauties holding fast" catch the oxymoronic sense of movement (fast-paced) that goes nowhere certain (holding-back) so that the pattern perpetuates patriarchal imperatives in its logical impossibilities and parodies Petrarchan denials in its fruitful inevitabilities. The "stiff beauties holding fast" are pinned down from the very beginning, locked in place by the economic desire of the "pruners" who cut them to size so that they will propagate more fully. Rich's "stiff trees" yield to the rancher's reality, as they fulfill his lust for patriarchal fruition. The ranchers use the doctrine of Petrarchan sublimation economically, turning the body of the violated woman into the medium for financial gain just as the poet redacts the traditional laurel into the vehicle for literary fame.

Rich's trees are peculiarly bookish, already laurelized. The narrative follows a camera motion—"heartsick within and filmed in heartsickness around you"—that records no e-motion. The landscape seems psychological ("heartsickness without you") but is hostile to the pathetic fallacy ("with or without your passion"). That movement toward stillness and death (winter stiff) and stillness awaiting movement and birth (gelatin cocoon) encapsulates the self-canceling process of the poem. One season inevitably over-rides the other. The feminine resistance to masculine power values that Daphne represents in the Petrarchan ethos is subsumed by the deliberate obviation of female iniative in the patriarchal ranch Rich images.

Paralleling the shift in the landscape from one that seems sympathetic ("filmed in heartsickness around you") to one that persists indifferently ("with or without your passion") is the strange relationship of the narrator to the "you" throughout all of "Through Corralitos": at first sympathetic, then malignant, then sympathetic again and, finally, indifferent. Withdrawing from the "you" in poems I and II, the narrator rubs salt into the wound of the resistant and dying self. In poems III and IV, she shifts gears and speaks on behalf of the "you" injured by her initial commentary, her acidity sharpened into the venom of Medusa, this time directed against the survivor. Such shifts also work against the reading audience that is first included in the sympathy, as the "I" speaks for an implied "you"; and then is implicated in the villainy, as the "I" asks accusatory questions of the reading "you."

At first, in poem I, the narrator seems to include the "you" in her assessment, arguing that the world resonates with "your" pain. By the end of poem I, she maintains, contrarily, that the world wags on without "you" too. That shift is recorded through the changing meaning of the thrice repeated "stiff" ("winter stiff . . . stiff beauties . . . strange stiff"). Transforming the agency of the tree from victim, to survivor, to ghost, Rich plays on *stiff*: as seasonal (and therefore temporary) state; as the constant condition of self-preserving womanhood; and, finally, as a dead body in a bizarre *film noir*. Each of the meanings of stiff depends on its modifier. "Winter stiff" depicts a self frozen by its position in time; "stiff beauties" are frigid in their unresponsiveness and defiant in their refusal to yield to passion; "strange stiffs" are psychological corpses that haunt the living. Those reversals follow a three-part split in the narration from sympathetic, through anti-poetic, through spectral that prepares for the split in the second poem, where the speaker describes a simple feeling, recovery after sickness, that separates the "you" from its past ("uncertain who she is or will be without you," p. 47) as, in the first poem, she had severed the "you" from the landscape ("with or without your passion," p. 46). With the "strange stiffs," Rich enters the nether world as her critique moves from an examination of patriarchy to an indictment of the surviving self, who turns out to be no different in her indifference from the ranchers.

In the guise of the spectral "stiff," she challenges the notion of survival after the horrors twentieth-century life produced. Bringing the political into the poetic, Rich takes off from a prose thought found in a 1984 essay and brought to fruition in her work of the nineties, "Notes Toward a Politics of Location":

> The growing urgency of an anti-nuclear, anti-militarist, movement must be a feminist movement, must be a socialist movement, must be an anti-racist, anti-imperialist movement. That it's not enough to fear for the people we know, our own kind, ourselves.[14]

In the prose passage, Rich calmly arrives at an assessment of political movements based on identity politics to say "it's not enough." "Through Corralitos" questions the sufficiency of "mere" survival by progressively changing its levels of intensity and complexity. First there is the simple recovery after illness in poem II; then there is the question of community survival in poems III and IV. Finally, there is the question of self-survival in poem V. Can the poet who sacrifices a self for the poem subsequently recall the self who died? Or does her recovery in the poem place her so far out of touch with her earlier self that return is impossible? The voice of the earlier self cannot even be fathomed. In poem II, the "you" recovers callously; in poems III and IV, the callous recovery is named. But in poem V, recovery itself seems impossible. Medusa torments the surviving Perseus. The repressed self haunts the forgetter.

First, the body's survival is presented by the narrator as a stab-in-the-back to the dead:

> this other who herself barely came back,
> whose breath was fog to your mist, whose stubborn shadow
> covered you as you lay freezing, (p. 47)

The embryonic and initially protective other ("whose breath was fog to your mist, whose stubborn shadow / covered you") is dismissed, as the body—in its drive to survive—seems utterly indifferent to its earlier com-

forter. In the narrator's indictment, the ritualized motion of survival surfaces as an act of deliberate cruelty to the dead. The subtle rhyme between
the "barely" of poem II and the "bearing" of poem I links the future survivor to the fruitful trees. As the "strange stiff" shapes are estranged from
the "stiff beauties," so the "other" who "barely came back" feels no remorse
for her dead self. The field of difference between life and death is hardly
there as the field of difference between *bearing* fruit and holding fast
seemed *barely* there in poem I. Yet it makes all the difference. The shadow
self is the Medusa who, in poems III and IV, takes over the central voice.

In poem III, the narrator begins by attacking the surviving "you" for not
realizing herself except in contrast to the other she left behind:

> what do you know
> of the survivor when you know her
> only in opposition to the lost? (p. 48)

She then complicates the question by arguing that the presumed survivor
only escapes by a narrow-minded reading of the self:

> What does it mean to say *I have survived*
> until you take the mirrors and turn them outward
> and read your own face in their outraged light? (p. 48)

Light—the objectively illuminating source that focuses indiscriminately on
whatever catches it—becomes the subjectively speaking mirror that turns
the focus on the guilty originator. The shadow this time becomes the
inquisitor. In "Through Corralitos," the mirror finally produces a point of
view—outraged light—through which the survivor reads her own face to
learn that she survives over her own dead body, at the expense of her dead
body. When Rich's outraged mirror speaks, it turns the survivor into a
Claudius who kills his brother, a Perseus who beheads Medusa. The outraged light in the mirror speaks on behalf of the double, the other who is
victimized by what the survivor determines. To read the image from the
point of view of the outraged light in the mirror is to see the originating
self as repressive and to read survival as a victimization of the represented
other. The light and sound gradually merge so the mirror (a source of
light) becomes a point of view (the voice of Outrage) reflecting a disembodied person that finally becomes an embodied voice, a speaker in the
poem punctuated (as in a Ben Jonson play) as a humor. The voice brings
the Lyotardan forgotten to life again.

Finally, the voice of Outrage emerges as a full-blooded character in the play, having progressed from the third poem, where it is a reflective visual mirror, to the fourth poem, where it is the subjective auditory point of view. The named Outrage asks questions that traditional discourse—and even the radical feminist rhetoric of Rich's earlier poetry—cannot bring itself to ask. As in "Final Notations," the "I" and the "you" join together in the face of a common enemy. But that union lasts only until Outrage breaks through the glass and speaks on her own behalf:

> Outrage: who dare claim protection for their own
> amid such unprotection?   What kind of prayer
> is that?   To what kind of god?   What kind of wish? (p. 49)

Outrage's questions point to the contrast between the vastness—the utter ruthlessness—of the "such" as measured against the vulnerability—the extreme defenselessness—of "unprotection." Guarding the victimized in their fragility, she also points an accusatory finger at people who do nothing but protect "their own." The chiasmic relationship between Outrage's identification of the marginialized and denouncement of the repressors renders her simultaneously defendant and prosecutor. She facilitates the revival of those repressed in the past even as she represents the gathering force of those who previously had no voice of their own.

Rich's device—the setting apart of lines of the poem to be spoken by a feeling that emerges a fleshed out character in the poem—is part of her conspiracy to turn on safe assumptions. In the fourth poem, those safe assumptions have a poetic history in the *locus amoenus* the narrator uses to define the sense of security she shatters in three stages: (1) through the myths of Diana and Actaeon; (2) after the death of Narcissus on behalf of Echo; and finally (3) through the voice of Outrage who speaks of the original Medusan violation as another version of the story of Actaeon and Diana and of the interiorization of Echo by Narcissus. The narrator describes Outrage:

> That light of outrage is the light of history
> springing upon us when we're least prepared,
> thinking maybe a little glade of time
> leaf-thick and with clear water
> is ours, is promised us, for all we've hacked
> and tracked our way through: to this: (p. 49)

She draws two mythological circles, one menacing and the other comforting, and then contracts them so that their dark end precedes their innocent beginnings. The glade is first Diana's pool, the safe harbor invaded by Actaeon, "springing upon us when we're least prepared," and then the false/safe feeling such places encourage ("thinking maybe a little glade of time . . . is ours"). Then it is Narcissus's pool, with its mirror of clear water, and the place of death, leaf thick, with its already growing and entangling narcissi. Time past—"hacked / and tracked" our way through—and time present—the point of final epiphany—coalesce in the "this." Like Stevens's Narcissus confronted with what he "did not expect,"[15] Rich's Narcissus is already ensnared by his own desire. In the landscape of repression and revenge, there is no clear picture. Blurred from the start, the mirror is "leaf-thick," assuming the foliage of Narcissus's metamorphosis.

In the safety of the imagined enclave, the poem becomes a duet of politeness:

> What will it be?   Your wish or mine?   your
> prayers or my wish then: that those we love
> be well, whatever that means, to be well. (p. 49)

With the casualness of conversation, the prayer and the wish occupy the scene of the glade, as the "I" and the "we" join together at the wishing-well, throwing platitudes at each other. The wishing-well is the well-wisher. Time becomes place. Place becomes person. Noun (wishing-well) merges with verb (well-wishing). Everything is an image that turns into a mirage. If the water has no margin, the glade evaporates. The end is an image without a body: Narcissus in the water; Medusa on the shield. The glade and pool become the scene where Outrage speaks. The false safety, of Diana, Narcissus, and Perseus, emerges the harsh reality of Medusa, Echo and pointed accusation.

In response to the shallow conversation of hollow embodiment, Outrage speaks. The source of light in III turns into the voice of thunder in IV. Breaking all bounds, Outrage fleshes itself out in shattering words:

> who dare claim protection for their own
> amid such unprotection? (p. 49)

The speech not only unsettles the goddess Diana for whom the nymphs claim protection in the Actaeon myth, it also deconstructs the representation of Diana as female goddess whose vengeance for the shattered glade bifurcates the world into hunted and victims. Similarly, Medusa, whose presence in the poem conflates warrior and enemy, demonstrates that there are no shields. But more than that, it dismisses the territorial claim of the enclave. Inside the mirror is Echo who, in the end, voices her revenge by turning Narcissus into her. Rich's questions resonate from the myth to the twentieth century. After Auschwitz and Hiroshima, how can there be a protected place "amid such unprotection"? How can we draw a ring around "our own" when such circles leave the "unprotected" outside? And what of the very idea of "our own" and the exclusionary reality that brands those not "our own" vermin? If Outrage shatters boundaries to speak her question, she also questions the boundary-making impulse, which is hierarchical and hegemonic, on behalf of the avenging victim. The made-up word "unprotection" (which suggests total vulnerability), like the made-up body "Outrage" (which represents unbridled anger), reiterates that time differences vanish as mythic violations bring on contemporary horrors. Crashing through the protected enclave of the glade, the unsponsored Medusa undermines the accepted forms of social difference and the binary differences of literary forms to disrupt all conventions.

Finally, the tiny wishing well emerges, in poem V, the whole ocean in the "boom of surf . . . the undertow . . . the reef" that undo safety. The narrator assumes Medusa's revenge and cancels survival:

> She who died on that bed sees it her way:
> She who went under peers through the translucent shell
> cupping her death and sees her other well,
> through a long lens, in silvered outline, well
> she sees her other and she cannot tell
> why when the boom of surf struck at them both
> she felt the undertow and heard the bell,
> thought death would be their twinning, till the swell
> smashed her against the reef, her other still
> fighting the pull, struggling somewhere away
> further and further, calling her all the while:
> she who went under summons her other still. (p. 50)

The poem recalls both the bed of poem II, where the primacy of the "she" who died is asserted as memory, and the glade of poem IV, where the assumptions of those who survived are undone as possibility. "Well" is repeated as adverb (seeing well) and adjective (well other) until finally, it becomes a noun (like the watery wishing-well of poem IV). As the water becomes a mirror, the dead self sees her double—well enough—and finds her whole—well again: Perseus as triumphant and callous warrier.

The sub-marine periscope becomes the super-terrestial telescope as the victim sights the survivor through the Earth's distance. Outlined in silver, the well "she" assumes the remoteness of a star. The rhyme of well with swell and bell again mingles sight and sound as the waves "tell" and the telling waves surface as inevitable death knells. The end is inexorable in the mistaken thought—"death would be their twinning"—and unfinal. "She who went under summons her other still." The opening sense of movement without body in the personless participles of "Corralitos I" climaxes in the closing frame of body without movement: "she who went under summons her other [to] still[ness]" ("Corralitos, V"). If the *light* of Outrage scatters the obsessive image of one other, it also shatters the poetical belief in artistic mastery.

The *voice* of Outrage reflected in poems III-V seems an answer to the calm complacency of Stevens's "rage for order" in the "Idea of Order at Key West." Rich's poem functions as a postmodernist rebuttal of Stevens's modernist triumph:

> Ramon Fernandez, tell me, if you know,
> Why when the singing ended and we turned
> Toward the town, tell why the glassy lights,
> The lights in the fishing boats at anchor there,
> As the night descended, tilting in the air,
> Mastered the night and portioned out the sea,
> Fixing emblazoned zones and fiery poles,
> Arranging, deepening, enchanting night.
>
> Oh! Blessed rage for order, pale Ramon,
> The maker's rage to order words of the sea,
> Words of the fragrant portals, dimly-starred,
> And of ourselves and of our origins,
> In ghostlier demarcations, keener sounds. (*Collected Poems,* p. 130)

In Stevens, the singing woman inspires the feeling that men can conquer the mysteries of nature, and ominous night, through the mastery of art, and glassy lights. Stevens's oxymoron—"rage for order"—exceeds the natural cancellations of the ebbing and flowing sea and the waxing and waning night. The hierarchy of poetry, with its "ghostlier demarcations" and "keener sounds," outdoes the dominion of origins in the sea and the prophecies of doom in the skies. All "things" are annulled by the rage, as they are sucked back into the "*idea* of order." The rage for order of Stevens's poetic insists that the body of art precedes the world's body in nature. In the beginning was the word.

When Rich turns to the light of Outrage, her victim has no words. While the Stevens of "Idea" never questions why the singing woman stopped, the Rich of "Through Corralitos" speaks on behalf of the silent woman until, finally, she acknowledges the impulse to repress the inspiring other that haunts all poetic distillations. In Stevens's "Idea," the woman disappears as she is replaced by her song. In "Through Corralitos," the woman refuses to disappear. Stevens invites Ramon Fernandez to tell, as he is *already* telling, why art seems to master nature. Rich's "she" "cannot tell" why the "she" [who went under] "summons her other still," why death invokes silence, not words. In Rich's poem, Medusa turns the surviving Perseus to the stillness of stone. In Stevens, the call to language continues as an infinite incantation to fluidity. The woman's song stirs the poet who, in turn, challenges Ramon Fernandez to the words that might, at some future time, answer his questions. Male poet calls to his successor across the continents to continue the male quest. Rich's "she" breaks the connection. Her "she" is condemned to silence. Isolated, the dead "she" can only summon her other to a similar death.

The repeated phrase—"her other still"—frames life in terms of a battle against death—"fighting the pull, struggling somewhere away." Finally, everything is constricted by the unremitting pull of death calling the other [to the] "still[ness of immobility]." We know that the surviving other fights the pull of death and struggles "further and further" as the "she" who died is left (in remoteness) far behind. But what remains ambiguous is the subject of "calling her all the while":

> her other still
> fighting the pull, struggling somewhere away
> further and further, calling her all the while:
> she who went under summons her other still. (p. 50)

Does the survivor "fight, struggle, and call" or is it the dead "she" who continues to recall her live self while the "other" struggles and fights somewhere away out of earshot? Do the living recall the dead or are the dead silenced because, unheard, they are forgotten?

Is the "she" who survives, like the nurturing Demeter to the overcome Persephone, or the poet Orpheus to the stung Eurydice, the subject of the calling? The myths of Demeter and Orpheus center on the active desire of those who survive to keep seasonally or poetically "calling" for the missing child and wife. Demeter and Orpheus never give up on the dead. Their myths are commemorative and poetic. Does the call here reverse the myth with Eurydice pulling Orpheus back to the underworld again, Persephone beckoning her mother to "still" life, and Medusa turning Perseus to the "stillness" of stone? Or, like the Elusinean mysteries and Athena-Medusa-Perseus, does the calling suggest that other and self are the same? In the end, the call for a response results in silence. The call to movement ends in paralysis. If the "she" who died summons the survivor, then the myths are reversed. It is the dead who pull the survivors to them and, hence, recall what the living repress. Thus the dead deaden the living because there is no surviving if living means denying the existence of the selves who "went under." The clear demarcations are muddied. In poem IV, space converges as the protective enclave is haunted by those it excluded. In poem V, time collapses as the survivor is haunted by the self it repressed.

What has Rich imagined here in this "pas de deux" that questions the survival of: the chosen people; the beloved other; the living self? The command to stillness brings on the silence of the end of the poem even as the light of Outrage disorders the stratifications structuring the beginning of the poem. And, where Stevens ends with the "blessed rage for order" that confirms the melodious song, Rich's poem is haunted by the harsh voice of Outrage. In that echo, she negates Stevens's "ghostlier demarcations" that outline origins of difference somewhere in the past and the "keener sounds" that speak to destinies of power somewhere in the future. Rich renders the "idea" of order obsolete. Stevens's "ghostlier demarcations" merely reiterate the long history of repression. The demarcating mechanism ties the "keener sounds" to the violative impulse at the beginning. Where Stevens ends in the oxymoronic "rage for order" that preserves the male hierarchies of Petrarchan form, Rich's Outrage breaks the form and pushes out the center to reveal the Medusa as form shatterer. In Stevens's "Idea of Order," the woman disappears as the male poets toss her inspirational resources between them, in a game of catch-up that finally abjects her completely. Deprived of the consolations of kind, Rich's self is left in the terminations of stillness. The other "stills" the self away from the sentimentalization of poetry and the idea of its redeeming power. Unlike Ramon Fernandez whom Stevens commands to "tell," the dead self "cannot tell" herself apart from the living self who, nevertheless, moves further and further away. Her recovery is signified by her refusal to listen. The self who survives is one dimensional. Her "stillness" in persistence speaks to a hollowness reflected in an essential indifference to the calling. Like Elmer's ciborium, the form is an empty shell whose distillations speak of the *ghastliness* of demarcations.

"Through Corralitos" chronicles the history of the dead "she" by bearing witness to what Lyotard calls the immemorial, "that which can neither be remembered (represented to consciousness) nor consigned to oblivion."[16] The shattering question—"who dare claim protection"—points toward the "unprotection"—the silence—that implicates a culture that denies the repressed other a narrational place. While the Stevens of "The Idea of Order at Key West" glories in the culture he inherits, Rich insists that that very culture may have played a role in the unspeakable events of the century. When Memory speaks in "Eastern War Time," the poem that precedes "Corralitos," it turns the mirror on the survivor to say that no poem can "do right" by the dead:

> Memory says:　Want to do right? Don't count on me.
> I'm a canal in Europe where bodies are floating
> I'm a mass grave (p. 44)

> I am standing here in your poem　unsatisfied
> Lifting my smoky mirror (p. 44)

Like the mirror in "Through Corralitos," Memory returns in infinite regression to the fires of the past. But it is a history of violation. And, like the amassing ocean in "Through Corralitos," the mass grave in "Eastern War Time" makes "doing right" in the poem somehow massively wrong. Lifting the "smoky mirror" to reveal an emptiness at the origin, Memory turns form into a deformation. In Stevens, the "blessedness" of the oxymoron "rage for order" produces an art that justifies the necessary repressions. In Rich, the voice of Outrage commands the Medusan stillness that ends poetic distillation. What survives is ultimately turned to stone. If the self merely assimilates the other, the future is condemned to repeat the past in the way that Perseus mirrors Medusa. And, if the future repeats the past, then what Lyotard calls the process of "appearance" and "disappearance" simply allows for replacement: the well self takes over for the victim; the healed society forgets the past; the poem sublimates the life. Memory cannot be relied on because the forgotten never had a narrative place. In "Through Corralitos," Outrage protests the dehumanizing, deindividualizing, massive lunge toward survival that folds (and so suppresses) the other into the self. Her unanswerable questions smash mirrors to "contest" the force of the representations Rich uses and to destabilize the traditional sites of poetic usurpation. In "Eastern War Time," as in "Through Corralitos," time and space converge. The mass graves of Europe spill over from the continental canals of the forties to flood the room of the nineties poem.

Travailing after Outrage:
"For a Friend"

In "For a Friend in Travail," Rich asks questions which can be answered. Focusing directly on the other and rearticulating the *aubade* tradition, Rich encourages a friend to "tell" her suffering.[17] In "Corralitos," the other is silenced and distant, overcome by the waves. In "For a Friend," the other seems right there in her self-consciousness:

> *What are you going through?* she said, is the great question.
> Philosopher of oppression, theorist
> of the victories of force.
>
> We write from the marrow of our bones. What she did not
> ask, or tell: how victims save their own lives.
>
> That crawl along the ledge, then the ravelling span of fibre strung
> from one side to the other, I've dreamed that too
> Waking, not sure we made it.   Relief, apallment, of waking.
> Consciousness.   O, no.   To sleep again
> O to sleep without dreaming.
>
> How day breaks, when it breaks, how clear and light the moon
> melting into moon-colored air
> moist and sweet, here on the western edge.
> Love for the world, and we are part of it.
> How the poppies break from their sealed envelopes
> she did not tell.
>
> What are you going through, there on the other edge? (p. 51)

The lady in Donne's *aubade*, "Breake of Day," accuses the man of having a "businesse" that takes him away from her.[18] In "For a Friend," Rich's "I" makes the other's business her own. Unlike Donne's lady who dreads the death day brings, the "I" of "For a Friend" speaks of daylight as a precursor to night, "moist and sweet." After the difficult night, difference is at once shattering—"how day breaks"—and nothing—"how the moon melts into moon-colored air." In "Through Corralitos," the terrible end of the myth circles round to the innocent beginning so that death triumphs. In its three repetitions, the "break" of Rich's *aubade* calms the separation anxiety of Donne's "Breake of Day" because its harshness is softened by the melting moon and absorbed by the moony air. Already colored sympathetically, the air *breaks,* and thereby softens, the fall. Nothing is final. Here, Rich draws *this circle,* as she did in "Twenty-One Love Poems," to say something else: "in this round world the corners are imagined." The difference of difference is less significant than being "part of it." In *extremis,* the precarious western ledge (the dark night of the soul) merges with the saving eastern edge (the bright light of waking). To break the "sealed envelope" may not be to tell. It may be to listen. The poppy heralds a red-lettered day. The poet who meets a friend in "travail" facilitates a birth into the other, not a separation (as in "Twenty-One Love Poems") but a joining. Unsealing the envelope and penetrating beyond the sound barrier are acts that also open the self up to the other's expressiveness: "what are *you* going through?" Victims save their own lives by keeping the narrative thread alive: the "ravelling span of fibre strung."

In the responding letter, the other "tells." The self listens. Like a hand reaching across an abyss, the question forms a connection to the other that spans the difference to open the possibility for dialogue. That connection suggests that the envelope can spontaneously open to reveal new life inside rather than to shatter the life outside. The allusion to dream and sleep again, like Hamlet's "consummation / devoutly to be wished" (3.1. 63–64)[19] speaks to the death-wish—the appallment—in day's pale light, the "death-drive" that connects the postmodern to the early modern and Rich's *aubade* to Donne's "Breake of Day."

The moon colored sky is both comforting and draining: yet another replication of an already known pallor. Rich's "appallment" condenses Hamlet's "pale cast of thought." But her "consciousness," a heroic waking to the other, is not quite Hamlet's conscience, a cowardly quaking in the self. The "undiscovered country" that gives Hamlet pause is the other-discovered country language bridges in Rich's poem when it unseals the edges. For Hamlet, the question centers on the self in isolation. For Rich, it moves the self into the community: "what are you going through?" If Hamlet's alternatives in the "To be or not to be" speech are indistinguishable from each other, Rich's *what* is answerable. It provides a safety net where language can soften into meaning. Like daylight fusing with moon-colored air and like Lowell's crocus in "The Day" (*Day by Day,* p. 53), the poppies "break" from their sealed envelopes to open up meltingly and to begin the quiet discourse that comes after the voice of Outrage. The question casts the extending rope, dangling a poetic line that heals the self, angling a political line that imagines the other. Like Donne's "inward narrow crooked lanes / [that] Do purge sea waters fretful salt away" ("The Triple Foole," p. 52), the question—"what are *you* going through?"—intimates that the difficult tunnel has the light of articulated language at the end. Asking the question presupposes an answer, one not yet formulated but still possible.

In "Final Notations," Rich echoes the Marvell of "Damon the Mower" to demonstrate how language and its necessary formulae overtake self and its presumed independence. When the self projects itself as other, the other, in turn, endangers the self: "it will become your will." In "Through Corralitos," Rich argues that language and what she calls mere "containment" (*Points of Departure*, p. 7) confine both the depicted other and the depicting self. But, in "For a Friend," she goes beyond the breaking point and over the edge to speak, as Donne appears to in "A Valediction: Forbidding Mourning," against "the breach." Her line, "the ravelling span of fibre strung / from one side to the other," seems at first glance to be an equivalent of Donne's "an expansion / Like gold to ayery thinnesse beat" (p. 63). But, while Donne's solid gold fades into vaporous thinness, Rich's ravelling span weaves itself back again, forming a solid bridge to the saving "ledge." Rich speaks beyond the inevitably of the chasm and in the hope of an "expansion" that commemorates the possibility of return. Her language spans the distance between self and other to "see how words come down to us and how we can go on with them" (Montenegro, *Points of Departure*, p. 7). The present tense of "what are you going through" has a future end in sight. The travail of death pain fuses with the travail (in its obsolete sense) of birth pain and thereby becomes the means to a rebirth in a place "where the end of suffering will begin."[20]

In providing the substance for an answer by phrasing the question in answerable terms, the inquisitor of "For a Friend" also assures the future of narrative. "Final Notations" dictates the last word. "For a Friend" assumes another story, one contained within the letter of the sealed envelope. Through the encirclements of internal rhyme, that letter moves away from the abyss of self to turn the corner from the "outer edge" and to find poetic footing in the containing—hence saving—inner ledge. The reified "you" in "For a Friend" goes beyond the invented other of "Twenty-One Love Poems" to focus on something not yet drawn there: the future possibility of an other who escapes Petrarchism's other-denying forms, an Eve with a life of her own. That Laura-Eve is palpably present, as she is in those rare moments in *Rime sparse* 181, 188, 237, and 354, where the woman seems to return the poet's desire with a desire of her own. The overwhelming difficulty in *Atlas* is the horror of the past that remains "unsatisfied / lifting [its] smoky mirror" (p. 44). In "Through Corralitos," the mirror

176 ᴖ *The American Love Lyric after Auschwitz and Hiroshima*

reflects "outward/in outrage" to point toward "such unprotection" (p. 49). In "For a Friend," the victim is given a voice and a body, though the answer to the question—"what are you going through?"—is not yet given. In *Atlas*, Rich "opens" the way to what will be her continuing "transformation" and "rearticulation" ("Against Proper Objects," 20) of the forms she inherits. In her next book, the 1995 *Dark Fields of the Republic*, Rich "goes on" despite her sense that "this life of continuing is for the sane mad / and the bravest monsters" (*Dark Fields*, p. 71) to stretch the boundaries and the oxymoron still further. Entering the interspace of the oxymoronic sensibility she inherits from her Petrarchan predecessors, she moves inside and outside of the margins to accommodate the form to the other in the self and the selfhood of those others expropriated by the repressions she so "monstrously" and "bravely" identifies in *Atlas*.

Chapter 7 ✑

"AT LONG LAST FIRST":
ADRIENNE RICH'S *DARK FIELDS*
AND SAMUEL BECKETT'S
COLORLESS CLIFF

Un dévoilement sans fin, voile derrière voile, plan sur plan de transparences imparfaites, un dévoilement vers l'indévoilable, le rien, la chose à nouveau.

An infinite unveiling, veil behind veil, plane upon plane of imperfect transparencies, an unveiling toward the unveilable, nothingness, the thing, again.
—Samuel Beckett[1]

In the 1991 *An Atlas of the Difficult World,* Rich's Laura-Medusa haunts the poet, crashing through the restrictive wall at the edge of the form to challenge its defining mechanisms. Four years later, in the 1995 *Dark Fields of the Republic,* the still-troubled poet moves from the center she herself inhabits and implodes the form from within. Tinkering with the characteristic oxymoron, Rich shifts the balance from the "either/or" of the conventional *impossibilia,* to the "both/and" of her revisionism. The new poetic she evolves seems more attuned to the marginalized and to the anxieties of post–World War II reality. As Rich's recent work inclines more deeply inward, she also moves more courageously backward to reassess her prewar life, to the thirties that fed into the forties and to the culture that shaped her.

In fact, there is a curious parallel between her "recovered" oxymorons and recent scientific discoveries that (like her poetry of the nineties) attempts in very concrete terms to address issues raised before the war. In language that seems remarkably similar to the "both/and" toward which Rich's revisions aspire, Malcolm W. Browne describes how physicists at the National Institute of Standards and Technology have used the beryllium atom to document the feasibility of occupying two states at once:

The main object of the institute's experiments was to create the atomic equivalent of "Schrodinger's cat"—the hypothetical victim of a whimsical "thought experiment" devised in 1935 by the German quantum theorist Erwin Schrodinger to illustrate one paradox of quantum theory.

Schrodinger suggested that a box might be built and a live cat and a capsule of poison gas put inside. The capsule could be broken, and the lethal poison released, by a trigger mechanism actuated by the decay of a radioactive atom. The experiment would be conducted during a specified period of time in which there could be a precisely 50–50 chance that the atom would decay, killing the cat, or would not decay, leaving the cat alive.[2]

That the psychological suspension of states—dead and alive—is as old as the oxymoron, poets since Petrarch have long accepted as a given. In the typical Petrarchan poem, the poet seems victim of a Laura remarkably like Schrodinger, an *inamorata* who casts her would-be lover into a terminally indeterminate position while she resists, through a variety of dodges, all closure. The oxymoron represents the *impossibilia* as a tease, promising everything in the expectation, eliminating everything in the negation. In the traditional poem, "dead and alive" comes to mean "dead." By heightening the impossibility (the feeling that no alternative is possible and that nothing is settled) the oxymoron erodes the form from within, undoing confidence at the very moment of expectation. When practical physicists resolve the uncertainty in the thought problem by proving that it is indeed possible to occupy two states at once, they tilt the balance in favor of life and perhaps to a new understanding of the split as a necessary beginning. Recalibrating the metaphysical contradictions of Petrarchism to take into account the destabilization she sees as inherent to the poetic, Rich can be linked to Samuel Beckett who, earlier than other writers of his generation, seems to have come to terms with the "endgame[s]" of post-Hiroshima reality.

Both writers seem intrigued by the undecidability of the poetic and the tease of deferral. Both invent a way to have it both ways—to define what was wrong in the forms and to redirect them to answer the very problems they pose. Though Beckett's primary medium is prose, his thinking, like Rich's, is Petrarchan both in its reliance on a dyadic structure and its predilection for metamorphosis. In their reservations about the sublimation factor that defines the poetic, Beckett and Rich similarly express an ambivalence that seemed all the more urgent to convey in the post-Hiroshima, post-Holocaust, years so central to their literary coming of age. In *Dark Fields,* as in *Atlas,* Rich keeps coming back to those years, as if—in returning to them—she might revise the self she finds there.[3] Both Beckett and Rich share a sense of dissatisfaction with the limitations of the "received . . . forms"[4] they inevitably follow. Both indict themselves for using them in earlier work and, at a later stage, return to the same poetic to answer their own accusations. The self-critical Beckett and Rich can be compared through his 1949 French essay that comprises an introduction to a book about his contemporary, the Dutch painter, Bram Van Velde (first appearing in France in 1958, later translated to English by Beckett and published by Grove Press in 1960), and her *An Atlas of the Difficult World* of 1992, respectively. The revisionist Beckett emerges in the 1975 piece entitled "The Cliff," dedicated to Bram Van Velde and translated in 1996 by Edith Fournier, the revisionist Rich in the 1995 "Inscriptions" from *Dark Fields of the Republic.*

For both writers, the later works chronicle recognizable returns to representational failures that each catalogued earlier. In the earlier works, both seem unable to define themselves outside of conventional—what Beckett explicitly labels bourgeois, what Rich calls utterly selfish—terms. In the later works, both enter the very spaces—Beckett the "verge upon verge,"[5] Rich the "thinnest air" (*Dark Fields*, p. 75)—that, at first, seemed closed off: zones impossible to enter and remain alive. In the 1949 essay, Beckett depicts himself as inadequate to the heroic artist he describes. Viewing a Van Velde painting, he feels unable to know what "this coloured plane, that was not there before is."[6] Contrastingly, when he writes *to* Bram Van Velde in 1975, Beckett merges with the artist and moves with him "from thence away" ("The Cliff," p. 257). In the 1991 *An Atlas of the Difficult World,* Rich points an accusatory finger at herself, the "I" who, in the 1978 "Twenty-One Love Poems," inscribed the "circle"[7] of her exclusiveness. But in the last poem of the 1995 *Dark Fields of the Republic,* she slips into the mode of her denouncer and—with the ragged edges of "Inscriptions"—includes the "extremes" (p. 73) that exceed the boundaries of the poetic she had earlier embraced.

In "The Cliff" and in "Inscriptions," Beckett and Rich enter the "undiscovered country," between decay and being alive, self and other, impasse and exhilaration which, in earlier works, each had claimed inaccessible. Both writers set up heroes—Beckett, Van Velde, Rich her actual lover and various avatars who are known political activists (Ethel Rosenberg, Rosa Luxembourg)—next to whom they feel inadequate. Both first define their own lack through the counter example of the admired other. Both later (Beckett in 1975, Rich in 1995) move into the narrow space their heroes inhabit, a space that first reduces, and subsequently frees, them to "the elements." Like *The Tempest's* Ariel, they follow their deforming impulses even as they shape seemingly solid forms. Both similarly begin with Hamlet's remembered ghosts, Beckett with a skull like Yorick's in "The Cliff," Rich with the old Hamlet's beyond-the-grave imperatives in "Inscriptions." Both similarly end with Ariel's dematerializing self, moving (as Beckett writes) "from thence away from it all" ("The Cliff," p. 257). In the 1988 "She," Rich also sets out to evade the detritis of old forms, alluding to the over-stuffed images she escapes when she is "not there" (*An Atlas of the Difficult World*, p. 29). In 1995, she specifies what "not being there" in the impris-oning forms might mean. In the arena between the haunting of Hamlet and the desiring of Ariel, Beckett and Rich work toward a reassessment of the real, lapsing into an anamorphic image where a second vision wipes out the first one. Finally, bypassing the "either-or" of anamorphism, they make way for the "both and" of a newly situated "old" poetic, what Louis Marin calls "the movement of a momentarily suspended transition."[8] The revital-izations enable them to view Petrarchism from the perspective of the desired other in the dyad.

Petrarchan poems are built, as Gordon Braden puts it, on the "prolonged elaboration . . . [of] an erotic trance,"[9] the desire for an object that perpet-ually refuses to yield. But the trance itself proves so exhilarating that the poet sees it as a way of sustaining two things at once: first, the heightened excitement stimulated by desire and, second, the comforting replacement afforded by sublimation: poem for body. In the 366 poems of the *Rime sparse*, Petrarch settles for "the laurel of poetic achievement and glory" (Robert Durling, *Petrarch's Lyric Poems*, p. 27) but returns, each time when he begins again, to a newly aroused state of expectation about the body he can't have. The rejection of one poem serves as the occasion for the next one. From the point of view of poetry, the woman silenced by the Petrar-chan tradition is desired for what she won't say. Hinting at an arena not yet named even though the formula for naming has been dutifully evoked, her "no" means more than her "yes" might. Within Petrarchism itself is an acknowledgment of a shortcoming actually prolonged by the repeated elaboration. Something about the other is unattainable; that's a given. But something about the other is also uncontainable in a form accessible to the poet. As woman, Daphne sees what the poet can't have. As laurel, she gives him something else instead. But the sublimation of form actively represses what both poet and woman want: the "something" that eludes representa-tion.

And it is the excess of the "both and" that Beckett and Rich seize on when they assert that the abstracting impulse of the other (Laura's resis-tance to being confined to forms not her own) is in some way akin to the amorphous state in the self (the originating excitment that started the chase) and the consequent admission that the forms that confine the other also constrict the self. They define desire not so much as a Lacanian lack but as a poetical doubling, a state beyond division (and yet before it), a state resolving contradiction (by embracing inwardness). Seeking access to that excess, Beckett and Rich return to a time before language and its normative strictures to revitalize precisely the arena that Lowell awakens in the "child's daubs" ("The Day," *Day by Day*, p. 53), the moment when the representational matrix is unfettered by the historical bind. In the undecidability of the oxymoron lies the possibility for realizing the excitement the poet originally felt. By reworking the extremes of the oxymoron so that they are no longer self-canceling, Beckett and Rich join with the other effaced in the typical dyad to change the order of things: "at long last first." Rendering the annulments of the oxymoron as additions, they overcome the history of repression to make the other absented in the beginning present now. Beckett and Rich share a sense that the terms of relation they use point (as Beckett puts it) to "the acute and increasing anxiety of the relation itself, as though shadowed more and more darkly by a sense of invalidity, of the inadequacy of existence at the expense of all that it excludes."[10] Rich is forced by the voices she invents to acknowledge her own lapses, her past failures to protect the unprotected or to honor the unnamed. Beckett is less explicit about identifying the connections between a narrow and therefore "inadequate" art and an ideology based on exclusionary practices. Yet both struggle through the problematics of erasure in remarkably similar ways and both return therefore to the post–World War II moments when the so-called progress of enlightened culture seems most to have failed.

With her references in *Dark Fields of the Republic* to biographical activists—her lover (pp. 59–69), Rosa Luxembourg (p. 5), Ethel Rosenberg (pp. 23–4, 65)—Rich seems more directly political in her models of social activism. But, in choosing Van Velde as the artist who is the "first to submit" (*Bram Van Velde*, p. 10) wholly to "the absence of terms or if you like the presence of unavailable terms" (pp. 10–13), Beckett defines the conditions under which the "fidelity to failure" makes it necessary to work through the old forms to uncover—the hint of a face, the face of a hint— what the old forms repressed: the other on its own terms. Van Velde indicates the inadequacy of representation as the right side of his paintings renders the left side in doubt. Beckett similarly emphasizes his remoteness from the creative matrix when he identifies Van Velde's mind as a "warren" (*Bram Van Velde*, p. 9) he can't readily enter; and Rich, when she speaks of history as an unfolding and a folding over: "It moves / in loops by switch-backs loosely strung" (p. 63). The "switchbacks" repeat the repressions of the past, covering over and thus distending the original violations. The loose string eventually hardens into a whipping "switch" as the historical connection swings around and catapults an earlier violation into being again. Reopening old wounds, such "switchbacks" fuse the torture instru-ment with its scarring effect and then extract a revenge based on an initial violation. Petrarch himself sometimes "switches back" in those rare *Rime sparse* places where Laura describes her wound and in turn wounds Petrarch, engraving him in stone. Similarly, Beckett's oxymoronic rephras-ing—"the absence of terms or the presence of unavailable terms"—under-scores the limitations of "terms" and refers to a double repression. Sublimation fails at the very point that it is conventionally expected to suc-ceed. The terms keep slipping away, always revealing something that can't quite be saved. The "switchback" points to a lesion there from the start. Like Laura-Mercury who stresses the difference between what she is and what Petrarch *says* she is, Beckett turns on language itself. The "terms" point to a vortex of inaccessibility, indicating their past failures, present inadequacy ("absence of terms"), and a future of missed or continually deferred connections ("presence of unavailable terms").

Absent-presence is a familiar Petrarchan oxymoron, usually used to describe either the living death of the artist or the elusive aura of the woman. But, for Beckett and Rich, the oxymoron describes the insuffi-ciency of art itself, an insight Beckett claims is contained in the work of Van Velde, Rich in the active politics of those (like her lover) braver than she. For Beckett and for Rich, the right terms are somehow just beyond reach. They seem to be owned by others (for Beckett, by Van Velde; for Rich, by her lover) who have already seen the desired matrix as an arena where new life might incubate.

Painting Petrarchan Pursuit, Pursuing the Painter's Vision

Van Velde in fact illustrates something about the divisions of Petrarchism that excites both Beckett and Rich. In his paintings, the simultaneous anx-iety and possibility of Petrarchism appear as echoes of landscapes, hints of portraiture that progessively undermine the connection to recognizable forms. A Van Velde "landscape" could as easily be a Van Velde "portrait," the fusion suggesting a mythic connection in the same way that suns and trees in the Petrarchan landscape (of, for example, Rich's "Through Cor-

ralitos under Rolls of Clouds") refer back to portraits of the poet and
Laura in the retelling of the Ovidian story of Apollo and Daphne.

In an early work "Nu aux arums," done between 1915 and 1920, the
artist establishes the right/left division that would be a benchmark of his
work.[11] The lilies on the left side mirror the woman's breasts on the right,
suggesting that it is possible to read backward from the portrait to the still
life. The pendular breasts of the woman repeat the phallic lilies on the left;
her two arms parallel the stems. The lilies work as symbols of sexuality and
death, strewn, as lilies are, on marriage and death beds.[12] They seem identical to the breasts, forming with them a circle of repetition simultaneously
as they invite the viewer into their central mysteries. But the woman's face
breaks the circle. Her eyes avoid the gaze, her head pointing downward and
away, reflecting an indifference, an aversion even, a desire to escape the circle of bodies and flowers. Though her body is gendered female, her elon-
gated and angular face resembles Van Velde's portrait of his brother, done
during the same year.[13] The resistance renders the lilies and breasts less
receptive, too aggressive in their lines to offer the expected maternal comfort. The face forces us to look at the lilies differently. The inward turning
denies the initial sense of opening; the masculine presence overtakes the
feminine, the woman absented and, hence, unavailing. The lilies as symbol
of death detract from the sustenance the breasts offer. In Kleinian terms,
the breasts become threatening in the same way as Rich describes the erotically feminine as phallic hazards to the desirer. In the culture of Petrarchism,
for men and for women, "lips were knives breasts razors" ("Inscriptions," p.
64). The desired object represented by the split is simultaneously the cutting agent defining the split. Projecting only an inner lack, the body simultaneously signifies the mirage of comfort and the menace of desire itself.
Like Daphne as laurel, the woman's metamorphosis in the Van Velde flowers renders her unavailable: "mains tenant le vide." When, in his later work,
Van Velde moves steadily away from recognizable forms, the rupture suggests the "lesion" or "locus of pain"[14] of the Lacanian void and becomes
more acute. The cut in the middle renders both sides equally cold, the mirror returning the self to itself.

In the postwar and increasingly abstract compositions, there are orbs and
lines that allude obliquely to female bodies and male linear forms as well as
still vaguer suggestions of mountains and moons, the phallic projections of
landscape tearing up against the circular organization of lunar and solar sky,
less and less certainty of form in contrast to bolder demarcations of formlessness. Moons and heads, suns and ovaries, seem interchangeable as inscape

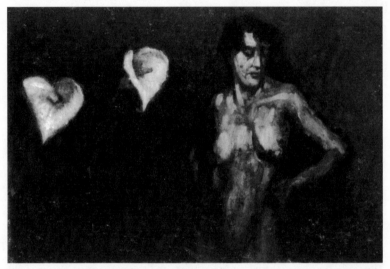

Bram Van Velde, "Nu au Arums," La Haye(?), 1915-1920. Photograph courtesy of Rainer Michael Mason, Musée Rath, Geneva. Permission granted by Catherine Putman, Paris.

and landscape fuse. Repeated in a different form as the viewer moves from left to right, those shifting images work through a dyadic structure to suggest that behind the metamorphosis is the dead end of the mirror. What is always there in Van Velde's work until the end is the right/left division of the canvas and the presence of a tension on both sides of the divide, a problem presented and resolved if you look one way, a solution denied in the undecidability of the other. In the 1970 painting where sandy colored projectiles might be the cliffs to which Beckett alludes in 1975, the lunar circle in the upper right seems poised to escape. Does it elude the slings at the lower left or repeat the sense that it is framed by shapes that imprison and impelled by the projectiles that render connection impossible? Is the left enclosed circle with the sandy background a precursor to the sepulchral (and black shadowed) noose at the right? Is the line in the center of the canvas permeable or are the two sides forever unanswerable to each other? Do the sides correspond at all? Is the shape at the upper right a sun, and in the mid-left a feminine triangle, a reversal of the line of pursuit or a sense that, read backward or forward, the forms, like the lilies and breasts in "Nu aux arums," are unavailing?

Van Velde's dyad is Petrarchan in the way it counters loss with discovery and threatens expectation with disappointment. Attempting to "render visible what is not originally represented,"[15] Van Velde pursues, as Beckett puts it, the "total object, complete with missing parts" ("Three Dialogues," p. 227). In pointing to the repressions inherent to forms, Rich and Beckett lament the void the forms reveal at their base. In demanding the "total object," Beckett names the lost synthesis simultaneously as he admits to the impossibility of any unification. Like Van Velde, Beckett and Rich are Petrarchan in: (1) their insistence on chase even as they resist closure; and (2) their constancy in revisiting the site of desire even as they point to the ineluctability of that site. But they are most united in the way they connect the landscape of desire to the very real scenario, brought out in the war, of the end of landscapes. Rich in America in the late 1990s and Beckett in France in the early 1950s seem to be inching toward the same new opening, one based on a recognition that the forms of love are very closely connected to the forms of war. Both concur in their assessment that there is a causal connection between what we thought before the war and what we did in the war. It is their mutual insistence on facing the dead ends of art and on finding at the edge the saving ledge of new language that links Beckett and Rich to each other and to the central concerns of this study.

For both, Petrarchism is the poetic medium for persistence and for the

Bram Van Velde, "Composition 1970." Carnegie Museum of Art, Pittsburgh; Purchase, Patron's Art Fund.

repetition of loss. Apollo endlessly pursues Daphne despite the fact that he inevitably confronts a dead end: lilies for Van Velde, laurel for the poet. Both recognize that Petrarchism is about what gets away. Apollo comes to Daphne from behind. In his desire to overtake her, Apollo also wants to become her, a transformation that would allow him to see what she sees, precisely what, in reducing her to an image and in remaining therefore loyal to his own aroused emotions, he could never have envisioned on his own. In the second instance, Daphne's sightlines are the lost landscape of Petrarchism: what looms before her as she runs to the other side of the Van Velde divide. Awaiting her of course—since we all know the outcome of the story—is death as metamorphosis. She becomes a different object. Her absence as resistant other calls the matrix into being; her presence as the new thing suggests the inadequacy of the matrix, a blankness Beckett evokes by playing on invisibility, Rich by playing on inaudibility. Beckett cites the "verge upon verge" ("The Cliff," p. 257) that obscures visual borders, Rich the "thinnest air" ("Inscriptions" 73) that in musical terms evokes a barely perceivable volume.

In the 1948 passage prefacing this chapter, Beckett describes the interval—the desired space—as the place between "le rien" (his failure to see) and "la chose à nouveau" (Van Velde's vision). Using the ambiguous phrase "la chose à nouveau," Beckett raises a problem for the translator: Is he stuck in "the [old] thing, again," enclosed in a self defeating circle? Or does "la chose à nouveau" suggest "the thing, anew," the possibility that the object might be reconstructed from the point of view of the other? In 1948, certain that what is represented is not the desired other but the desiring self, Beckett saw only the "thing, again."

From the Thing, Again / Toward the Thing, Anew

In the 1949 English translation, Beckett valorizes Van Velde's willingness to face the "absence of available terms. . . his fidelity to failure" (p. 13) while confessing his own confinement in the old forms of representation Van Velde leaves behind :

> My case since I am in the dock is that Bram Van Velde is the first to desist from . . . estheticised automatism, the first to submit wholly to the incoercible absence of relation, in the absence of terms, or if you like in the presence of unavailable terms, the first to admit that to be an artist is to fail, as no other dare fail, that failure is his world and to shrink from it desertion, art and craft, good housekeeping, living. I know that all that is required now, in order to bring even this horrible matter to an acceptable conclusion, is to

make of this submission, this admission, this fidelity to failure, a new occasion, a new term of relation, and of the act which, unable to act, obliged to act, he makes, an expressive act, even if only of itself, of its impossibility, of its obligation. I know that my inability to do so places myself, and perhaps an innocent, in what I think is still called an unenviable situation. For what is this coloured plane, that was not there before. I don't know what it is, having never seen anything like it before. It seems to have nothing to do with art, in any case, if my memories of art are correct. (*Bram Van Velde,* pp. 10–13)

Prisoner of his inability to see, Beckett is "in the dock," the anti-hero locked within his own memories of what art was. He is victimized by "estheticized automatism," what Rich defines as the unavoidable "will" of form in "Final Notations," and Stevens describes as the industrialized pressure of "things alike" in his essay on Marcel Gromaire. Like Hamlet haunted by the ghost, Beckett is unable to move beyond what he remembers. Contrastingly, in full recognition of his limitations, the Van Velde Beckett describes feels only the futility of action as he submits [himself] wholly to the "incoercible absence of relation." Beckett describes Van Velde's rejection of the old forms as necessary to the discovery of a depth—something hidden behind the veil of form—that was never allowed to surface, something that the form covered over and rendered invisible. The "warren" where creativity takes place is gendered as a feminine secret Beckett cannot penetrate. As Beckett writes, "if the occasion appears as an unstable term of relation, the artist who is the other term, is hardly less so, thanks to his warren of modes and attitudes" (p. 9). The "warren" in this case is the half-hidden subterranean space that seems inaccessible because of "modes and attitudes" as yet undefined. In the warren is "the thing, anew" that Beckett cannot reach. Incubated by the warren, the "new thing" exists in potential. Protected from his gaze, the "new thing" is the other repressed in the history of representation by the imposing forms of the past.

To define the artist's mind as a rabbit warren is to see it as the inaccessible safe haven where production takes place invisibly beneath the surface. A labyrinth Beckett cannot enter, the warren is teeming with a life of its own. As minotaur on the edge, Beckett sees "nothing." Associating the warren with Van Velde renders the artist protective mother, presiding over a mysterious network, a creative matrix, Beckett cannot fathom. Linking the line of vision to sexual and maternal desire, Antonio Saura describes the relationships among Van Velde's orbs: "circles like eyes, eyes like breasts."[16] Beckett remains the hungry self unable to penetrate the veil or to tap the source of his desire. Conflating the object of desire with the desiring subject, Van Velde's circle suggests the return of Petrarchan images to the originative self.

That sexualization also casts the viewer as hunter, seeking access to the inviolate "new thing." Redeploying in subterranean unrecognizability the Petrarchan *impossibilia* of Sir Thomas Wyatt's translation from Petrarch, "Whoso List to Hunt," Beckett locates beneath the earth what Wyatt describes in terms of atmospheric heights. Wyatt struggles to hold "the wind in a net"[17] without losing its exciting momentum, Beckett to uncover the light that shines inwardly without dulling its inspirational impulse. And, like the Petrarchan Wyatt, who "may no more" (p. 77), the 1949 Beckett gives up the chase even though, like Wyatt, he knows "where is an hind" (p. 77). He has identified its warren. Like the wind and the woman, the vision Beckett seeks to contain, domesticate, and tame resists his shaping eye. In important ways, then, Beckett's relationship to Van Velde mirrors the painter's relationship to the real and the poet's relationship to the woman: there are recognizable signs of a figure or a landscape but it is a body or a scene most desired in its vagueness. As soon as the form materializes as breast, the other slips away. The "I" is an "eye" that sees what it wants but can never possess what it sees. Van Velde becomes the other Beckett seeks to contain, not the colleague in art he can emulate. For Beckett, held back in the dark, Van Velde's vision, is "le rien," what Luce Irigaray calls, the "zero of the [prenatal] infant's nocturnal abode."[18] For Van Velde, presiding over the warren, it is "la chose a nouveau," a possibility still to be enacted.

Despite his assessment of Van Velde as unfathomable in 1949, Beckett nevertheless penetrates the "thing, anew" envisioned by the artist in the brief tribute he wrote to Van Velde in 1975. Hovering between landscape and portrait, Beckett's sketch undoes both. His "portrait" is a skull; his cliff "vanishes," as the anamorphic images erase earlier signs and prepare for his entrance to the space between signs. From the piece itself, it is impossible to know whether Beckett describes a cliff in the landscape as the "window between earth and sky" (p. 257), a painting through whose frame (window) Beckett sees, or the eye that opens up to imagined possibility. His words set the lure for the painting that isn't as a Van Velde painting depicts a landscape that "vanishes." Asking "what do pictures want," W. J. T. Mitchell imagines a "thought experiment"[19] that we might similarly perform on Beckett's homage. Mitchell transfers to inanimate objects the question Frantz Fanon asked of blacks and Freud asked of women. In answer to his own question, Mitchell argues that "abstract paintings are pictures that want not to be pictures" (80). Similarly, Beckett's picture, neither painting nor cliff, fulfills the picture's desire *not* to be even as it evokes the viewer's desire to mimic the desiring picture's unlocatability and therefore similarly to escape the demands of the objectifying eye. In the viewer's desire to see and the picture's desire not to be, we have a play by play enactment of what it means to represent the desire of the other if the desired other desires not to be represented. Beckett gives us *ekphrasis* without a visual antecedent: the specter of a double with no original.

As Beckett's tribute proceeds, the eye gets lost and is absorbed by a skull. The unseen object reflects backward on the seeing subject, who becomes ghost to his own quest. In those terms, visual obsession can be termed a perpetual state of deforming, a desire, as Rich puts it, to "gaz[e] at the wildest light" (*Dark Fields*, p. 72), the very opposite of the pictorial impulse that seeks to capture or, in Lowell's terms, to "caress" the light ("Epilogue," *Day by Day*, p. 127). Beckett slowly unravels the forms he sees, removing "veil upon veil" until he arrives at the "unveilable," the "verge upon verge," the moment where figure and ground overlap and where the difference between them is rendered nonexistent. Verge *toward* verge leads to Petrarchan deferral. "Verge upon verge" signals post-Petrarchan convergence. In 1949, Beckett is unable to penetrate the "warren" though he recognizes that it is there. In 1975, Beckett is delivered through the "window" to an outer space through which he hopes to gain access to the inner space of the artist he pursues:

The Cliff[20]

Window between sky and earth nowhere known. Opening on a colourless cliff. The crest escapes the eye wherever set. The base as well. Framed by two sections of sky forever white. Any hint in the sky at a land's end? The yonder ether? Of sea birds no trace. Or too pale to show. And then what proof of a face? None that the eye can find wherever set. It gives up and the bedlam head takes over. At long last first looms the shadow of a ledge. Patience it will be enlivened with mortal remains. A whole skull emerges in the end. One alone from amongst those such residua evince. Still attempting to sink back its coronal into the rock. The old stare half showing within the orbits. At times the cliff vanishes. Then off the eye flies to the whiteness verge upon verge. Or thence away from it all. (*The Complete Short Prose*, p. 257)

When he begins with the "window," Beckett shifts between gerund (describing the inside act of seeing) and adjective (describing the scene seen outside), using "opening" partly as a means toward the end, veering forward to the cliff, partly as the source of discovery, referring backward to the eye, which, in yet another remove, turns back to the "I" ambiguously. Is the mysterious "I" the painter, represented by the painting, or the viewer seeking the painting and the self it represents? Does a window let you see in or out? If the cliff is colorless, does it exist, the way vaporous air does, invisibly? Or does it exist as yet another eye, the source of vision merging with the desire to see? What you begin with in the Beckett image is a window that opens to nothing solid: landscapelessness; what you end with is a skull that closes in on nothing gelid: eyelessness. Thus the eye tracks its own disappearance. Eyelessness mirrors the nothing seen. Between those poles, Beckett arrives, first, at an anamorphic image, exchanging skull for cliff, and, second, at an oxymoronic image (merging remaindered skull with his remaining eye). The skull/cliff confusion is anamorphic in the way that Salvador Dalí used the term: "something seen only through the modality of misrecognition."[21] In this sense, the anamorphic is the thing not originally seen, but there. The oxymoronic is the thing there and not there, a space represented by the slimmest possible margin, a margin that turns out to be both an originary ambivalence and a desired state.

Making its way toward what will end up as an anamorphic image, the eye attempts to find a point of departure. Forming the Van Velde "line," the window reflects the described scene and the originating seer. The eye is represented by its mirror image, the window, and mirrored by its function, seeing. At the same time, the eye is blinded. As mirror of the landscape, its colorlessness merges signifier with signified. If René Magritte's famous eye is "the false mirror," the mirror that trades eye for sky, Beckett's mirror is faithful to both word and image, reflecting an eye for the savage bite of truth. The "verge upon verge" merges tooth to tooth, as the whiteness silences, the unyielding eye the equivalent of the closed bite. The window refuses to open; the mirror gives us back to ourselves: whiteness to no end. Clenched together, the teeth emit no sound. Gazing at a blank space, the eye sees nothing. In the face of a vast emptiness, in the space of absence, there is neither image nor sound. Thus, the eye mirrors and is unable to fathom what impresses it in a chiasmic replay of the active-passivity suggested by Ferdinand's command to Bosola in *The Duchess of Malfi*: "cover her face: mine eyes dazell" (4.2.251).[22] Where Ferdinand's eye "dazzles" in response to the Duchess's face, Beckett's eye is whitened, reflecting, in the "verge upon verge," the colorless cliff. If Ferdinand is stupefied by the implied Petrarchan sun of the Duchess's face, Beckett is blinded by the undifferentiated colorless cliff. It's not just that he gets what he sees; it's that he becomes what he sees. His white eye reflects the nothing that is, just as Ferdinand's eye reflects and therefore cannot bear everything the Duchess was.

The narrative question—do we have a story—fuses with the ocular question—do we have a "proof of face"? When Beckett details the scene anamorphically, he makes out a second vision that erases the first one, moving steadily through the window frame until, at the end, the cliff disappears. Using the "eye" instead of the "I," Beckett gives to the orb a psychological power it otherwise might not have. When it moves through the window, Beckett's eye is bodiless, Narcissus's mirror image in absolute attenuation, Echo's bones suggesting the absolute absence of self. When it actually is outside the window, Beckett's body is virtually eyeless: "The old stare half showing within the orbits." Losing its power to fix the other, the "old stare" is only half showing. Similarly, the cliff is absorbed by the sky: "the crest escapes the eye wherever set," the *crest* of the cliff, an anachrostic opposite of the imposing *set*. While the eye attempts to find a point of rest in the "crest," that ending is elusive, the internal rhymes (crest, rest, and set[23]) an effort to bridge the failure of visual closure to "no end." The landscape refuses to produce "a land's end," either vertically as the border between earth and sky, or horizontally as the border between sea and shore. The eye can never find a point of rest.

Yet in the middle of the journey, when the eye gives up it proprietariness "the bedlam head takes over." The picture turns around as the eye enters an anamorphic space. The ambiguous it—eye or crest, sight or seer—is promised a life that is itself a knowledge of death, the moment of beginning ("enlivened") arriving at the moment of ending ("mortal remains"). The eye gets a point of view just as it loses direction and gives up control: "Patience it will be enlivened with mortal remains." The scene comes to life when the anamorphic image of the death's head takes over: "At times the cliff vanishes," in the way that the skull in the Holbein portrait undermines the stability of the Ambassadors and their artifacts. When the cliff becomes a body's end (a skeleton), then it ceases to be a land's end (a crest). "Patience" yields what "setting" lost. Skull takes the place of cliff in the anamorphic image. The cliff—a land's end—is composed of skulls—body's ends.

But then the eye penetrates further, finding in the skull another version of its present quest. If the skull is "still attempting to sink back its coronal into the rock" and the "old stare half shows," then we are back at the beginning, only this time, bridged by a double oxymoron: "at long last first looms the shadow of a ledge." At the center of the oxymoron, the eye finds the little gap that then fosters the hoped for completion. That moment ends the cliff-hanger: the story only becomes possible through a letting go of possibility. *Patience*, to let happen, is the opposite of *setting*, to make happen. The voice ceases to describe the eye's failures. It issues a commanding prophecy phrased in terms of the oxymoron. The eye will find a point of life in the signifier of death's presence, "mortal remains." When the shadow seems a ledge, it erases the security of sanctuary. As a shadow, the ledge does not exist: the haven is a hoax, only an illusion of support.

Recovering his initial desire at the end of the piece, Beckett has come close to the edge, to the "shadow of a ledge," where a safe landing seems assured and the last vestige of the house of forms produces the first evidence of a launching ground. "The *shadow* of a ledge" ("l'ombre d'une corniche") is, however, insecure: a place (ledge) where possibility is infinite and annihilation (shadow) evident. Is a shadow the last residue of a shape once embodied or the preliminary sketch for a shape still to come? As it does for Stevens in the "shade" of "An Ordinary Evening" and for Lowell in "the glow shadow" of "The Downlook," Beckett's shadow land is half remnant of what came before and half new life. For Stevens and Lowell, the retrospective shadow is the past haunting back. For Beckett, the ledge is a retrospective glimmer of hope and a contemporaneous trick of despair, evoked as wished-for mirage simultaneously as it is retracted as physical support. It is a ledge but only the shadow of one, a treacherous trick of relief (shadow) and the imagined possibility of a start (ledge). At the edge is the jumping off point into the "bedlam head," just as, at the ledge, is the uttermost point of full desire.

Beckett's "bedlam head" is both currently dead, a skull, and a reminder of the "seething brain" that once was. Infinite possibility in the bedlam; definitive end in the skull. In the frenzy of "bedlam" Beckett sees the possibility for life in death: chaos yields to the "warren." As counter to the skull, "bedlam" evokes a teeming vitality. Choosing shadow and ledge, Beckett is dead and alive. Reversing the order and turning the chase around, his first comes last, the way Marvell's does in "To His Coy Mistress": "Thus, though we cannot make our Sun / stand still, Yet we will make him run."[24] With "Time's winged Charriot" subjected by their chase, rather than at their back, the embracing lovers of Marvell's poem change the linear into the circular: "Let us roll all our Strength and all / Our sweetness, up into one Ball." In Marvell's pun on sun/son, Apollo (mythic evocation of the pursuing male sun) becomes an egg (psychic symbol of the son-producing female). As Marvell's sun is forced, like Daphne, to run from its pursuers, so Beckett's eye—the last thing seeing—becomes the first object seen—an "opening" to the female matrix, a receptive crack in the egg.

If, as Timothy Bahti contends, a lyric is *"a role offered a reader,"*[25] then

Beckett offers his tribute for Van Velde to read and thereby asks the artist to follow him following Van Velde. Van Velde is invited to read Beckett's reading and, hence, to become Beckett. What Van Velde admires—the unavailable—is cast forward yet again as an object not yet formed—the invisible. Instead of a painting, we have the absence of a painting. Imbricated in the text is the desiring other whose absence undermines objectification and whose presence veers toward erasure. At the end, as the last sign, is the beginning: the painting remains to be painted, open to both Van Velde and Beckett. The denuding of the landscape is triumphant, a sense of freedom that comes from passing through the window and leaving behind the house of forms altogether. "Thence away from it all" takes us back to the beginning, an oxymoron that turns the chase around as Beckett allows Van Velde to read him reading Van Velde.[26] With that reversal, the oxymoron shifts ever so slightly from shadow onto the ledge. Rich similarly turns the chase around as she seeks climax after climax in a never-ending pursuit of what she calls the "extremes" (p. 73), her version of Beckett's overlapping "verge upon verge." Like Beckett, Rich inverts the order and offers to her reader the role she herself plays. In that offering, difference vanishes into "thinnest air" (p. 73).

Still Roaring: The Thinnest Air

With *Dark Fields of the Republic*, Rich again takes up the themes that haunt the 1991 *An Atlas of the Difficult World*, setting her love poems and the privileging of a special place for the "ones we love" (*An Atlas of the Difficult World*, p. 49) against the accusation that such protection is utterly selfish. When Rich returns in the later book to the forms she earlier condemns, she retraces the territory uncovered in *Atlas* and the horrors of World War II superannuated by the still greater guilt of having survived the war unscathed and of going on to live and write afterward. Rich's strategy for dealing with her inadequacies is twofold in *Dark Fields*. It involves first uncovering an earlier self, as if to find the moment when she might confess her complicity in the process she condemns, and then becoming her accuser, so that, having touched the bottom, she can use the voice of the other against the self. That process works, the way the voice of Outrage does in "Through Corralitos under Rolls of Cloud," to change the picture we think we see and to expose the weakness of the self. But, in "Inscriptions," it also forges an opening that allows the "I," confessing the excess of its desire, to use the condemned form as the vehicle of escape.[27] In this last phase, the "I" becomes the unyielding other it invents—just as Beckett, in the 1975 Van Velde tribute, moves with the artist into an obscurity that represents what he defines as the only possibility for being. Situating her at the maximum of the minimum, such a transformation allows Rich to dissolve. Rich enters the birth canal of the warren and uses it as a hiding place. By the end of "Inscriptions," she is at the center of the oxymoron.

In this series, Rich complicates the political scene with the love scene, contrasting the socially committed lover to the poetry-committed self. Poem ONE: "COMRADE" opens expectantly, lover and other engaged in a process of mutual discovery: "it's the one known and unknown / who stands for, imagines the other   with whom faith could be kept" (p. 59). Like chemists measuring carefully hefted test tubes of self, the "I" and the "you" exchange places, trying to fathom what the other sees and hears: "my testimony: yours" (p. 59). Studying the "you's" line of vision, Rich renders her "inscription" both a dedication to the other and an attempt geometrically to slide into her by writing about her. The first and second stanzas of poem ONE are homages to the beloved who sees her role as charter and reliever of others' pain. In poem ONE, the "you" is the socially active, political other whom the "I" wishes to become.

The third stanza of poem ONE is a devastating answer, as if the "you" sent back the "ethical flowers" (p. 59) the "I" had offered in the second stanza, the rejection indicating that it is impossible to know self or other. Ridiculing the idea of becoming the other, the retorting "you" argues that it is impossible to know the self. What began as chiasmic possibility—knowledge as a transferable commodity, sliding from one vessel to another—ends as a closed circuit—the self repeating itself to no end:

> The self unlocked to many selves.
> A mirror handed to one who just released
> from the locked ward from solitary from preventive detention
> sees in her thicket of hair her lost eyebrows
> whole populations.
> One who discharged from war stares in the looking-glass of home
> at what he finds there, sees in the undischarged tumult of
>   his own eye
> how thickskinned peace is, and those who claim to promote it. (p. 60)

The anarchy set loose by the "unlocked self" and the "undischarged tumult" links an already destructive anteriority to a still-to-be-experienced explosion. The past is guilty as charged. The thicket and the tumult contain a murderousness waiting to be disclosed. In "Inscriptions," there is no state of recoverable innocence. Like Beckett's "bedlam head," the "undischarged tumult" refers to a seething excess pressing against the iron bars of preconceived forms. "Peace is thickskinned," covering over a deeply repressed rage. The last stanza of poem ONE reveals a lion in the other Rich pursues, as the mirror person leaps out at the original to break the boundaries between self and other, present and past. Subverting the good intentions of poem ONE is the resistant other who undoes her idealization by proclaiming her ferocity and defies her representation by emphasizing her spatial and temporal unlocatability. Like Medusa on Perseus's shield, the anamorphic blur in the mirror is a monster. The future becomes a not-yet-completed past as unlocked selves and undischarged tumult reveal a bestiality at the core. The "you" resists the "I's" effort to compartmentalize, lionize, and become her.

Having failed—in the first poem—to present the self *as* the other, the "I" tries, in poems TWO through FIVE, to present the self *to* the other. That presentation involves a series of rhetorical questions put to the "you," which the "I" struggles nevertheless to answer, and a series of questions put to the "I," which the "I" seeks, in various ways, to evade. As if in response to the impossibility of knowing the other, the "I" responds by representing herself. Twice she asks:

Should I simplify my life for you? (pp. 63, 64)

Partly that question is an answer to the tumult and thicket—the complexity—of poem ONE and partly a desire to separate out two forms of the "I's" history, as social political self, as sexual poetical self. But, mostly it involves a shift from the "either or" of anamorphism to the "both and" of the oxymoron. At first, life's possibilities are open to interpretation, as one mood overcomes another, and Rich fluctuates between a feeling that political involvement is "a movement" that might buoy her and the fear that it might open a deep current, a "*terror [she] couldn't swim with*" (p. 61). Still lingering in anamorphism, Rich characterizes the alternatives as "a black or a red tulip opening" (p. 61). But when she uses the same colorings oxymoronically, she moves through two stages. In poems TWO through FOUR, she switches from the "either or" of the anamorphic image into the cancellations of both in the oxymoronic image, as the hopeful beginning inevitably leads to a dark end. She repeats the red-black oxymoron three times (pp. 61, 64, 65), unfolding a biography that ends in the death of her expectant self. In poem SIX: "EDGELIT," when she alludes to yet a fourth use, she turns the oxymoron around, stoking the black ashes of her desire until it results in the red blaze of an inner fire. For the red-black of the impossible alternatives, poem SIX offers the black-red of poetic rebirth, one that both takes the failure of representation into account and reshapes the form that encodes the failure. Like Beckett's, her reversal turns the dead-end of the poetic into the first arrival of the phoenix. Rising from her ashes, Rich emerges in poem SIX beyond the forms of her confinement.

In poem TWO: "MOVEMENT," the double possibility merely reverts to a dark field:

> one mind unfurling like a redblack peony
> quenched into percentile, drop out, stubbed-out bud. (p. 61)

Spring is immediately outdone by winter; bloody vitality turns into its remaindered failure. The quantifiable certainty of death wipes out the expectant growth of spring: "when I consider everything that grows / Holds in perfection but a little moment" (Shakespeare, "Sonnet 15"[28]). What begins as alternative possibilities—a black *or* a red tulip—becomes, with the peony, a single flower: redblack. The dark underside of death is apparent from the first bloom. Retrospectively, the peony is erased before it opens up.

Later in the series, Rich tells her history as a writer in terms of the same self-canceling matrix. She refers to a "red-and-black notebook" (p. 64) and a "red-and-black enamelled coffee-pot" (p. 65) at key junctures where writing and love enter the realm of death, the way bud reverts to its opposite, stubbed-out. In Poem FOUR: "HISTORY," she thickens the expected black and white (of the Hollywood mythos; the stenciled school book; the household commonplace, pp. 64–65) into three dimensional blood and death, the rush of red expectancy drained by the black lines of conformity. When she returns to her beginnings in love, she refers back to the dark spring of the peony. Repeating the question she asked in poem TWO, the "I" discovers yet again the violent end of beginnings. The "I" opens Poem FOUR once more with the question she has already asked:

> Should I simplify my life for you?
> Don't ask how I began to love men.
> Don't ask how I began to love women. (p. 64)

In the first questions about simplification, she inverts what she had closed off in the "Final Notations" of *Atlas*: "it will not be simple" (*Atlas*, p. 57), just as, in the last question, she affirms what "Final Notations" had already decreed: the unspecified "it" (the normative form of desire) will "become your will" (*Atlas*, p. 57):

> (*When shall we learn, what should be clear as day,*
> *We cannot choose what we are free to love?*), p. 65

The poem answers the question (when do we learn about our lack of freedom) first by describing the social construction of self; then by analyzing the psychic destruction of self; and, finally, by acknowledging the generic constraints on the poet.

Poem FOUR is premised on comedy as commanding patriarchal form. The young heroine is shaped by the society—music, films, teachers—who offered, by example or counter-example, ways of being happy. Marriage is the objective of the forms that culturally determine and socialize the self. The poem ends with a wedding and begins with the courtship rituals leading up to it; the "I" streaks the silver-gray Hollywood image with the red lipstick of Hollywood "dreams":

> Dreaming that dream
> we had to maze our way through a wood
> where lips were knives breasts razors and I hid
> in the cage of my mind scribbling
> *this map stops where it all begins*
> into a red-and-black notebook. (p. 64)

Here the red-and-black notebook returns to the self-canceling peonies. The "I" is lost in the thicket, where lips sever, and, as they do in the Van Velde portrait, breasts cut. The source of womanly nurturing becomes phallic knife and razor to the self. When the mind takes over the instruments of male inscription, it becomes a threat to the female body.

The self canceling imagination can describe only the origin of its own imprisonment in "the cage" of the mind. Thus the scribbling act of liberation gets stuck in the inscriptive trap and the "I's" dreams of patriarchal love, framed by Hollywood and family, end in the perpetuation of deadening conventions. The map of possibility stops where "it"—the culturally determined form that converts all possible selves into the mold—takes over. The forest is a maze in which female images are both erotically evoked and psychically dangerous. That destruction spills out into the social and historical context where the beginnings of World War II peace signify the end of life: "*this map stops where it all begins.*" Moving through nuclear fallout to the danger of nuclear secrets, Rich fuses her own wed-

ding with that of the accused spies, Ethel and Julius Rosenberg. Opening
the self-canceling notebook with the unconscious dream work, Rich con-
cludes it with the self-canceling waking reality:

> and the red-and-black enamelled coffee-pot dripped slow through the dark
>   grounds
> —appetite terror power tenderness
> the long kiss in the stairwell the switch thrown
> on two Jewish Communists married to each other
> the definitive crunch of glass at the end of the wedding?
> (*When shall we learn, what should be clear as day,*
> *we cannot choose what we are free to love?*), p. 65

As the "I" turns the haze of the dream into clear day and the coffee stim-
ulant, she still works through the same "dark grounds," merging the personal with the societal, the definitive crunch of the broken wedding glass
sending back the shattered image of a self in the shards, freedom to love
stymied by lack of choice. The dark grounds repress the self as the origin
of the desired other is defined by society. The clear glass image of the day
turns back to the dark ground rules of the imperious society. This time, the
passion of beginning is cancelled with the thrown switch of electrocution,
just as peace rained with the knowledge that the "world could end" (p. 64).
The oxymorons—appetite-terror, power-tenderness—annihilate feeling, as
the pressure to conform and the power of convention spoil appetite and
bully tenderness. The symbol of beginnings (peace raining down) merges
with the symptom of endings ("Hiroshima Nagasaki Utah Nevada," p. 64).
The "quality" of savagery rains down. Solids shatter and simplification
means acquiescing to acceptable forms. In the fourth poem, the "I," offering herself to the "you," commands the "you" to remember a self overcome by postwar social pressures, the red of her awakened passion
dampened by the black of her subdued performance. Stubbed out, the bud
of her initiative yields to the force of predetermined expectations.

With poem SIX, the "I" returns to her life as poet-lover. In her guilty
pleasure, she works toward another sense of the oxymoron:

> In my sixty-fifth year I know something about language:
> it can eat or be eaten by experience (p. 71)

Experience makes us eat our words. We regret what we said. But language also
preempts experience. As an end in itself, it satisfies and therefore virtualizes the
actual hunger. The conscious participation in the language game is partly a

Woody Allenesque "the food is terrible and the portions so small" love of complaint and partly a Petrarchan feeding on absence: "language / can eat or be eaten by experience." Experience—the having that renders poetics unnecessary—eats the impetus for words. The impetus for words feeds on the absence of experience, the fertile lack that sets it into being. The red-black embers she stokes at the end are implicitly turned around (like Beckett's "at long last first") to the black-red of "sunklight of bloody afterglow," (p. 72).

When she vows, however, to "go on," Rich continues to seek sustenance in words:

> This week I've dredged my pages
> for anything usable
>   head, heart, perforated
> by raw disgust and fear
> If I dredge up anything, it's suffused
> by what it works in, "like the dyer's hand"
> I name it unsteady, slick, unworthy
>
> and I go on. (pp. 70–71)

Choosing to stick with the incorrect "suffused" she had imprecisely remembered, rather than the "subdued" of the text, she deliberately misquotes the Shakespearean line of sonnet 111.[29] To be *subdued* by what one works in "like the dyer's hand" is to be, as she was at the end of "Final Notations," controlled by the poetic medium: "it will become your will" (*An Atlas of the Difficult World*, p. 57). But to be *suffused* by what one works in is to be fed and strengthened by the self-absorbing material. Despite the fact that Rich confesses the "unworthiness" of her appetite for the forms that erase her, she finishes the lines by simultaneously extending their absence (going on) and denying it (moving forward). Rich suggests that beyond expectation the medium offers the warren of a new life. She is nurtured by resources that exceed the forms, even though going through the forms is somehow necessary for the realization.

In the poem's final images, Rich reaches the full potential of the oxymoron, as she continues the Shakespearean play,[30] moving from the "remember me" of *Hamlet* (1.5.90),[31] through *The Tempest's* song and Ariel's thinnest air, to incorporate the "dream" of Sonnet 129 (*Shakespeare's Sonnets,* p. 373). She begins with the imploring ghost and works her way to the despairing Prospero without voicing any of Prospero's panic:

> *Remember me . . . . O, O, O,*
> *O, remember me*

. . . .
this my irreplaceable
footprint vanishing from the air (p. 72)

First, she describes the inherited burden of Shakespearean tragedy. The
Hamlet answer is to reembody, to remember by becoming the stricken
father. The cry for help from the dead, "O, O, O," is also an apostrophe to
the living. "Be thou me," cries the father, demanding that the son similarly
relive his life. In the piteous cry for help—the "O, O, O," of "remember
me"—is the insidious demand that turns the young Hamlet into hapless
mirror of his father's helplessness. When she refers to yet another father
(Miranda's), Rich's last lines pick up (in their melting, vanishing, and thin
air) Prospero's famous lines:

> These our actors
> As I foretold you, were all spirits, and
> Are melted into air, into thin air. (4.1.149–51)[32]

Contemplating his mind and its creation, Prospero sees them as extensions
of a process leading only to evaporation. Noting the wisp of air into which
his pageant has faded, Prospero reasons by analogy that all forms will so dissolve and "leave not a rack behind." Hamlet's "O" equals Prospero's dissolution into zero. Hamlet's answer to past murders is to become his father
now; Prospero's answer to present melting is the comic promise of children
still to come. In the dynasty it anticipates, the marriage he arranges at the
end of the play leaves something, at least, behind. But, as we have already
seen in poem FOUR, for Rich the marriage "map stops where it all
begins" (p. 64). Comedy and its patriarchal closure shatter the selves they
define, leaving the same cipher that sucked in Hamlet. If the *Hamlet* allusion prompts Rich to recalibrate memory, the *Tempest* allusion allows her
to turn anticipation around. The reversals come as Rich doubles Shakespeare, repeating the ghost's "remember me" twice and outdoing Prospero's
"thin air" by exceeding it with her own "thinnest air" (p. 73). Her doubling
involves a series of distorted oxymorons that tilts the balance toward addi-
tion and a new life in the forms.

While Hamlet is wiped out by memory and Prospero mourns the lost
object ("the palaces . . . the great globe itself"), Rich revels in her "irreplaceable foot*print* vanishing into air." Setting the footprint in the air
instead of the earth, she anticipates that the index and the self it organizes
will also disappear. Her visual absence determines her auditory presence.

Air becomes not vapor but song. Letting go of signs (in the footprint) of the poem, she seeks instead the excitement generated by what poetic feet sublimate: desire itself. When the "remember me" is no longer situated in the command of a ghostly father and the prospect of vanishing is no longer abstracted in disembodied thought, then arousal itself becomes the desired state. "Remember me" emerges not the dead father but the repressed self.

To "die in full desire" (p. 72) is to move into the "verge upon verge" ("The Cliff," p. 257), the interval between nothingness and "the thing, anew" that defines the arena of excess. "Dying in full desire" pushes the life-death oxymoron toward sexuality, as it turns the absence of Petrarchan denial into the substance enriched by desire: "solid with yearning" (*Day by Day*, p. 127). In poem THREE: "ORIGINS," Rich describes her sense of history as an unfolding and a folding over: "it moves / in loops by switch-backs loosely strung" (p. 63). Here, she applies that theory to language itself, creating two pairs of circular oxymorons that lead to, and "switch back" from, the complications of a "labyrinthine filmic brain" to bring out, rather than repress, the self form covers over. In poem THREE, the "switch-backs" into the labyrinth of history reveal the same foundational empti-ness. Here the labyrinth is both complex and permeable, rendering the inside, at last, recoverable. In between Hamlet's trap and Prospero's com-promise, Rich's use of the oxymoron unhinges the left/right direction of the lines, the way Van Velde's painting does, when he questions, in the sec-ond image, what he had asserted in the first:

> these vivid stricken cells
> precarious living marrow
> this my labyrinthine filmic brain
> this my dreaded blood
> this my irreplaceable
> footprint vanishing from the air (p. 72)

As she moves steadily inward toward the brain, from skin cell to bone marrow, Rich diverts the flow toward denial and circles round to an affir-mation. The fluctuation between "precarious" and "living" is a reverse mirror of "vivid" and "stricken." Rich preempts the after-effects of blows (stricken) with the before-effect of risk (precarious) and then leaves the "vivid" and "living" at the outside of her circle, transforming the expected oxymoron—vivid stricken, precarious living—into a double life. In the final pair, she reverses yet again, as the dreaded blood and its appearance are cancelled by the irreplaceable footprint vanishing, sign immediately unsigned by design. In the second pairing, the blood-letting folds into a letting go. If the footprint disappears, so does the blood. The self's desire for forms yields to the other's desire for formlessness as form opens itself up to the repressed. Letting go of the irreplaceable, Rich casts herself to the wind, turning the impulse to assert and insinuate the self into a willingness to lose and transform the self. Where Prospero climbs from height to height (the gorgeous palaces the cloud-capped towers) in his terror, Rich moves from the earthly bottom to the topless air in her desire. Like Prospero, she anticipates disappearance. But the dread is erased:

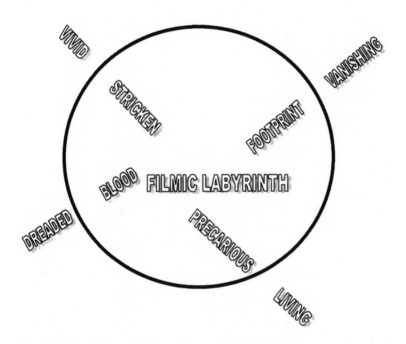

What makes the difference is the release afforded by the central indeterminacy. When the brain is seen as at once complexly deep (a labyrinth) and as easily penetrable (filmic), the expected rupture becomes not a break but an extension. Yet Rich's "airyness" is pleasure bound. The unravelling of the film is an infinite regression, just as, in the prefacing passage, Beckett unveils "veil upon veil toward the unveilable." As she sees through the density of the labyrinth by turning it into the diaphanous veil of the film, Rich enters the "warren" that frees her. Forfeiting the irreplaceable, she lets go of signs. And, recognizing that the space between nothingness and "the thing, anew" is absence itself, she chooses absence. The "missing parts" are absorbed by the flowing element, as blood and air become part of a liquid consciousness, and as the permeable film softens the walls of the labyrinth. To be labyrinthic *and* filmic is to render the repressed inner self transparent in the viscous film and to establish a record of the repression in the celluloid film. Finally, to accept the matrix of the unconscious is both to recognize the desire behind the form and the vaporousness of form itself.

Rich now defines full desire as a way of moving into the "verge upon verge" of "at long last first":

> dying in full desire
> thirsting for the coldest water
> hungering for hottest food
> gazing into the wildest light (p. 72)

When Rich turns the oxymoron around, she also reverses sexual climax and anticipation, the way Shakespeare does in sonnet 129 with the line "before a joy proposed behind a dream" (*Shakespeare's Sonnets,* p. 373). Like the appetite for food (hunger and thirst), an experienced sexual pleasure feels as if it had never happened. It seems a dream rather than a reality. Expectation ("a joy proposed") is at both ends of the experience, since the "behind" is as arousing as the "before." "Dying in full desire," the "I" embraces the physical. Instead of a poetic based on absence, Rich suggests a poetic based on presence. A sexual experience remembered stimulates the desire to have it happen again, turning recollection into anticipation, partly because the "dread" of "vanishing" has been subsumed by the pleasure of becoming. To die "in full desire" is to pursue the extreme beyond the end.

As Rich moves away from the realm of the visual, she similarly opens up the end of the Petrarchan dyad to the beginning, freeing the gaze so that the aroused emotion of her extremes mirrors the anticipated climax of her pursuit. In seeking the "wildest light," she confirms that the abstracting impulse of the other flows into her own desire for arousal. Surrendering forms ("the irreplaceable footprint"), she chooses the wildness of the not-yet-formed. For the fluctuating space of the Stevensian "wild wedges" in "Auroras of Autumn," Rich offers the "wildest light." While Stevens's "wild wedges" describe a conflict between the heavy form and the excitement of release, Rich's "wildest light" synchronizes Apollonian form and Dionysian exuberance. Her "light" suggests a lightness of being as, wafted by the "thinnest air," Rich moves into the exaltation of the updraft. Stoking the fire that eats self and its enclosures, Rich conflates bodily extremities (footprint with writing hand, toes with brains) to reach beyond the vanishing point:

> These are the extremes I stoke
> into the updraft of this life
> still roaring
>
> into thinnest air. (p. 73)

Moving from water, through fire, from "this life" (of earth) into another life of the "thinnest air," Rich does Prospero one better. As she melts in the fire, she approaches "still roaring" into the oxymoronic zone. The oxymoron "still roaring" does not end (with Prospero's fading pageant) in a self-canceling image. Quite the opposite. "Still" is used in the Elizabethan sense of "always" to suggest that the voice of poetry will prevail because it has moved beyond the burned out form. In "For a Friend in Travail," Rich doubled back to the supporting ledge with the "ravelling span of fiber strung," finding a way to bridge the gap between other and self. But in the "extremes" of "Inscriptions," she forfeits the traces of foothold or footprint and moves beyond visual proof, out onto the least substantial element.

The "thinnest air" is at once the smallest song and the center of the oxymoron, the point where life and death touch each other without eradicating either possibility. Like Beckett who disappears with Van Velde in "The Cliff," Rich herself is untraceable. Evaporating into the "thinnest air," she also moves into the vaporous "warren" where form incubates, the space between the black embers of an old fire and the red blood of a new life. Her pen is no longer a knife or razor. When the red-black notebook succumbs to the black-red of the blaze, Rich finds the interval where her "stoking" fills in the void, turning up the weak volume of "O, O, O," into the substance of her roaring, allowing the image of her disembodied self to be replaced by the sound of her full bodied song. She is Echo with a difference, having found her voice through the indulgence of her body. Merging with the escaping other and getting by on the thinnest air, she prevails and walks the line that allows her, like Schrodinger's cat, to be "both and." Roaring, the cat is a lion. "Still," the lion is approachable. The poetic medium of the lionized forms is hers to reshape.

In these last lines, Rich reverts again to Shakespeare's sonnet 129. "Had, having and in quest to have," she is "extreme" (*Shakespeare's Sonnets,* p. 373). As she slides between the bars of the oxymoronic cage, she pulls one step further: "from thence away from it all" ("The Cliff," p. 257). Stoking beneath and above the surface, she aligns herself—the amphibious salamander feeding on fire[33]—with the "missing parts." "Dying in full desire," she links climax to expectation. Returning as the repressed other, she emerges simultaneously fully herself, hovering on the border and maximizing the slim margin that allows her to be both dead and alive: "at long last first." Those expansions, in turn, change the poetic to render it responsive to the cultural agony of the postwar period, a response she demanded when she asked in *Atlas of the Difficult World*, "Who dare claim protection for their own / amid such unprotection?" (*An Atlas of the Difficult World*, p. 49). With the oxymoronic "still roaring," she simultaneously cries out as the monster and pacifies the self she exposes to the "extremes"—the "violent unspeakable underside"[34]—of the abject. Her persistence in becoming the other (still in its retrospective and projective sense) allows her to revel in her inflamed self, "roaring" and pushing beyond the "extremes" of the desired form. Like Beckett, Rich enters the "verge upon verge," heightening the remarkable convergence that makes room for "both and."

and consumed by body, I sit like you
on the rocky shore   (like you, not with you)

A windmill shudders, great blades cleave the air and corn is ground
For a peasant century's bread and fear of hunger
(like that, but not like that)

Pewter sails drive down green water
Barges shoulder fallowing fields
(Like then, not then)

If upstairs in the mill sunrise fell low and thin
on the pierced sleep of children hidden in straw
where the mauled hen had thrashed itself away

if some lost their heads and ran
if some were dragged

if some lived and grew old remembering
how the place by itself was not evil
had water, spiders, a cat

if anyone asked me—

How did you get here anyway?
Are you the amateur of drought? the collector
of rains? are you poetry's inadmissible
untimely messenger?

By what right?
In whose name?
Do you[2]

Transporting herself imaginatively to the nightmare of "unthinkable" Europe (*Einstein's Monsters*, p. 18), Rich emphasizes the overly expansive and ultimately disappointed expectations of the simile-making mechanisms endemic to Petrarchism: how love pain feels like a body blow; how yearning for emotional support is like hunger for alimentary sustenance; how our times mirror other times in their spoiled innocence and recovered purity. She sketches a landscape, almost a Dutch painting, of a Europe that seems eternal: "pewter sails drive down green water / Barges shoulder fallowing fields" but that, in 1941, was shattered by "the pierced sleep of children hidden in straw." The three parenthetical pairs ("like you, not with

Chapter 8 ✌

AFTER-WORDS

It is astonishing how little the mainstream has had to say about the nuclear destiny—a destiny that does not want for complication, inclusiveness, pattern, paradox, that does not want for *interest*. (Nuclear weapons have many demerits but drabness is not one of them.) And yet the senior generation of writers has remained silent; prolific and major though many of them are, with writing lives that straddled the evolutionary firebreak of 1945, they evidently did not find that the subject suggested itself naturally. They lived in one kind of world, then they lived in another kind of world; and they didn't tell us what the difference was like . . . It could be argued that all writing— all art, in all times—has a bearing on nuclear weapons, in two important respects. Art celebrates life and not the other thing, not the opposite of life. And art raises the stakes, increasing the store of what might be lost.

—Martin Amis, *Einstein's Monsters*[1]

Telling Differences

With a poem from her latest book, called simply "1941," Adrienne Rich still questions her earlier confidence that small-scale late nineties private suffering privileges her understanding of the enormous cataclysm that went on in mid-century Europe. Can "the handbook of heartbreak" (Wallace Stevens, *Collected Poems,* p. 507) or the body "consumed" mindbreak Rich describes in the poem connect us to the qualitatively different breaks and their eventuation into the "evolutionary firebreak" (which Martin Amis insists was) brought into being during the second World War?:

1941
In the heart of pain where mind is broken

you . . . like that, but not like that . . . like then, not then") argue for both the unchanging human condition and the extraordinary situation of the war. What remains the same is the neutral landscape—"the place by itself is not evil"—restored on both sides of the Atlantic shore. But the three negations qualifying the metaphors emphasize that, in valorizing our introspective "heart of pain" as the connective link to the brutally desecrated "mauled," we undercut our empathy for the unrecoverable victims of the war. Are our body-broken minds adequate to imagine the "pierced sleep of children"? Is being "*like*" the same as feeling "*with*"?

The Medusa who challenges the speaker in the italicized questions at the end does away with the false modesty of metaphor ("like you, not with you") to expose the unqualified presumptuousness of the simile-maker: "*How did you get here anyway?*" Laura-Medusa's *how* is at once an indictment of the process and a measure of the intrusion. It is not, as Amis proposes, that "art raises the stakes, increasing the store of what might be lost." Art *sets* the stakes, and, in defining what constitutes the "store," separates out what seems not worth saving. When Medusa asks "*in whose name*," she undermines the aggressive supposition of "naming" as a process that determines differences and then claims (through simile) to bypass the very differences it constructs. Medusa's rage upsets all assumptions of poetic kinship: "*By what right? / In whose name?*" Identifying the peremptory constructions of metaphor, Medusa's last question, "do you," is, first, the conversationally polite "*really*" thus intimating (with raised eyebrows) that simile is always fiction. The narrator can never put herself in the place of the victims. But, second, the "do you?" is also overtly accusatory, implying that what the poet *does* (in the present tense) is still cathected to what was *done* in the war. The open-ended question emphasizes the ongoing process of desubjugation that renders poetry part of the "doings" and "deeds" that were so terrible in 1941. The presentness of the doing indicates that Rich can avoid neither the splittings that propel desire nor the forms that define the split. She cannot stop herself from wanting both.

What she resists through metaphor is simultaneously what she "harbors in the being that [she is]."[3] Despite the fact that lyric divisions are dangerous, the danger itself is compelling. In this recent poem, Rich rests with the accusations of Laura-Medusa and thereby questions the terms of her confidence in the forms through which she comes into being. The only real alternative to Medusa's stone throwing lies with the woman who speaks to the possibility of another "doing," one that puts an end to the repetitions inherent to the rhetoric of desire. And the principal proponent for such loosenings is Laura-Mercury who advocates the form-challenging strategies that save Petrarchism from itself. In some of Rich's poems, Laura-Mercury withholds an unformed vision from the poet that defies poetry's usual "doings," just as the same evasive woman resists the poet in the confrontations of "Inscriptions," in Stevens's "An Ordinary Evening in New Haven," and in Lowell's London and New York series in *The Dolphin*. In those poems, the beloved "other" challenges the forms that define her. But in a few poems, the three poets uncover for themselves what Laura-Mercury only hints at, an escape from the constricting confines of what *they* are supposed to be. Each of the poets celebrates something pulsing behind the words: the fluidity and openness that the lyric sometimes confers through its rhythms. Rich names that force "the music [that] always ran ahead of the words" ("Late Ghazal," *Dark Fields of the Republic*, p. 43), Lowell the "genius [that] hums the auditorium dead" ("Fishnet," *The Dolphin*, p.15) and Stevens, in a very late poem, the "intelligible twittering of the birds" ("Hermitage at the Center," p. 505).

Poets know there is something that gets away and that what gets away might save us in the end. One reads because the "hum . . . the music . . . [and] the twittering" release the other denied by the forms and reveal a harmony that was there before the forms or apart from them. Freed of the automata—the unstoppable machine—of our times and its connection—in "flocks and herds and shoals" (Stevens, *Opus Posthumous*, p. 250)—to things mechanically alike, such music allies itself with the unnameable to suggest that it has yet to come into being. For all three poets, the form is end-stopped—"the line must terminate" (Lowell, *The Dolphin*, p. 15)—and the source of release. But the release comes only after the forms are identified as stifling, the reflections as menacing, the thought as inadequate. Siding with what gets away at the end, Stevens, Lowell, and Rich admit to the repression at the beginning. If the Petrarchan poem involves the "desubjectification" that triggers the genocidal mentality, its rhythms defy the containments it crystallizes. Lowell categorizes both the repressions and the release:

> Music,
> its ever retreating borderlines of being,
> as treacherous, perhaps, to systems,
> to fecundity,
> as to silence. ("In the Ward," *Day by Day*, p. 39)

Lowell's odd triad of constrictions ("systems . . . fecundity . . . silence") defines the normative bind in terms of forms and their restraining language, families and their reproductive pressures, and the societal with its "silencing" modes of censure. At the same time, the music, with its "retreating borderlines," suggests a "child's daubs" (*Day by Day*, p. 53) as it loosens the very separations upon which it depends. Lowell's word "treacherous" speaks to the surrealist *informe*: "what form itself creates, as logic acting logically to act against itself, form producing a heterologic . . . as a possibility working at the heart of form to erode it from within."[4] Music operates internally to render its pathways slippery. In Lowell's poem, the "treachery" moves outward as well and takes music into a realm that approaches the political in the sense that Judith Butler means "as an unanticipated appropriation and perversion of its own mandate."[5] Similarly in "Late Ghazal," when Rich's skin "[runs] with blood" (p. 43), the running evokes both a spilling over—with the surging blush of sexuality—and a thrusting forward—with the rushing lilt of the music—that stretches beyond the splittings of her own forms. In its erasures, Lowell's treachery "retreat[s]"; in its bypassing, Rich's "run[ning]" advances.

Stevens's "Hermitage at the Center" combines Lowell's retrospect and Rich's prospect. In his tribute to music and its border crossings, Stevens offers an alternative to the retractable "gestures" of "So-and-So Reclining on her Couch." Trading the private for the communal, Stevens calls the center a hermitage, a refuge ordinarily outside in lonely, single, isolation. This time, "the desired" also reclines but declines the abstractions of the poet's ideas:

THE HERMITAGE AT THE CENTER

The leaves on the macadam make a noise—
    How soft the grass on which the desired
    Reclines in the temperature of heaven—

Like tales that were told the day before yesterday—
    Sleek in a natural nakedness,
    She attends the tintinnabula—

And the wind sways like a great thing tottering—
    Of birds called up by more than the sun,
    Birds of more wit, that substitute—

Which suddenly is all dissolved and gone—
    Their intelligible twittering
    For unintelligible thought.

212 ⌐ The American Love Lyric after Auschwitz and Hiroshima

> And yet this end and this beginning are one,
>> And one last look at the ducks is a look
>> At lucent children round her in a ring. (pp. 505–506)

In "So-and-So Reclining on her Couch," Stevens acknowledges the Lacanian anamorphosis, the black hole, in the connection between the denying woman and the withdrawing mother. In "Hermitage," Stevens again merges the desired *inamorata* with the desired mother, a union that makes possible the extraordinary vision at the end. "The desired" and the children are part of a concentric circle. In one sense, Stevens's music (the tintinnabula . . . the noise . . . the twittering) is entirely unmelodious, a clamoring as annoying as a child's cry. But Stevens's "temperature of heaven" is like Rich's "thinnest air" in "Inscriptions." It can take, and sustain, all that "roaring." Such a hermitage offers "a deep-founded sheltering" ("The World as Meditation," *Collected Poems*, p. 525), the softness of response to "tintinnabula . . . macadam . . . and intelligible twittering." The source of the tintinnabula is the ring of children as they emerge the bell ringers who account for the air of expectancy. Instead of running away, "the desired" waits for them. Since the birds, too, are "called up by more than the sun," the "tales" offer an alternative to Apollo and his unrequited love.

In "Three Academic Pieces," Stevens evokes a history that leads only to the explosive eventuation of the bomb. "Yesterday birds sang preludes" that were Petrarchan in the chase they recorded, as the hunter pursued the male bird who, for his part, was stalking the female, and as Apollo turned Daphne into the occasion for song. But here, Stevens returns to the "day *before* yesterday" and its mythologies, to something older, prelapsarian, that seems simultaneously ancient and still unformulated. In "The Hermitage at the Center," Stevens calls Apollonian sublimation "that substitute" and dissolves it. While the Petrarchan poem seems self-satisfied in its embodiment, it never is. Its failures generate a fragmentation that mirrors its initiating appropriation. But in this poem, the excitement and fluidity are shared. The rupture is unnecessary because nothing is embalmed as a solid. Everything "sways," revealing only an "unnamed flowing" an aimlessness that (like "The River of Rivers in Connecticut") "flows nowhere, like a sea" (*Collected Poems*, p. 533). Swaying hints at impressionability and dislocation. Because nothing is permanently immobilized, nothing is totally committed. The undoer of things—the wind—is "*like* a great thing" undone. The great thing—the readily recognizable solid—merges with the loosening force. Nothing in this poem is self-contained; each part seems somehow contingent, attached in a mutual dependency. In the "ring," the resonance of sound and sight is immediate, as the rustling wind is activated by the "sway" of the implied dance and, as the form, which insists on one, relaxes in the plenitude that frees the many. The agency of everything is abdicated in the sway and imprecise in the "noise." It is unclear which is the origin and which is the destiny. The children in a ring are circling in a ring-around-a-rosy and the rose is, in her "natural nakedness," the "desired" in the middle. Stevens's ring, with its play on sight and sound, appears at once as a musical calling and a visual reflection. The "toddling" of a little thing standing up becomes the "tottering" of the great thing bending down, a movement between rise and fall, that augurs a connection between first and last.

Why are Stevens's ducks interchangeable with children in a ring? To make such an assertion is to return to the sea, to choose a creature at home in water, on land, and in the air, one that, like Lowell's dolphin, traverses the elements. And, like Lowell's "unrealism"—with "the husband swim[ming] like vagueness on the grass"[6]—Stevens's children ring round to connect shore and sea. Stevens, too, resorts to a quackiness, a surrealist movement that, after all that twittering, tintinnabula, and mic-macking on the tarmacadam, leads beyond expectation to a "lucent ring." In canto XII of "An Ordinary Evening in New Haven," nothing escapes the "said words of the world" as the "leaves whirling in the gutters". . . resembl[e] . . . the presences of thought" that keep returning to the Apollonian "reverberations" (p. 474). Here, Stevens begins with the "leaves on the macadam" and their "noise," the same gutteral of gutter sounds. But when the desired retreats from the couch of "So-and-So" to the grass, she returns to an arena before pavements or gutters and before the "guilt [that] lies buried / beneath the innocence of autumn days" (p. 504). In "the temperature of heaven," seasons remain the same and sound and sight coalesce. As geometrical circle and musical echo, the "ring" to which the desired attends is based, finally, neither on the compulsions of the marriage plot and its familial bind nor on the violations of Petrarchan plot and its empowering voice. Instead, the last look is of something provisional, casual, accidental, something that almost doesn't happen, a bit like the sleight of hand trick on the shadow of the wall. Rabbit or duck. We are no longer in the Vienna woods with a bird at the end of the hunter's gun barrel and Daphne as the origin of Apollo's "substitute." The birds of "Hermitage" are "called up by more than the sun," the excess beyond the forms of Apollonian convention.

If the last look at the ducks is a look at lucent children, then the object at the end of the look is as innocent as a child's "daubs . . . one sex, one herd, / replicas in hierarchy" ("The Day," *Day by Day*, p. 53). Open, the children are clear, and clear, they are subsequently receptive. Ringing round, the lucent children return to the mirroring element of their origin in desire. Equal, the children are also in tune with "the desired." Brought back from the empty reflection of the Lacanian irretrievable, she is restored.

Since we wait until the end of the poem to find the source of "the tintinnabula," and since even then it could as easily be something else, we're not sure that what we wait for—at ends—isn't what we offer at the beginning—*at-tendre*, in the tenderness of childhood. Stevens answers his hesitation about form by working through the self-cancellations of "So-and-So," to the desired in the grass, a woman whose reclining is a response to the desires of children, a mother whose fullness answers need. But she can be understood only by moving backward and beyond "the tales that were told yesterday" to a beforeness that does away with the divide. How is that possible? How can there be an after-words that retrieves the oneness of before-words? Such a vision overcomes the darkness by moving *through the divisions* that enable us linguistically to be. It comes miraculously and casually, like day after night. If the underside is brought round and the last look returns to a first glance, then the borders of division are negotiable and the music [that] "runs ahead of the words" reveals what we needed at the start. This very late Stevens poem acknowledges the anamorphic vision and its necessary double takes, rendering the split that inspires language the source of recovery, like Beckett's "at long last first."[7]

Stevens's belated knowledge in words parallels, almost uncannily, the sightlines of Charlotte Salomon's prescient certainty in painting, producing in language what she evoked in pictures: the lucency and permeability of the divide that defines. I cite Salomon, who died in Auschwitz in 1943 at age 26, because of the striking resonance between Stevens's "last look" in "Hermitage at the Center" and the final gouaches in her *Life or Theatre*. Both are "last" statements that could emerge only, as in Rich's "Inscriptions" and Lowell's "Epilogue," by "stealing" over and beyond the boundaries that divide. After the war, Stevens also moves toward a return that might correct or make amends for what was lost from the start. Stevens's two-pronged ring, hovering between infant noise and ancient vision, and Salomon's circles, alternating between written text and painted image, allow us to link the sheltered American poet to the wore-torn European painter. Both circles and rings portend the possibility of *responsiveness*. Both bend or slant the rigid divisions of Petrarchan form so that "the ever retreating borderlines of being" might reach a point where a new beginning—that of lucent children—can evolve.

Foam Dreams and Lucent Children

In Stevens's "ringing" children, the mirroring silvery double floats into the multiple, like the amazing first gouache in Salomon's "Epilogue" where she paints herself in the plural, rendering the panel both an allusion to the past and a reference to her multiple—and complex—present selves. Her oeuvre, *Life? or Theatre?*, which she called an "operetta," is a unique form. Consisting of nearly 800 unbound gouaches, it describes her life and bleak family history (her mother, aunt, and grandmother committed suicide) first, in Germany, and, later, in France where she was sent into exile until she was arrested in 1943. As Mary Lowenthal Felstiner writes:

> The first painting announces a formal title, *Life? Or Theatre? An Operetta,*
> inviting a viewer into a new performing art, one that mixes pictures and
> music and talk: Your eyes take in the images, page by page, then read the
> words, while you imagine the melodies suggested in the scenes. . . . Only an
> offstage narrator, a kind of ironic chorus, keeps the story moving along. . . .
>
> Overlays are purely Charlotte Salomon's invention—a unique storytelling
> site. They let you imagine you're watching a play while the script scrolls in
> front of the stage, on a scrim. The overlays keep reminding you that these
> pictures are not the life she lived but the one she thought about for years.
>
> No artwork or artifact has ever looked like this one. An autobiography
> without an *I*, a chronicle with visuals, an operatic memoir: "Something so
> wildly unusual," as Charlotte Salomon called it.[8]

Like Stevens's "wild wedges" (*Collected Poems,* p. 416) and Rich's "wildest light" (*Dark Fields of the Republic,* p. 72), Salomon's quest to make something "wildly unusual" pushes the forms inside out, and exposes them to an energy that was there before they ever came into being. Simultaneously over the edge and beneath it, that energy is subtle and untamable: "a force that traverses a shade" (*Collected Poems,* p. 488). The first and last paintings of Salomon's "Epilogue" seem remarkably like Stevens's "Hermitage at the Center." In the inscriptions of the first painting, the visual ring of the small silvery leaves suggests an oral ringing as well, both the bell that calls and the circle that beckons. Out of the darkness of the war, the artist sees not one other to mirror the self, but infinite selves on the sea shore. In the projection of her present selves, Salomon recollects her earlier selves as, freed from the death-dealing sublimations of form, she evolves into something new that includes them. Like Stevens's "last look," the small ducks at the upper right become the sighted objects that complete the circle.

Emerging from an Ibsenite past, the Charlotte Salomon of *Life? or The-*

atre? invents her own mythology, one that is the visual equivalent of Stevens's hermitage. In the three potential circles of the scene in France that begin the "Afterward," the ring of girls on the shore, the younger children happily painting in the woods, and finally, the bathing-suited figures in the sand, Salomon depicts the artist coming into her most recognizable clarity. The three images represent various stages of her life: her beginnings as a painter, her early childhood in Berlin, and herself, alone, painting in France. There, she delineates the silvery leaves of a tree, swaying in the wind, as she lets go and finds herself through a loosening that allows for such inversions. Salomon's ring is lucent in the anticipation of things still to come, while Stevens's ring is already rounded in the memory of a yielding center in the past. For Stevens, the lucency returns to the desired in the expectation of her answer. Salomon's past is less certain. With a suicidal mother and a self-absorbed family, she is left on her own. But, for both Stevens and Salomon, the fertile soil is at the edge of a sea that goes "nowhere" but to the rhythms of a constant becoming: "Foam dreams— my dreams on a blue surface. What makes you shape and reshape yourselves so brightly from so much suffering? Who gave you the right?"[9]

Salomon asks her questions of nature in the same year as Rich appoints Laura-Medusa to ask them of art: "1941." But in both cases, the questions implicate the "user" who blithely turns suffering into beauty. On the one hand, the "foam dreams," as Rich writes of the California landscape, "with or without [her] passion" (*An Atlas of the Difficult World*, p. 46). Salomon similarly cites the ultimate indifference of nature in its constant shaping and reshaping. Unaltered by human feeling, it continues in its unceasing course. Like Lowell's unavailing God who fails to react to earthly misery ("the heavens were very short of hearing then," *The Dolphin*, p. 45), nature follows its rites of passage regardless of our needs. In its constant becoming, it "dreams [her] dreams" because its essence is imminence. But Salomon's suffering privileges her voice and allows it to speak "beyond the genius of the sea" that Stevens so confidently intoned in "The Idea of Order at Key West" (*Collected Poems*, p. 130). It gives her the "right" to find in the sea a reflection of her own buried resourcefulness, an image clear and unmistakable and ringing in its shining rhythm with the "hum," the "tintinnabula," the "running music" of the irrepressible urge to be.

The many Salomons of the first epilogue painting are condensed in the one Salomon at the close of *Life? or Theatre?* In the final image of her collected work, Salomon positions herself on a rock, looking out into a sea that (as at the moment prior to the divisions of Genesis) merges with the sky, turning the likeness of resemblance into the oneness before separation.

Charlotte Salomon, JHM no. 4835, Collection Jewish Historical Museum, Amsterdam, ©Charlotte Salomon Foundation.

But, unlike Rich's rocky European shore in "1941," which is mirrored across the ocean in America, this rock seems to go "nowhere" but to the sea. The drawing board is translucent even as the artist begins to etch out the lines of herself painting. Significantly, her hand is seen somehow both in back of the painting—as an extension of the sea—and through it—as an extension of her body. It is impossible therefore to separate her body from the ocean's body, self from scene, drawing hand from painted image, inside from outside, the painter from the painting.

Using her body as a canvas for her words, she creates a *mise-en-abyme* with a series of canvases leading all at once to an origination that defies the binaries of difference. What looks like a line may be a paintbrush. What looks like something already drawn might be something not yet represented. What looks like a biological self—the painting body—may be a poster board—a body painting. What looks like a figure already there might actually be the instrument that will put it there. Finally, what looks like a hand connected to a body might be a hand connected (like the one snatching back Excalibur in *Le Morte d'Arthur*) to the sea. Yet, in all the scenarios, Salomon seems to be setting up a right/left division in her painting, evolving an anamorphic image (duck or children) still to come. As maiden painting, Salomon is a Lorelei, creature of land and sea, mermaid mother and desired end to her own work. Single self, she is at one with the sea and her own muse.

If the initial painting in Salomon's "Epilogue" is of the trees whose silvery leaves perpetuate themselves in multiple and discrete forms, the last image is of the unforming of ocean and sky into a contrasting vastness that both swallows and predates forms. Despite all that fusion, Salomon still divides her last painting in half, as if the only way to begin is by dividing again. But the division does not repeat the same old binary. Its slant interrogates the form, indicates a new way out of it, and projects a different take on its eternalizing practices. Like Stevens's "tottering" wind moving downward and the toddling children circling round-ward, her slant redistributes the agency of power. Is the image on the translucent canvas a landscape or a seascape? In hovering between the two, it aligns itself with what Stevens in "So-and-So" calls the "unpainted shore," an allusion to the borderland, the world before art came into being, and to the one that evolves when the old forms are subject to the very erasures they themselves effected.

Charlotte Salomon painted the story of her life in one intense year, 1941–42: "And with her dream-awakened eyes she saw all the beauty around her, saw the sea, felt the sun, and knew: she had to vanish for a while from the human plane and make every sacrifice to create her world anew

Charlotte Salomon, JHM no. 4925. Collection Jewish Historical Museum, Amsterdam ©Charlotte Salomon Foundation.

out of the depths" (*Charlotte Salomon: Life? or Theatre?* p. 822). In the oxy-moron of "dream-awakened eyes," Salomon fuses ends and beginnings. Like the Stevens of "Hermitage," Salomon senses that in order to "create her world anew," she had to "vanish" from the "plane" of history and everything that fed into the events that eventually killed her. In the last painting, she returns to something earlier, before the "depths" began. Finally, she lived according to the maxim, "One has to go into oneself—into one's childhood—to be able to get out of oneself" (*Charlotte Salomon: Life? or Theatre?* p. 819). In the connection she forges between "go[ing] in" and "get[ting] out," Salomon's explorations of the "depths" suggest three objectives: to express the depravity of the historical moment in the tem-poral sequence; to search the inwardness of the self as a psychological state; and to sound the bottom of the sea as the spatial origin of all things. That circular movement parallels the process of "Hermitage at the Center," where Stevens ends with children and opens with "the desired." Foraging to the root of "the depths" in his postwar poems, Stevens, too, finds some-thing that existed before the divide as he connects the reclining other to the couching mother through the ring that renders "this end and this beginning . . . one" (*Collected Poems*, p. 506).

Does Stevens—who situates "The Hermitage at the Center" very near the middle of the last section of *The Collected Poems*—have the right, as an American poet who remained physically protected from the war, to make and remake himself from "so much suffering?" I'm not sure he takes it as a right. Instead, he takes it as a responsibility: "The scholar of one candle sees / An Arctic effulgence flaring on the frame / Of everything he is. And he feels afraid" (*Collected Poems,* p. 416). When the poet imagines himself as the other and admits that the frames by which he invents himself depend on the unmaking of the other, he also confesses that the Petrarchan freez-ing fires (the "frigid brilliances," p. 413 and "Arctic effulgences," p. 416 of "Auroras of Autumn") may reflect the inner desolation that propelled the initial annihilations. And, when they challenge the privileging of "their own / amid such unprotection" (*An Atlas of the Difficult World,* p. 49), Stevens, Lowell, and Rich acknowledge the extent to which Americans are involved with the culture that went so terribly awry in the middle of the twentieth century. Recognizing that link, they turn the poetic inside out and reshape themselves. They thereby connect both to the young girl whose lucent form is so open to the world and to the sea in its endless becoming. Their risks involve putting themselves at risk. And that expo-sure uncovers the repressive self even as it allows the repressed other to sur-face. Like Salomon, Stevens, Lowell, and Rich return to an origin that unmakes the demarcating boundaries between self and other through which they so often found themselves.

When the desiring self on the shore meets the desired being in the grass, the anamorphic image yields to an alternative that is not a "death's head." Finally, when the end and the beginning are one, a last look, free of the desubjectivizing gaze, is merely a mistaken glance. We read for the shining accidence of such resemblances. And we read because those resemblances are not the same old "look alikes." The resignifications chronicle a swaying—"like a great thing tottering"—that loosens the "historically sedimented effect"[10] of culturally determined forms and that reveals, all at once, a clarity and a luminescence. In the light of such rings, yesterday's "preludes" revert not to the appropriations in the Vienna woods but to "tales that were told the day before [the] yesterday" (*Collected Poems,* p. 505) of "Three Academic Pieces."

Different Tellings

"Straddl[ing] the firebreak" Martin Amis describes in the epigraph, Stevens self-consciously writes in the face of his own death as he works against the firebreak in his late poems and Lowell doubles his love and kills himself in the transatlantic waverings of *The Dolphin* and *Day by Day*. But the firebreak is part of the self-awareness that casts him as the incendiary source of his own demonic drive. Rich, even younger than Charlotte Salomon was in 1941, is still coming back to that firebreak in her recent work and still returning to the *aubade,* with its sunrise and inevitable splittings:

and the day will break

as we say, it breaks
as we don't say, of the night

as we don't say of the night (*Midnight Salvage,* p. 50)

Petrarchism involves the break, both the initial split between self and other and the necessary parting heralded in the dawn song. Daybreak is a theme for Stevens in "The World as Meditation," for Lowell in "The Downlook," and for Rich both in "For a Friend in Travail" and the 1997 "The Night Has a Thousand Eyes" of *Midnight Salvage*. The dawn song refers forward to the inevitability of a love that will never last or backward to a love that was never fully realized. For these three writers, the Apollonian sun itself almost automatically conjures up images of breakage. Recognizing how the inevitable oppositions of the poetic (between self and other, word and word, line and line, day and night) may have contributed to the splittings that caused the "firebreak[s]" of Auschwitz and Hiroshima, all three turn the fires inward and outward at once. Yet (in the back and forth of their reinvented oxymorons, in the othered selves of different mythologies), all three find enough oxygen in the forms to "tell us," as Amis demands, "what the difference was like." Stevens, Lowell, and Rich venture one step further than Amis asks, as they carefully unhinge the fixed divisions to discover "some basis on which the symbolic in its hasty foreclosures might founder" (*Antigone's Claim*, p. 55). And they risk the break and the "foundering" in their own terrain, the lyric country simultaneously small enough to be workable and, as Lowell writes, responsible for the "gigantism" ("After-thought," *Notebook, 1970*, p. 263) of its cultural repercussions.

Like Molière's "bourgeois gentleman" and his prose, we find ourselves, in almost every aspect of our daily lives, speaking Petrarchanly. Our commonplace Petrarchisms—the oxymorons, the splittings—stem not from the refined world of an effete poetic but out of the European "militarist mindset" Doctorow's fictional Wittgenstein denounces at the end of the second millennium[11] and Withold Gombrowicz's narrator, on the eve of mid-twentieth-century conflagration, calls the same "power of form . . . [which] is the cause of wars."[12] The telling differences Stevens, Lowell, and Rich enact in their work challenge the preludes they inherited from the "Vienna woods" and Italian mountains of a beleaguered continent. In their different tellings, they simultaneously take into account our ancient desire for the poetics of desire and our urgent need to repair the divisions and consequential cultural inevitabilities its forms sanctify.

Notes ∽

Preface

1. E. L. Doctorow, *The City of God* (New York: Random House, 2000), p. 190.
2. As quoted by James Glanz, "Testing the Nation's Aging Nuclear Stockpile in a Test Ban Era," *New York Times*, November 28, 2000: D5.
3. Judith Miller, "At Bleak Asian Site, Killer Germs Survive," *New York Times*, June 2, 1999: A1.
4. Matthew L. Wald, "Step in Storage of Atom Waste is Costly Error," *The New York Times*, June 2, 1999: A1.
5. *Way Out There in the Blue: Reagan, Star Wars, and the End of the Cold War* (New York: Simon and Schuster, 2000), p. 498.
6. "Beam Me up Rummy," *New York Times,* May 9, 2001: A31.
7. Michael R. Gordon, "Rumsfeld Limiting Contacts with the Chinese," *New York Times,* June 4, 2001: A1.
8. Michael E.O. Hanlon's phrase. See James Dao, "Rumsfeld Seeking an Arms Strategy Using Outer Space," *New York Times,* May 8, 2001: A-10.
9. *Hystories: Hysterical Epidemics and Modern Culture* (London: Picador, 1997), p. 7.
10. *The Collected Poems of W. B. Yeats, Revised Second Edition,* ed. Richard J. Finneran (New York: Simon and Schuster, 1996), p. 294.
11. As quoted by Peter Haidu in "The Dialectics of Unspeakability: Language, Silence and the Narratives of Desubjectification," *Probing the Limits of Representation: Nazism and the Final Solution,* ed. Saul Friedlander (Cambridge: Harvard University Press, 1992) p. 287. Haidu writes: "Himmler's discourse is *unheimlich* because it reproduces, with all nuances and paradoxes in place, the discourses we know as the discourses of poetry, policy, of idealism and religion, of administration and bureaucracy," p. 292.
12. Adrienne Rich, "Notes Towards a Politics of Location," Blood, Bread and Poetry (New York: Norton, 1986), p. 225.

Introduction

1. "Three Academic Pieces," *The Necessary Angel: Essays on Reality and the Imagination* (New York: Knopf, 1951), p. 76.

2. Arguing that Lowell's politics over the years displayed "a lack of consistency" ("Robert Lowell and the Cold War," *New England Quarterly* 72.3 [1999]: 340), Steven Gould Axelrod writes that, "by the end of his career, Lowell's engagement with contemporary issues and discourse—and the hopefulness such engagement implied—had virtually disappeared," 360.

3. "Letter to a Young Poet," *Midnight Salvage* (New York: Norton, 1999), p. 29.

4. "The Garden," *The Poems and Letters of Andrew Marvell, Third Edition*, ed. H.M. Margoliouth, revised by Pierre Legouis and E. E. Duncan-Jones (Oxford: Clarendon Press, 1971), p. 52.

5. "Love and Fame, the Petrarchan Career," *Pragmatism's Freud,* ed. Joseph H. Smith and William Kerrigan (Baltimore: Johns Hopkins University Press, 1986), p. 128.

6. *Love in the Western World,* trans. Montgomery Belgion (New York: Pantheon, 1956), p. 8.

7. "The Bomb's Womb and the Genders of War (War Goes on Preventing Women from Becoming the Mothers of Invention)," *Gendering War Talk,* ed. Miriam Cooke and Angela Woolacott (Princeton: Princeton University Press, 1993), pp. 293–94.

8. Robert J. Lifton and Eric Markussen's term for the "cast of mind that created and maintains the threat of nuclear weapons" and that defines "the general nature of nuclear entrapment and then seeks insight from a major genocide that has already taken place." See *The Genocidal Mentality: Nazi Holocaust and Nuclear Threat* (New York: Basic Books, 1990), p. 1.

9. *The Differend: Phrases in Dispute,* trans. Georges Van Den Abbeele, *Theory and History of Literature,* vol. 46 (Minneapolis: University of Minnesota Press, 1988), p. 101.

10. Three collections of essays are vital to a consideration of gender issues as they relate to poetry: *Speaking of Gender,* ed. Elaine Showalter (New York: Routledge, 1989); *Shakespeare's Sisters: Feminist Essays on Women Poets,* ed. Sandra M. Gilbert and Susan Gubar (Bloomington: Indiana University Press, 1979); and, because it speaks to "the interplay of gender and genre," *Dwelling in Possibility: Women Poets and Critics on Poetry,* ed. Yopie Prins and Maeera Shreiber (Ithaca: Cornell University Press, 1997). See also *Desire in the Renaissance: Psychoanalysis and Literature*, ed. Valeria Finucci and Regina Schwartz (Princeton: Princeton University Press, 1994). Other relevant studies are: Ilona Bell, *Elizabethan Women and the Poetry of Courtship* (Cambridge: Cambridge University Press, 1998); Gordon Braden, *Petrarchan Love and the Continental Renaissance* (New Haven and London: Yale University Press, 1999); Sheila Fisher and Janet Halley, *Seeking the Woman in Late*

Medieval and Renaissance Texts: Essays in Feminist Contextual Criticism (Knoxville: University of Tennessee Press, 1990); Elizabeth Harvey, *Ventriloquized Voices: Feminist Theory and English Renaissance Texts* (London: Routledge, 1992); Nancy Vickers, "Diana Described: Scattered Woman, Scattered Rhyme," *Critical Inquiry* 8 (1981–82): 65–79; and Marguerite Waller, "Academic Tootsie: The Denial of Difference and the Difference it Makes," *Diacritics* 7 (1987): 2–20.

11. *The Rhetoric of the Body from Ovid to Shakespeare* (Cambridge: Cambridge University Press, 2000), p. 15.

12. *Heidegger and "the jews,"* trans. Andreas Michel and Mark Roberts, introduction by David Carroll (Minneapolis: University of Minnesota Press, 1990), p. 45.

13. *Postmodernism Across the Ages: Essays for a Postmodernity That Wasn't Born Yesterday*, ed. Bill Readings and Bennet Schaber (Syracuse: Syracuse University Press, 1993), pp. 1–2.

14. *Heidegger and "the jews,"* trans. Andreas Michel and Mark Roberts (Minneapolis: University of Minnesota Press, 1990), p. 48.

15. "Holocaust Consciousness in the 1990s: Adrienne Rich's 'Then Or Now,'" *Women's Studies* 27 (1998): 384.

16. "Afterthought," *Notebook* (New York: Farrar, Straus and Giroux, 1970), p. 263.

17. Irene Costera Meijer and Beaukje Prins, "How Bodies Come to Matter: An Interview with Judith Butler," *Signs* 23.2 (1998): 284.

18. *A History of the World in 10½ Chapters* (London: Picador, 1990), p. 181.

19. "Beween Image and Phrase: Progressive History and the 'Final Solution' as Dispossession," *Probing the Limits of Representation: Nazism and the Final Solution,* ed. Saul Friedlander (Cambridge: Harvard University Press, 1992), p. 184.

20. Peter Haidu, "The Dialectics of Unspeakability: Language, Silence and the Narratives of Desubjectification," *Probing the Limits of Representation: Nazism and the Final Solution,* p. 299.

21. "Round Table Discussion," *Writing and the Holocaust,* ed. Berel Lang (New York: Holmes and Meier, 1988), p. 281.

22. *Caught by History: Holocaust Effects in Contemporary Art, Literature and Theory* (Stanford: Stanford University Press, 1997), p. 7.

23. Robert Alter, "Who is Shylock?," *Commentary* 96.1 (July 1993): 30.

24. "Asphodel, That Greeny Flower," *Asphodel that Greeny Flower and Other Love Poems*, intro. Herbert Leibowitz (New York: New Directions, 1994), p. 19.

25. "Pre-empting the Holocaust," *The Atlantic Monthly* 282.5 (November 1998): 105. This essay forms part of the first chapter of Langer's book, *Preempting the Holocaust* (New Haven: Yale University Press, 1998), pp. 1–22.

26. Even as he disputes Theodor Adorno's dictum and therefore necessarily contests Langer, Daniel R. Schwarz writes: "after Auschwitz it is barbaric *not*

to write poetry." *Imagining the Holocaust* (New York: St. Martin's, 1999), p. 22.

27. "Cultural Criticism and Society," *Prisms*, trans. Samuel and Sherry Weber (London: Neville Spearman, 1967), p. 34.

28. "After Auschwitz," *Negative Dialectics*, trans. E. B. Ashton (New York: Seabury Press, 1973), pp. 362–63.

29. "Lyric Poetry and Society," *The Adorno Reader* (Oxford: Blackwell, 2000), p. 215.

30. Arno J. Mayer, *Why Did the Heavens Not Darken?* (New York: Pantheon Books, 1988), p. 17.

31. "How to Read *The Merchant of Venice* Without Being Hererosexist," *Alternative Shakespeares 2* (London: Routledge, 1993), p. 139.

32. Jacqueline Vaught Brogan is one of the few critics to note that Stevens's political position changed after the war and that this change coincides with Stevens's increased sensitivity to issues of gender. She doesn't, however, think that the war affected Stevens to the extent that it did Adrienne Rich. While maintaining that World War II "instituted a fundamental and on-going change in [Stevens's] relationship to language, one that will allow for the rich and more vulnerable poetry of his later years that many critics, including feminists, found to be his best," Brogan writes that, in contrast, the Adrienne Rich of "Eastern War-Time" is still more sensitive to the effects of the war. Rich, she insists, "vividly portrays the magnitude of her pain at the time, even if luckily an American girl, and her on-going pain, now, as a poet and as a woman of sixty remembering." See "Planets on the Table: From Wallace Stevens and Elizabeth Bishop to Adrienne Rich and June Jordan," *The Wallace Stevens Journal* 19.2 (1995): 257. In "Wrestling with Those 'Rotted Names': Wallace Stevens' and Adrienne Rich's 'Revolutionary Poetics,'" *The Wallace Stevens Journal* 25.1 (2001): 7–39, Brogan modifies her earlier assessment, arguing that, despite their differences, both poets "ultimately share the desire to create what Rich prophetically called *The Dream of a Common Language*": 36.

33. "Habermas, Enlightenment, and Antisemitism," *Probing the Limits of Representation, Nazism and the "Final Solution,"* p. 168.

34. "Vital Signs: Petrarch and Popular Culture," *Romanic Review* 77 (1988): 187.

35. *The Handbook of Heartbreak: 101 Poems of Lost Love and Sorrow*, collected by Robert Pinsky (New York: Morrow, 1998), p. xiii.

36. Judith Butler's summation of Gayatri Chakravorty Spivak's argument in "Against Proper Objects: Introduction," *differences*, 6. 2 and 3 (1994): 18.

37. *Excitable Speech* (New York: Routledge, 1997), p. 138.

38. "this is the oppressor's language / yet I need it to talk to you": Language a Place of Struggle," *Between Languages and Cultures: Translation and Cross-Cultural Texts*, ed. Anuradha Dingwaney and Carol Maier (Pittsburgh: University of Pittsburgh Press, 1995), p. 295.

39. "The Burning of Paper Instead of Children," *Collected Early Poems: 1950–1970* (New York: Norton, 1993), p. 364.
40. *The Dream of A Common Language* (New York: Norton, 1978), p. 34.
41. *The Tempest*, ed. Virginia Mason Vaughan and Alden T. Vaughan, *The Arden Shakespeare, third series* (London: Thomas Nelson, 1999), p. 254.
42. Most notably, Angus Cleghorn, *Wallace Stevens's Poetics: The Neglected Rhetoric* (New York and Houndsmill, England: Palgrave, 2000); William Doreski, *Robert Lowell's Shifting Colors: The Poetics of the Public and the Personal* (Athens: Ohio University Press, 1999); Alan Filreis, *Wallace Stevens and the Actual World* (Princeton: Princeton University Press, 1991); John Gery, *Nuclear Annihilation and Contemporary American Poetry: Ways of Nothingness* (Gainesville: Florida University Press, 1996); Andrew Lakritz, *Modernism and the Other in Stevens, Frost and Moore* (Gainesville: Florida University Press, 1996); James Longenbach, *Wallace Stevens: The Plain Sense of Things* (New York: Oxford University Press, 1991); Kevin Stein, *Private Poets, Worldly Acts: Public and Private History in Contemporary American Poetry* (Athens: Ohio University Press, 1996).
43. *Private Poets, Worldly Acts: Public and Private History in Contemporary American Poetry*, p. 7.
44. Like Stein, Thomas Travisano cites "For the Union Dead" as a statement against "the burgeoning of a callous and triumphant commercialism in the fifties and sixties." But he does say that "the age of nuclear anxiety that followed Hiroshima and Nagasaki (so vividly crystallized in Lowell's "Fall 1961") provides a backdrop for Lowell's mature poetry." See *Midcentury Quartet: Bishop, Lowell, Jarrell, Berryman, and the Making of a Postmodern Aesthetic* (Charlottesville: University of Virginia Press, 1999), p. 254.
45. "Introduction: Thinkability," *Einstein's Monsters* (London: Vintage, 1999), p. 17.
46. Melissa Zeiger's term. *Beyond Consolation: Death, Sexuality, and the Changing Shapes of Elegy* (Ithaca: Cornell University Press, 1997), p. 166.
47. *Modernism and the Other in Stevens, Frost and Moore* (Gainesville: Florida University Press, 1996), p. 20. Unlike Lakritz, Alan Filreis locates Stevens's postwar sensibilities in questions of practical, rather than theoretical, issues. Filreis is much more concerned with situating Stevens in the day-to-day political, rather than, as I am, with the connections between postwar nuclear buildup and prewar nationalism. The postwar poems become, in his reading, inquisitions not about what lead to the war but about how the country should work toward the rebuilding of Europe. The poems embed "Stevens assessment of the effort made by European generations to renew their world in an effort to contain the growing Russian power." *Wallace Stevens and the Actual World* (Princeton: Princeton University Press, 1991), p. 213. In that regard, Filreis is specific about his praise for Stevens's involvement in the world, as Marjorie Perloff is in her criticism of Stevens's indif-

ference to particular events in her "Revolving in Crystal: The Supreme Fiction and the Impasse of Modernist Lyric," *Wallace Stevens: The Poetics of Modernism*, ed. Albert Gelpi (Cambridge: Cambridge University Press, 1985), pp. 41–64.

48. *What is It Then Between Us?: Traditions of Love in American Poetry* (Ithaca: Cornell University Press, 1998), p. 185.

49. John Gery's *Nuclear Annihilation and Contemporary American Poetry: Ways of Nothingness* (Gainesville: Florida University Press, 1996) confronts more directly than any other work the problems I take up here to argue that, in the face of "an era in danger of initiating its own annihilation (p. 1) . . . poetry is a pertinent voice in the discourse of survival" (p. 4). In a similar vein to Gery, George Monteiro writes of the history of how "poets reacted to the bomb," citing Robert Frost, Daniel Hoffman, Richard Wilbur, Paul Roche, and Olga Cabral. See "Poets and the Bomb," *War, Literature and the Arts* 11.1 (1999): 152, 162.

50. *Of Spirit: Heidegger and the Question*, trans. Geoffrey Bennington and Rachel Bowlby (Chicago: University of Chicago Press, 1989), pp. 109–110.

51. Jonathan Monroe, "Poetry, the University and the Culture of Distraction," *Diacritics* 26.3 and 4 (1996): 4. For a summary of the arguments against Adrienne Rich's recent work precisely because "the intrusion of Rich's political concerns has spoiled and betrayed her artistic gift," refer to Peter Erickson's defense of Rich in "Singing America: From Walt Whitman to Adrienne Rich," *Kenyon Review*, n.s. 17.1 (1995): 114. If Rich is considered too political, Lowell is currently marginalized because he is too poetical. See Steven Gould Axelrod's introduction to *The Critical Response to Robert Lowell* (Westport, Conn.: Greenwood Press, 1999), p.18.

52. "Poetry in Theory," *Diacritics* 26.3 and 4 (1996): 160. Albert Gelpi writes of Adrienne Rich's affinities with the political causes of the Language Poets, but that, finally, she is committed to "using an admittedly impaired language as a medium of communication and so as a subversive vehicle for change." See "The Transfiguration of the Body: Adrienne Rich's Witness," *The Wallace Stevens Journal* 25.1 (2001): 8.

53. "Lyric Resistance: Views of the Political in the Poetics of Wallace Stevens and H.D.," *Wallace Stevens Journal* 13. 2 (1989): 195. On the question of Stevens's less theoretical political engagement, John Timberman Newcomb, for example, writes that "a dismissal of Stevens as apolitical or reactionary ignores his development of an intellectual basis for collective social responsibility through the critique and rejection of authoritarian modes of thought." See "Life Anywhere But on a Battleship: Stevens's Wartime Poetry and the Apolitics of Postwar Criticism," *Criticism*, XXXII, no. 1 (1990): 103. Of particular interest as well is his dismissal of Marjorie Perloff's "exposé of Stevens's ostensible fascist unconscious [in her "Revolving in Crystal: The Supreme Fiction and the Impasse of Modernist Lyric," *Wallace Stevens: The*

Poetics of Modernism, ed. Albert Gelpi (Cambridge: Cambridge University Press, 1985), pp. 41–64]. But, like Filreis and Perloff, Newcomb is more immediate and specific in his assessment of Stevens's wartime poetry, particularly in his analysis of "Life on a Battleship," a poem which first appeared in *The Partisan Review* in 1939. Arguing against such specific "event-related" readings, Steven Miskinis ("Exceeding Responsibilities, Politics, History, and the Hero in Wallace Stevens's War Poetry," *The Wallace Stevens Journal* 20.2 [1996]: 209) nevertheless takes issue with Jacqueline Vaught Brogan's carefully balanced essay, "Stevens in History and Not in History: The Poet and the Second World War," *The Wallace Stevens Journal* 13.2 (1989): 168–90. Brogan maintains that "a critical change in Stevens's aesthetics . . . occurred during World War II from that of a relatively private poet to one with a public voice and conscience," 185. Brogan expands that point when she writes in a recent article that, toward the end of his life, Stevens was genuinely concerned with the issue of "how to dismantle an abusive structure of power (whether Marxist, imperialist, religious, racist, sexist) without merely inverting the structure and keeping the abusive structure in place." See "Wrestling with Those 'Rotted Names': Wallace Stevens's and Adrienne Rich's 'Revolutionary Poetics,'" 33. In a similar vein, Angus Cleghorn argues against the traditional split in poetic criticism between those who read Wallace Stevens formally (Pearce, Riddel, Vendler, and Bloom) and those who read him polemically (Longenbach and Filreis). In *Wallace Stevens's Poetics: The Neglected Rhetoric*, he maintains that Stevens believed that "clever wordsmiths carried influence" (p.1) and that the influence has a rhetorical thrust, particularly in the way poems like "Owl's Clover" take issue with what Cleghorn calls a "monumental aesthetics" which "serves only the rigid program of its creators" (p. 86). Cleghorn charts Stevens's development as a "rhetorical force that writes history" (p. 190).

54. "Against Proper Objects," Introduction, *differences* 6. 2 and 3 (1994): 20.

55. "Courtly Love as Anamorphosis," *The Ethics of Psychoanalysis 1959–60: The Seminar of Jacques Lacan, Book VII*, ed. Jacques-Alain Miller, trans. Dennis Porter (London: Tavistock/Routledge, 1991), p. 140.

56. "The Poetics of Discovery: A Reading of Donne's 'Elegy 19,'" *Yale Journal of Criticism* 2 (1989): 133.

57. *Ferdydurke*, trans. Danuta Borchardt (New Haven: Yale University Press, 2000), p. 72.

58. "The Bride Stripped Bare, by Richard Hamilton, even," *Tate: Modern Special Issue* 21 (2000): 59.

Chapter 1

1. Arundhati Roy, *The God of Small Things* (London: Harper Collins, 1997), p. 33.

2. *The Handbook of Heartbreak: 101 Poems of Lost Love and Sorrow*, collected by Robert Pinsky (New York: Morrow, 1998), p. xiii.

3. On Stevens as love poet, see, for example, Mary Arensberg, "'A Curable Separation': Stevens and the Mythology of Gender," *Wallace Stevens and the Feminine*, ed. Melita Schaum (Tuscaloosa: University of Alabama Press, 1993), pp. 23–45; Jacqueline Brogan, "'Sister of the Minotaur': Sexism and Stevens," *Wallace Stevens and the Feminine*, p. 3–22; rpt. from *The Wallace Stevens Journal* 12.2 (1988): 102–117; Barbara Fisher, *The Intensest Rendezvous* (Charlottesville: University of Virginia Press, 1990); Mark Halliday, "Stevens and Heterosexual Love," *Essays in Literature* 13 (1986): 135–55 and *Stevens and the Interpersonal* (Princeton: Princeton University Press, 1991); Frank Lentricchia, "Andiamo," *Critical Inquiry* 14 (1988): 407–13; and *Ariel and the Police: Michel Foucault, William James and Wallace Stevens* (Madison: University of Wisconsin Press, 1987); Paul Morrison, "Fat Girl in Paradise: Stevens, Wordsworth, Milton and the Proper Name," *Wallace Stevens and the Feminine*, pp. 80–114. Rosamond Rosenmeir, "Getting Wisdom: The Rabbis Devotion to Weisheit and its Implications for Feminists," *Wallace Stevens and the Feminine*, pp. 140–54, rpt. from *The Wallace Stevens Journal* 12.2 (1988); Eric Murphy Selinger, *What is It Then Between Us?: Traditions of Love in American Poetry* (Ithaca: Cornell University Press, 1998); Mary Doyle Springer, "The Feminine Principle in Stevens's Poetry: 'Esthétique du Mal,'" *Wallace Stevens Journal* 12.2 (1988): 119–137; Helen Vendler, *Wallace Stevens: Words Chosen out of Desire* (Knoxville: University of Tennessee Press, 1984).

4. Lynn Enterline also connects Narcissus and Pygmalion in *The Rhetoric of the Body: From Ovid to Shakespeare* (Cambridge: Cambridge University Press, 2000), p. 97. Similarly, J. Hillis Miller discusses the relationships among Ovidian stories: "Some residue of unassuaged guilt or responsibility leads to the next story, the next story literalizing yet another figure, then to the next and so on." See *Versions of Pygmalion* (Cambridge: Harvard University Press, 1990), p. 2.

5. *Letters of Wallace Stevens*, ed. Holly Stevens (New York: Knopf, 1966), p. 289.

6. Lisa du Rose assesses Stevens's sense of superiority in: "Racial Domain and the Imagination of Wallace Stevens," *The Wallace Stevens Journal* 22.1 (1998): 3–22. Of Stevens's habit of thought, Rachel Blau du Plessis similarly writes, "The African trope aggregates the diverse elements of a whole continent into one unhistorical mass and then absorbs African Americans into that bolus of materials." See "'Hoo, Hoo, Hoo': Some Episodes in the Construction of Modern Whiteness," *American Literature* 67.4 (1995): 669.

7. "Rotted Names," *What is Found There: Notebooks on Poetry and Politics* (New York: Norton, 1993), p. 204.

8. "Petrarch's Beloved Body: 'Italia mia,'" *Feminist Approaches to the Body in Medieval Literature*, ed. Linda Lomperis and Sarah Stanbury (Philadelphia: University of Pennsylvania Press, 1993), p. 10.

9. *Excitable Speech: A Politics of the Performative* (New York: Routledge, 1997), p. 158.

10. *Revolution in Poetic Language*, trans. Margaret Waller (New York: Columbia University Press, 1984), pp. 59–60.

11. *Five Temperaments: Elizabeth Bishop, Robert Lowell, James Merrill, Adrienne Rich, John Ashbery* (New York: Oxford University Press, 1977), p. 6.

12. *Beyond Consolation: Death, Sexuality, and the Changing Shapes of Elegy* (Ithaca: Cornell University Press, 1997), p. 268.

13. "Consolation," *The Collected Poems of W. B. Yeats, Revised Second Edition*, ed. Richard J. Finneran (New York: Simon and Schuster, 1996), p. 272.

14. "Shakespearean Inscriptions: The Voicing of Power," *Shakespeare and the Question of Theory*, ed. Patricia Parker and Geoffrey Hartmann (London: Methuen, 1985), p. 121.

15. As explained and translated by Rosalind Krauss, *The Optical Unconscious* (Cambridge, Mass.: MIT Press, 1993), p. 167.

16. In "The Blue Nude and Mrs. Pappadopoulos" [*The William Carlos Williams Review* 18. 2 (1992): 27], Terence Diggory assumes that Mrs. Pappadopoulos is the model who longs to escape the studio of Stevens's painterly self-absorption.

17. *Ariel and the Police: Michel Foucault, William James, Wallace Stevens* (Madison: University of Wisconsin Press, 1988), p. 195. On the controversy over Lentricchia's thesis, see "Patriarchy Against Itself: The Young Manhood of Wallace Stevens," *Critical Inquiry* 13 (1987): 742–86; Donald Pease "Patriarchy, Lentricchia and Male Feminization," *Critical Inquiry* 14 (1988): 378–85; and Sandra Gilbert and Susan Gubar, "The Man on the Dump versus The United Dames of America; or What Does Frank Lentricchia Want?", *Critical Inquiry* 14 (1988): 386–40, as well as "Andiamo," *Critical Inquiry* 14 (1988): 407–13

18. Toni Stooss and Patrick Elliott, *Alberto Giacometti, 1901–66 Exhibit Catalogue for the Royal Academy of Art* (London, 1996), p. 154.

19. *The Originality of the Avant-Garde and Other Myths* (Cambridge, Mass.: MIT Press, 1985), p. 258.

20. *Alberto Giacometti: A Biography of his Work*, trans. Jean Stuart (Paris: Flammarion, 1991), p. 239.

21. "Marginal Comments," *The Ethics of Psychoanalysis, 1959–1960, The Seminar of Jacques Lacan*, ed. Jacques-Alain Miller, Book VII, trans. with notes by Dennis Porter (London: Tavistock/Routledge, 1992), p. 136.

22. "Courtly Love as Anamorphosis," *The Ethics of Psychoanalysis, 1959–1960, The Seminar of Jacques Lacan,* p. 143.

23. *The Mestastases of Enjoyment: Six Essays on Women and Causality* (London: Verso, 1994), p. 91.

24. "Certain Functions of Introjection and Projection," *Developments in Psycho-Analysis: Melanie Klein, Paula Heimann, Susan Isaacs and Joan Riviere*, ed. Joan

Riviere, with a preface by Ernest Jones (New York: De Capo Press, 1953), pp. 167–68.

25. *The Psychic Life of Power* (Stanford: Stanford University Press), p. 187.

26. "Iago's Alter Ego: Race as Projection in *Othello,*" *Shakespeare Quarterly* 48 (1997): 142.

27. *Why War? Psychoanalysis, Politics, and the Return to Melanie Klein* (Oxford: Blackwell, 1993), p. 176.

28. "The Garden," *The Poems and Letters of Andrew Marvell, Third Edition,* ed. H. M. Margoliouth, rev. Pierre Legouis and E. E. Duncan-Jones (Oxford: Clarendon Press, 1971), p. 52.

29. Slavoj Žižek, *The Sublime Object of Ideology* (London: Verso, 1989), p. 175.

30. "The Survivor," *Toward the Post-Modern,* ed. Robert Harvey and Mark S. Robert (Atlantic Highlands, N.J.: Humanities Press, 1995), p. 162.

31. *King Lear,* ed. Kenneth Muir (London: Routledge, 1992), p. 206.

Chapter 2

1. *Forms of Farewell, The Late Poetry of Wallace Stevens* (Madison: University of Wisconsin Press, 1985), p. 35.

2. "The World After Poetry: Revelation in Late Stevens," *The Wallace Stevens Journal* 23.2 (1999): 188. Longenbach argues that "we need to feel the poem's true horror in order to feel its tenuous consolation, its transformation of a future threat into a domesticated past," 189.

3. "Three Academic Pieces," *The Necessary Angel: Essays on Reality and the Imagination* (New York: Knopf, 1951), p. 79. For an analysis of the three parts of the essay that focuses on its "lesson of metamorphosis," see David Galef, "Resemblance and Change in Wallace Stevens's 'Three Academic Pieces,'" *American Literature* 58.4 (1986): 589–308.

4. For Stevens's relationship to Duchamp, see Daniel R. Schwarz, "Reconfiguring Modernism: Exploring the Relationship between Modern Art and Modern Literature (New York: St. Martin's Press, 1997), pp. 201–202. My connection of Stevens to Duchamp here is indebted to Rosalind E. Krauss's reading of the rotorelief in *The Optical Unconscious* (Cambridge, Mass.: MIT Press, 1993), p. 95–104. For a sustained interpretation of the ties between Jackson Pollock and "Auroras" see Glen MacLeod, *Wallace Stevens and Modern Art* (New Haven: Yale University Press, 1993), pp. 175–97.

5. Charles Altieri's phrase, *Painterly Abstraction in Modernist American Poetry: The Contemporaneity of Modernism* (Cambridge: Cambridge University Press, 1989), p. 403.

6. "White Mythology and the American Sublime: Stevens's Auroral Fantasy," *The American Sublime,* ed. Mary Arensberg (Albany: State University of New York Press, 1986), p. 159.

7. Harold Bloom calls this moment a passage "that would have moved the author

of Huck Finn." *Wallace Stevens: The Poems of Our Climate* (Ithaca: Cornell University Press, 1977), p. 211. But Bloom's "injuns" and garter snakes both misrepresent the novel and Stevens's own lack of romance about the indians.

8. *The Postmodern Explained*, tr. Julian Pefanis and Morgan Thomas (Minneapolis: University of Minnesota Press, 1993), p. 11.

9. Slavoj Žižjec, *The Mestastases of Enjoyment: Six Essays on Women and Causality* (London: Verso, 1994), p. 91.

10. Robert Lowell writes of a similar desolation in his anti-nuclear "Fall 1961": "A father's no shield / for his child," *For the Union Dead* (New York: Farrar Strauss, 1964), p. 11.

11. Rosalind Krauss argues that the effect of the rotoreliefs "produce a fairly explicit sexual reading," *The Optical Unconscious*, p. 96.

12. On Stevens and the Lyotardan "forgotten" or "unpresentable," see David Jarraway, "'Velocities of Change': Exceeding Excess in 'Credences of Summer' and 'The Auroras of Autumn,'" *The Wallace Stevens Journal* 15.1 (1991): 82.

13. *Antigone's Claim: Kinship Between Life and Death* (New York: Columbia University Press, 2000), p. 81.

14. *The Complete Poetical Works of Percy Bysshe Shelley*, ed. Thomas Hutchinson (Oxford: Clarendon Press, 1967), p. 579.

Chapter 3

1. *Fugitive Pieces* (London: Bloomsbury, 1996), p. 161.

2. My premise here, that "automata" includes the political, might be disputed by those who say that Stevens was only concerned with *artistic* conformity. But Gromaire's paintings are, in themselves often political commentaries, alternating between the same woman—a "So-and-So" reclining—and industrialized landscapes, peopled by sculptured industrial workers. Stevens describes them as intrinsic to what Gromaire "postulates [as] an 'art directement social' which transmits itself to the spectator without mediation or explanation." See "Marcel Gromaire," *Opus Posthumous*, ed. Milton J. Bates (New York: Knopf, 1989), p. 251.

3. Marjorie Perloff is the most consistently critical of Stevens's indifference to politics. Of the "major man" of "Notes," Perloff writes, "What does it signify, in the middle of World War II—when the real Major Men included such names as Hitler, Mussolini, and Stalin—to posit the desirability, however fleeting, of Major Man?" See "The Supreme Fiction and the Impasse of the Modernist Lyric," *Wallace Stevens: The Poetics of Modernism*, ed. Albert Gelpi (Cambridge: Cambridge University Press, 1985), p. 59. In answer to Perloff's accusations, Dean Rader maintains, "What remains troubling about comments . . . by Perloff and others is that they assume an undeviating Stevens; that is, they take for granted the assumption that Stevens never changes his mind, and they tend to ignore that Stevens develops and alters

his vision over time as America and Modernity change." "Wallace Stevens, Octavio Paz, and the Poetry of Social Engagement," *The Wallace Stevens Journal* 21.3 (1997): 181. On the question of Stevens and politics, refer also to James Longenbach, *Wallace Stevens: The Plain Sense of Things* (Oxford: Oxford University Press, 1991) and Alan Filreis, *Wallace Stevens and the Actual World* (Princeton: Princeton University Press, 1991).

4. Considering Stevens's relationship to the continent, Helen Vendler writes, "It is only after students understand that maximalist euphony and minimalist colorlessness, Euro-culture and American bareness, are aesthetically troubling and divisive issues for Stevens that the teacher can begin to show them why accuracy of representation must be the artist's standard of moral responsibility." "Wallace Stevens: Teaching the Anthology Pieces," *Teaching Wallace Stevens: Practical Essays*, ed. John N. Serio and B. J. Leggett (Knoxville: University of Tennessee Press, 1994), p. 10.

5. See David Jarroway, *Wallace Stevens and the Question of Belief: Metaphysician in the Dark* (Baton Rouge and London: Louisiana State University Press, 1993), p. 302 for a play on New Haven and old havens as well as Eleanor Cook *Poetry, Word-Play, and Word-War* (Princeton: Princeton University Press, 1988), p. 268.

6. Beverly Maeder writes of the way in which Stevens's experiments are often set in tercets. She concentrates there on Stevens's "Man with the Blue Guitar," but notes that Stevens uses the form in his major postwar experiments, "Auroras of Autumn" and "An Ordinary Evening in New Haven." See *Wallace Stevens's Experimental Language: The Lion in the Lute* (New York: St. Martin's Press, 1999), pp. 42–43.

7. *Forms of Farewell: The Late Poetry of Wallace Stevens* (Madison: University of Wisconsin Press, 1985), p. 92. Helen Vendler also reads the lines optimistically. *On Extended Wings: The Longer Poems of Wallace Stevens* (Cambridge: Harvard University Press, 1969), pp. 277–78. While Eleanor Cook regards canto XII as central and while she maintains that the sense of the canto "remains autumnal," she still argues that the canto "affirms . . . the enduring power of human words." *Poetry, Word-Play, and Word-War*, pp. 284–85.

8. "The *Canzoniere* and the Language of Self," *Studies in Philology* 75 (1978): 282.

9. *Shakespeare's Sonnets, The Arden Shakespeare, Third Series*, ed. Katherine Duncan-Jones (London: Thomas Nelson, 1997), p. 257.

10. See *Poetry, Word-Play, and Word-War*, p. 286 for a similar notation of the importance of this sonnet.

11. In some ways, what Michael Davidson calls the "palimpset effect"—the "productive apparatus of a set of variable fictions, each one layered on top of the last" coincides with the oral reverberations and the visual burnishings Stevens imprints in this poem. Davidson notes the importance of dada and surrealism on modern poetry for precisely its emphasis on materializa-

tions of this nature. *Ghostlier Demarcations: Modern Poetry and the Material World* (Berkeley: University of California Press, 1997), p. 5.

12. Alan Filreis complains that "the poem's bread may seem to simulate realism, but it is actually constructed of types: *the* (typical) plate, *the* (typical) loaf of bread and so on. It does not depict the observed scene. Definitive articles stand for the universal; '*the*' rather than pointing to misery points it away." Filreis reads the poem as Stevens's defense of *not* going to Europe. Relying on "post-card" images sent to him by Barbara Church, who went grandly to Europe but wrote accurately of postwar European deprivation, he was able to resist "the travel-writing cliché of the 'grand tour.'" *Wallace Stevens and the Actual World* (Princeton: Princeton University Press, 1991), p. 226. On Stevens as armchair traveler, see Alison Rieke, "Stevens in Corsica, Lear in New Haven," *The New England Quarterly* 62.1 (1990): 35–59.

13. *Camera Lucida: Reflections on Photography*, trans. Richard Howard (New York: Hill and Wang, 1981), p. 96. This quote is also in Ronald Schleifer and Nancy M. West, "The Poetry of What Lies Close at Hand: Photography, Commodities, and Postromantic Discourses in Hardy and Stevens," *MLQ* 60:1 (1999): 50–51. Schleifer and West argue that "the advent of photography transformed verbal descriptions and taught poets such as Stevens and Hardy to see the world differently, to notice things close at hand: both commodified facts and the institutions that condition their activity," 52.

14. On Stevens's capacity for Biblical word play, see Eleanor Cook, "Wallace Stevens and the King James Bible," *Essays in Criticism* 41.3 (1991): 240–52.

15. "Blankness as a Signifier," *Critical Inquiry* 24 (1997): 164.

16. *Painterly Abstraction in Modernist American Poetry: The Contemporaneity of Modernism* (Cambridge: Cambridge University Press, 1989), p. 344.

17. *Heidegger and "the jews,"* trans. Andreas Michel and Mark Roberts, introduction by David Carroll (Minneapolis: University of Minnesota Press, 1990), p. 5.

18. *The Winter's Tale,* ed. J. H. P. Pafford (London: Methuen, 1963), p. 98.

19. "The Theogeny of Hesiod," *Hesiod, the Homeric Hymns, and Homerica,* trans. Hugh G. Evelyn-White (Cambridge, Mass.: Harvard University Press, 1977), pp. 91–95.

20. James Longenbach argues that "regendering in the late Stevens is meaningful precisely because it comes out of an earlier insistence on the imperatives of masculinist invention." *Wallace Stevens: The Plain Sense of Things* (New York and Oxford: Oxford University Press, 1991), p. 225.

21. Angus Cleghorn writes that "in 'The World as Meditation,' Stevens gives 'The Idea of Order at Key West' back to its singer." See "And of that Other and Her Desire: The Embracing Language of Wallace Stevens," *Ethics and the Subject,* ed. Karl Sims (Amsterdam: Rodopi, 1997), p. 235.

22. *Erotic Dawn Songs of the Middle Ages: Voicing the Lyric Lady* (Gainseville: University Press of Florida, 1996), p. 31.

23. Elizabeth Harvey calls the process of male poets speaking through women a habit of "domesticating the alterity of female power sources and [turning] them into versions of male selves." See *Ventriloquized Voices* (London: Routledge, 1992), p. 132.

24. *Antigone's Claim: Kinship Between Life and Death* (New York: Columbia University Press, 2000), p. 3.

25. *Playing and Reality* (New York: Basic Books, 1975), p. 47.

26. For a discussion of Winnicott's theory in Wallace Stevens, and especially in "The World as Meditation," as a way of mediating between the internalized image and objective reality, see Mary Sidney Watson, "Wallace Stevens and the Maternal Art of Poetry," *The Wallace Stevens Journal* 22.1 (1998): 72–82.

27. See Louis Martz's definition of the meditative tradition in *The Poetry of Meditation* (New Haven and London: Yale University Press, 1954), p. 1. Martz recognized the scope of "The World as Meditation" early on. "Wallace Stevens: The World as Meditation," *Yale Review* 47 (1958): 517–36.

28. For Loren Rusk, "Penelope is the counterpart of the poet" and Stevens comes close—with her inventiveness—to suggesting that the creative mind has an "androgynous center." "Penelope's Creative Desiring: 'The World as Meditation,'" *The Wallace Stevens Journal* 9.1 (1985): 16, 23.

Chapter 4

1. "On Robert Lowell," *Salmagundi* 37 (1977): 54–55.

2. *Shakespeare's Sonnets, The Arden Shakespeare, Third Series*, ed. Katherine Duncan-Jones (London: Thomas Nelson, 1997), p. 373.

3. *Notebook 1967–1968* (New York: Farrar, Straus and Giroux, 1969), p. 16

4. "Afterthought," *Notebook* (New York: Farrar, Straus and Giroux, 1970), p. 263.

5. "Courtly Love as Anamorphosis," *The Ethics of Psychoanalysis 1959–60: The Seminar of Jacques Lacan, Book VII*, ed. Jacques-Alain Miller, trans. Dennis Porter (London: Tavistock/Routledge, 1991), p. 140.

6. In the 1969 version, this sentence reads "A poet can be intelligent and on to what he does; yet he walks, half-balmy, and over-accoutered—caught by his gentle amnesia, his rude ignorance, his too meticulous education." *Notebook, 1967–68*, p. 160.

7. *Discours, figure* (Paris: Klincksieck, 1971), p. 378 [trans. Bill Readings, *Introducing Lyotard* (London: Routledge, 1991), p. 26.]

8. Despite her reservations about the wisdom of publishing *The Dolphin*, Bishop praises its poetry three more times in the letter, calling it alternately "magnificent," "honest, almost" and a "great poem." See *One Art: Letters*, selected and edited by Robert Giroux (New York: Farrar, Straus, Giroux, 1994), p. 561.

9. In an essay largely critical of Lowell's "naming names" in *The Dolphin,* John Ward writes, "I infer that [Lowell] finally decided that in disembowelling

himself it was acceptable, even unavoidable, to disembowel others, as long as he did so within the confines of the honourable sonnet form." See "'Not Avoiding Injury': Robert Lowell," *American Declarations of Love*, ed. Ann Massa (New York: St. Martin's Press, 1990), p. 53. Steven Gould Axelrod views this fusion positively: "Lowell sees that his life and his art have a coextensive existence. The life gives birth to the art and the art completes the life for it culminates his consciousness of that life." *Robert Lowell: Life and Art* (Princeton: Princeton University Press, 1978), p. 25.

10. Paul Mariani quotes Ian Hamilton on Lowell's odd comment to Jonathan Miller when he met him at Idlewild Airport and saw four Hassidic rabbis walk by. "Cal winked and told Miller that it was not the Germans who had been responsible for World War II." *Lost Puritan* (New York: Norton, 1994), p. 329–330. See also Hamilton, *Robert Lowell: A Biography* (New York: Random House, 1982), pp. 314–315. About Lowell's Hitler fantasies, see Hamilton, pp. 209–212.

11. Of Lowell's "aggrandized and merciless masculinity" in *Dolphin*, Adrienne Rich writes:

> I sense that the mind behind these poems—being omniverously well read—knew that "someone who suffered"—the Jews . . . his own wife—but is incapable of a true identification with the sufferers which might illuminate their condition for us. The poet's need to dominate and objectify the characters in his poems leaves him in an appalling way invulnerable. And the poetry for all its verbal talent still remains emotionally shallow.

"Carydid: A Column," *American Poetry Review* 2 (1973): 42–43. Rich is, of course, on to Lowell's game.

12. Steven Gould Axelrod writes of Lowell's obsession with the mixture of "self and trope" as typically American and argues that Lowell's sense of poetic prerogatives—his feeling that poetry mattered more than life—renders Ian Hamilton's failure to talk about poetry in his biography a critical shortcoming (*Robert Lowell: Essays on Poetry*, ed. Steven Gould Axelrod and Helen Deese [Cambridge: Cambridge University Press, 1986], pp. 14–25). The same shortcomings are true of the most recent biography, Paul Mariani's *Lost Puritan* (New York: Norton, 1994). Though reviewers note that the biographers "haven't shown us the depths of the poetry," they seem equally drawn in by the poet's life. In a review of *Lost Puritan*, David Bromwich projects a collection of letters: "Lowell's collected letters ought to prove enormously interesting to judge by the samples quoted by Mr. Mariani." See "I Myself Am Hell." *New York Times Book Review* November 20, 1994: 41. Bromwich fails to note that thus far there is no *Collected Poems*. In his review of *Lost Puritan*, Michael Hofman anticipates the rumored

arrival of a *Collected Poems* in "two or three years." See "Rescuing a Reputation from Poetic Injustice," *The London Times*, January 19, 1995: 40. On the reasons for the delay and the problems of editing Lowell, Geoffrey Lindsay writes, "Pity the poor editor entrusted with putting together Lowell's poems." "Drama and Dramatic Strategies in Robert Lowell's *Notebook 1967–68*," *Twentieth-Century Literature* 44.1 (1998): 53. Harold Bloom, however, assumes in the Bibliography to *The Western Canon* that a *Collected Lowell* already exists. *The Western Canon: The Books and School of the Ages* (New York: Harcourt Brace, 1994), p. 563. On the question of the biographical in Lowell's work, Frank Bidart (who is working on *The Collected Poems*), quotes the famous passage from "To Speak of the Woe that is in Marriage" of *Life Studies* where the wife voices her desperation to keep her husband from driving drunk: "Each night now I tie / ten dollars and his car key to my thy." Bidart writes, "I once brought this passage up with Lowell. He smiled rather sheepishly and said that his wife had never done that, that it was told to him by the wife of Delmore Schwartz." See "Panel: Lowell on the Page," *The Kenyon Review, New Series* 22.1 (2000): 239.

13. *The Good Soldier* (New York: Signet, 1991), pp. 221, 223.
14. As David S. Gewanter writes: "Lowell's ambivalence about his wives reflects finally on his own self-doubt." "Child of Collaboration: Robert Lowell's *Dolphin*," *Modern Philology* 93.2 (1995): 183.
15. *Moses and Monotheism*, trans. Katherine Jones (New York: Knopf, 1939), pp. 128–129.
16. "The Laugh of the Medusa," trans. Keith Cohen and Paula Cohen, *New French Feminisms*, ed. Elaine Marks and Isabelle de Courtivron (New York: Schoken, 1981), p. 254.
17. For the connections between Athena and Medusa, see Tobin Siebers, *The Mirror of Medusa* (Berkeley: University of California Press, 1983), p. 14 and Roberto Calasso, *The Marriage of Cadmus and Harmony*, trans. Tim Parks (London: Jonathan Cape, 1993), p. 228.
18. *The Merchant of Venice*, ed. John Russell Brown (London: Methuen, 1961), p. 73.
19. *The Poems and Letters of Andrew Marvell, Third Edition*, ed. H. M. Margoliouth, rev. Pierre Legouis and E. E. Duncan-Jones (Oxford: Clarendon Press, 1971), p. 28.
20. *Collected Prose*, ed. Robert Giroux (New York: Farrar, Straus and Giroux, 1987), pp. 37–38.
21. *The Marriage of Cadmus and Harmony*, p. 3.

Chapter 5

1. Peter Shaffer, *The Gift of the Gorgon* (London: Viking, 1993), p. 84.
2. On the contrast between the "laurel-wreathed Lowell as a bodiless iconic

head" in the cover portrait and the "out-of-date" male dominated tribute to Lowell in the actual story, see William Doreski, *Robert Lowell's Shifting Colors: The Poetics of the Public and the Personal* (Athens: Ohio University Press, 1999), p. xiii.

3. In a biography of the family that is part memoir, Sarah Payne Stuart speaks of the Lowell family legacy:

> In my family you are either crazy or built to stand those who are. The two extremes do not understand each other at all and yet seem to fit together in a larger dynastic sense like a cog and a wheel. They are deeply attracted to each other—the strong nonneurotics and the clinically insane—subconsciously wishing to compensate for traits lacking in themselves.

My First Cousin Once Removed: Money, Madness, and the Family of Robert Lowell (New York: Harper Collins, 1998), p. 236. But the book chronicles the family's sense of itself as inheritors of an aristocracy from both sides of the family, particularly from that of Lowell's mother: "We were brought up being told we were 'Winslows,' as if this information alone should make everything clear in our lives" (p. 19). As Winslows, they were descendants of Mary Chilton: "the first white woman to come to America and settle in Boston" (p. 20).

4. Payne Stuart argues that Lowell's trouble making caused his mother's sister to disinherit him. *My First Cousin Once Removed*, p. 215.

5. Ian Hamilton's *Robert Lowell: A Biography* (New York: Random House, 1982) is mostly a record of Lowell's psychic and amorous escapades. While claiming that the purpose of his biography is to "recognize Lowell as a major poet at every step of his development" (*Lost Puritan: A Life of Robert Lowell* [New York: Norton, 1994], p.13), Paul Mariani similarly spares us no detail of Lowell's struggles as a "thorazined fixture" (p. 19). M. L. Rosenthal writes that Lowell encourages the biographers as he "becomes one of those candid-camera figures . . . treating himself and his parents and the women he has loved and married and divorced and his children in the same way . . . a kind of diabolism in a minor key." See "Our Neurotic Angel," *Agenda* 18. 3 (1980): 35. Even the defenders of Lowell's poetry can't resist dragging in the biography. Anthony Hecht agrees that Lowell's manic cycles almost always "involved episodes of sexual adventurism," but maintains that the poetry must be separated out from the life and that the critical task is to "guard against the difficulty of confusing celebrity with achievement." See *Robert Lowell* (Washington: Library of Congress, 1983), pp. 7, 9. The strongest anti-biography critic is Steven Gould Axelrod who argues: "Hamilton's 'Lowell' is a problem child who never grows up, never can keep himself out of scrapes, never accomplishes anything of lasting value. . . .

His book reads less like a literary biography than a probation report."
("Lowell's Living Name: An Introduction," *Robert Lowell: Essays on the
Poetry*, ed. Steven Gould Axelrod and Helen Deese [Cambridge: Cambridge
University Press, 1986], p. 15.)

6. For an extended discussion of exactly which Vermeer painting, see Helen
   Deese, "Lowell and the Visual Arts," in *Robert Lowell: Essays on the Poetry*,
   pp. 180–216.

7. *Bodies that Matter: On the Discursive Limits of Sex* (New York: Routledge,
   1993), pp. 7–8.

8. Frank Bidart argues that re-writing was an ingrained habit in Lowell: "from
   the very beginning until the end . . . [It] proceeded very deeply from the
   nature of what he was doing as a writer, what he imagined his work as a
   writer to be." See "You Didn't Write, You Rewrote," *The Kenyon Review,
   New Series* 22.1 (2000): 206.

9. "Afterthought," *Notebook* (New York: Farrar, Straus and Giroux, 1970), p.
   263.

10. "Antebellum Boston," *Collected Prose*, ed. Robert Giroux (New York: Far-
    rar, Straus and Giroux, 1987), p. 292.

11. In a letter to Blair Clark, Lowell speaks of the "downlook" as an inward
    feeling of depression (the aftermath of manic attack):

    I've been home a month now, rather down looking at first, then
    thawing, all the while writing with furious persistence.

    Ian Hamilton, *Robert Lowell: A Biography*, p. 453. Helen Vendler ("Lowell's
    Persistence: The Forms Depression Makes," *The Kenyon Review, New Series*
    22.1 [2000]: 217) writes of Lowell's depression and the way in which he "per-
    sist[ed] in writing poetry concerning, and enacting, crushing depression."

12. *Antony and Cleopatra*, ed. M. R. Ridley (London: Routledge, 1988), p.
    201–202.

13. "Last Days and Last Poems," *Part of Nature, Part of Us: Modern American Poets*
    (Cambridge: Harvard University Press, 1980), pp. 165–166. Reprinted from
    Robert Lowell: A Tribute, ed. Rolando Anzilotti (Piza: Nistri-Lischi Editori,
    1974).

14. *Collected Prose*, ed. Robert Giroux (New York: Farrar, Straus, and Giroux,
    1987), pp. 37–38.

15. *King Henry V,* ed. J. H. Walter (London: Routledge, 1987), p. 141.

Chapter 6

1. "The Survivor," tr. Robert Harvey and Mark S. Roberts, *Toward the Post-
   Modern*, ed. Robert Harvey and Mark S. Roberts (Atlantic Highlands, New
   Jersey: Humanities Press, 1995), p. 162.

2. "Against Proper Objects," *differences*, 6. 2 & 3 (1994): 20. Future references are cited in the text.

3. "Inscriptions," *Dark Fields of the Republic* (New York: Norton, 1995), p. 71. In a note to *Dark Fields*, Rich writes:

> I had written "suffused," later began looking up the line I was quoting from memory: was it Coleridge? Keats? Shakespeare? My friend Barbara Gelpi confirmed it was Shakespeare, in his Sonnet 111: *Thence comes it that my name receives a brand / And almost thence my nature is subdued / To what it works in, like the dyer's hand.* I have kept "suffused" here because to feel suffused by the materials that one has perforce to work in is not necessarily to be subdued, though some might think so. (pp. 78–79)

4. Jane Hedley, "'Old Songs with New Words': The Achievement of Rich's 'Twenty-One Love Poems.'" *Genre* 23 (1990): 351. Refer to Alice Templeton, "The Dream and the Dialogue: Rich's Feminist Poems and Gadamer's Hermeneutics," *Tulsa Studies in Women's Literature* 7 (1988): 295. Hedley and Templeton anticipate Kevin McQuirk in "Philoctetes Radicalized:'Twenty-one Love Poems' and the Lyric Career of Adrienne Rich," *Contemporary Literature* 34 (1993): 61–87 as well as Thomas Byers, "Adrienne Rich: Vision as Rewriting," *World, Self, Poem*, ed. Leonard Trawick (Kent, Ohio: Kent State University Press, 1990), pp. 144–52 and Lorrie Smith, "Dialogue and the Political Imagination in Denise Levertov and Adrienne Rich," *World, Self, Poem*, pp. 155–62.

5. For a summary of the poetic dismissals, see Craig Werner, *Adrienne Rich:The Poet and Her Critics* (Chicago and London: American Library Association, 1988), pp. 37–41. Gayle Rubin and Judith Butler object to Rich's theory but see it only in terms of where Rich was at an earlier stage in her career. "Sexual Traffic," *differences* 6.2 & 3 (1994): 74-76.

6. *The Dream of a Common Language* (New York: Norton, 1978), p. 36.

7. Sandra Runzio writes that "Although the word 'choice' does not appear until Poem XV,'choice' as a premise lingers in virtually all of the poems [of 'Twenty-One Love Poems']." See "Intimacy, Complicity, and the Imagination: Adrienne Rich's 'Twenty-One Love Poems,'" *Genders*, 16 (1993): 71.

8. See Rich's interview with David Montenegro, *Points of Departure: International Writers on Writing and Politics* (Ann Arbor: University of Michigan Press, 1991), p. 7.

9. *Bodies that Matter: On the Discursive Limits of Sex* (New York: Routledge, 1993), p. 242.

10. "Defy the Space that Separates," *The Nation* 263. 10 (1996): 34.

11. For a discussion of the pivotal connections between Rich and "The Idea of Order at Key West" that cites *What is Found There*, see Jane Hedley, "Reforming the Cradle: Adrienne Rich's 'Transcendental Etude,'" *Genre* 28.3

(1995): 348–350. On other connections between Rich and Stevens, refer to Jacqueline Brogan "'I can't be still': Or Adrienne Rich and the Refusal to Gild the Fields of Guilt," *Women's Studies* 27.4 (1998): 311–30 as well as "Wrestling with Those 'Rotted Names': Wallace Stevens' and Adrienne Rich's 'Revolutionary Poetics,'" *The Wallace Stevens Journal* 25.1 (2001): 19–39.

12. Slavoj Žižek, *Tarrying with the Negative* (Durham: Duke University Press, 1994), p. 44.
13. Andrew Marvell, *Poems and Letters, Third Edition*, ed. H. M. Marguliouth, rev. Pierre Leguois, and E. E. Duncan Jones (Oxford: Oxford University Press, 1971), p. 48.
14. *Blood, Bread and Poetry* (New York: Norton, 1986), p. 225.
15. "Three Academic Pieces," *The Necessary Angel: Essays on Reality and the Imagination* (New York: Knopf, 1951), p. 79.
16. Bill Readings, *Introducing Lyotard* (London: Routledge, 1991), p. xxx.
17. For a sustained discussion of the way in which Rich writes of, and communicates, pain in her poetry, see "The 'Possible Poet': Pain, Form and the Embodied Poetics of Adrienne Rich in Wallace Stevens's Wake," *The Wallace Stevens Journal* 25. 1 (2001): 40–51. There, Cynthia Hogue writes that "as a feminist, Rich asserts, inserts, a suffering woman's body into the Canonical body of Western poetry surely in some sense as an audacious revision . . . of the blazon," 44.
18. *The Elegies and Songs and Sonnets*, ed. Helen Gardner (Oxford: Oxford University Press, 1965), p. 36.
19. *Hamlet*, ed. Harold Jenkins (New York: Routledge, 1982), p. 278.
20. Nadine Gordimer, *Burgher's Daughter* (New York, 1979), p. 356.

Chapter 7

1. Samuel Beckett in Samuel Beckett, George Duthuit, Jacques Putman, *Bram Van Velde* (Paris: La Musée de Poche, 1958), p. 7. This preface (written in 1948) appears only in the French version. Translations mine, unless otherwise indicated.
2. "Physicists Put Atom in Two Places at Once," *New York Times*, May 28, 1996, natl. ed.: C5.
3. Beckett's work has always been recognized as a commentary on postwar realities. In Rich's recent poetry, her subject often returns to the war and its aftermath. See *Atlas*: "Eastern War Time," pp. 35–44, "1948: Jews" p. 52; *Dark Fields*: "Food Packages: 1947," p. 27, "Revolution in Permanence (1953, 1993)," pp. 23–24, "Inscriptions," pp. 57–73; *Midnight Salvage*: "Char," pp. 16–17; "1941," pp. 23–24; "Letter to a Young Poet," pp. 24–29; "Seven Skins," pp. 38–42.
4. "Defy the Space that Separates," *The Nation* 263.10 (1996): 34.

5. "The Cliff, " tr. Edith Fournier, *Samuel Beckett: The Complete Short Prose*, ed. S. E. Gontarski, (New York: Grove Press, 1996), p. 257.

6. Samuel Beckett, Georges Duthuit, Jacques Putman, *Bram Van Velde* (New York: Grove Press, 1960), p.13. Future references are cited in the text.

7. *The Dream of a Common Language* (New York: Norton, 1978), p. 36.

8. "Topic and Figures of Enunciation: It is Myself that I Paint," *Vision and Textuality*, ed. Stephen Melville and Bill Readings (Durham: Duke University Press, 1995), p. 213.

9. "Gaspara Stampa and the Gender of Petrarchism," *TSLL* 38.2 (1996): 115.

10. Samuel Beckett, and George Duthuit. "Three Dialogues," *Critical Essays on Samuel Beckett*, ed. Patrick A. McCarthy (Boston: G. K. Hall, 1986), p. 232.

11. On the right/left division of Van Velde's work, see Gabriel Ramin Schor "L'Ultime Solitude" *Bram Van Velde: Rétrospective du centenaire* (Geneva: Musée Rath, 1996), pp. 293–94.

12. In Shakespeare's *The Winter's Tale*, the ambivalent role of lilies is clear.

> *Perdita.* lilies of all kinds . . .
> the flower-de-luce being one. O these I lack,
> To make you garlands of, and my sweet friend,
> To strew him o'er and o'er!
> *Florizel.* What like a corse?
> *Perdita.* No, like a bank for Love to lie and play on;
> Not like a corse; or if, not to be buried,
> But quick and in mine arms. (4.4. 126–132)

The Winter's Tale, ed. J. H. P. Pafford (London: Methuen, 1963), pp. 96–97.

13. See Michael Rainer Mason, *Bram Van Velde 1895–1981, Rétrospective du centenaire*, p. 57.

14. "Courtly Love as Anamorphosis," *The Seminar of Jacques Lacan: The Ethics of Psychoanalysis 1959–60, Book VII*, ed. Jacques-Alain Miller, trans. Dennis Porter (London: Tavistock/Routledge, 1991), p. 140.

15. Gabriel Ramin Schor, "L'ultime solitude," *Bram Van Velde: Rétrospective du centenaire*, p. 291.

16. "L'infaisable miroir," *Bram Van Velde: Rétrospective du centenaire*, p. 264.

17. *Sir Thomas Wyatt: The Complete Poems,* ed. R. A. Rebholz (New Haven: Yale University Press, 1978), p. 77.

18. *An Ethics of Sexual Difference*, tr. Carolyn Burke and Gillian C. Gill (Ithaca: Cornell University Press, 1993), p. 252.

19. "What Do Pictures Really Want?" *October* 77 (1996): 72

20. The French original is untitled, as are VanVelde's paintings. See *Celui qui ne peut se servir des mots* (Montpellier: Éditions Fata Morgana, 1975), p. 17

21. As translated by Rosalind Krauss, *The Optical Unconscious* (Cambridge, Mass: MIT Press, 1993), p. 149.

22. John Webster, *Works*, ed. David Gunby, Antony Carnegie, Antony Hammond (Cambridge: Cambridge University Press, 1995), p. 547.

23. The French has a similar internal rhyme ("crete," "mette," and "restes"). *Celui qui ne peut se servir des mots* (Montpellier: Éditions Fata Morgana, 1975), p. 17

24. Andrew Marvell, *The Poems and Letters, Third Edition*, ed. H. M. Margoliouth, rev. Pierre Legouis and E. E. Duncan-Jones (Oxford: Clarendon Press, 1971), p. 28.

25. *Ends of the Lyric* (Baltimore: Johns Hopkins University Press, 1996), p. 6. Bahti shares Helen Vendler's position: "Lyric offers itself as potential speech for its reader to utter, or *lied* for its hearer to sing." See "*Tintern Abbey:* Two Assaults," *Bucknell Review: Wordsworth in Context*, ed. Pauline Fletcher and John Murphy (Lewisburg, Pa.: Bucknell University Press, 1992), p. 184.

26. The French original for "thence away from it all" is more obviously circular: "ou se de detourner de devant," See *Celui qui ne peut se servir des mots*, p. 17.

27. Of Rich's revision of earlier work, Peter Erickson writes, "the mid-career shift in emphasis from rewriting the masters to rewriting herself helps to explain the reflexivity of Rich's subsequent work, the way it seems to be turning in on itself. The new, more difficult challenge is posed by the questions: What would it mean to rewrite *The Dream of a Common Language?* How can a volume that functions so strongly as the culmination of a whole phase of development also serve as a new, genuinely open-ended beginning?" See "Singing America: From Walt Whitman to Adrienne Rich," *The Kenyon Review*, n.s.17.1 (1995): 117.

28. *Shakespeare's Sonnets, The Arden Shakespeare, Third Series*, ed. Katherine Duncan-Jones (London: Thomas Nelson, 1997), p. 141.

29. See the Notes to *Dark Fields of the Republic*, pp. 78–79.

30. Peter Erickson ("Start Misquoting him Now," *Shakespeare-and-the-Classroom* 5 (1997: 55–56) similarly identifies the Shakespearean connection here.

31. *Hamlet*, ed. Harold Jenkins (New York: Routledge, 1982), p. 221. Peter Erickson cites Othello's "shock of insight" as the source of "O, O, O, / O." Erickson describes Rich's ambivalent connection to Shakespeare in terms that parallel what I name her vexed relationship to Petrarchan form: "The contrast between Rich's resistance to Shakespearean inscription—to being inscribed by Shakespeare's language . . . affords entry into the most far-reaching issues of inherited literary tradition—in particular the doubleness of how we are bound by it and how we are changing it." See "Start Misquoting Him Now," 56.

32. *The Tempest*, ed. Virginia Mason Vaughan and Alden T. Vaughan, *The Arden Shakespeare, Third Series* (London: Thomas Nelson, 1999), p. 25.

33. On the salamander as Petrarchan elider, see Gordon Braden, "Gaspara Stampa and the Gender of Petrarchism," 134.

34. Irene Costera Meijer and Beaukje Prins, "How Bodies Come to Matter: An Interview with Judith Butler," *Signs* 23.2 (1998): 284.

Chapter 8

1. "Thinkability," *Einstein's Monsters* (London: Vintage, 1999), pp. 18–19.
2. "1941," *Midnight Salvage* (New York: Norton, 1999), pp. 23–24.
3. Judith Butler, *The Psychic Life of Power: Theories in Subjection* (Stanford: Stanford University Press, 1997), p. 2.
4. As explained and translated by Rosalind Krauss, *The Optical Unconscious* (Cambridge, Mass: MIT Press, 1993), p. 167.
5. *Antigone's Claim: Kinship Between Life and Death* (New York: Columbia University Press, 2000), p. 54.
6. "Afterthought," *Notebook* (New York: Farrar, Straus and Giroux, 1970), p. 262.
7. "The Cliff," trans. Edith Fournier, *Samuel Beckett, The Complete Short Prose*, ed. S. E. Gontarski (New York: Grove Press, 1996), p. 257.
8. *To Paint her Life: Charlotte Salomon in the Nazi Era* (New York: Harper Collins, 1994), p. xi. See also Ernst van Alphen's reading of Salomon's work, as "the history of her gendered and her artistic becoming." *Caught by History: Holocaust Effects in Contemporary Art, Literature and Theory* (Stanford: Stanford University Press, 1997), p. 89.
9. *Charlotte Salomon, Life? or Theatre?*, ed. Judith C. E. Belinfante, Christine Fischer-Defoy, Ad Petersen, Norman Rosenthal; trans. Leila Vennewitz (London: Royal Academy of Arts, 1998), p. 722.
10. Judith Butler, *Excitable Speech* (New York: Routledge, 1997), p. 159
11. *The City of God* (New York: Random House, 2000), p. 190.
12. *Ferdydurke*, trans. Danuta Borchardt (New Haven: Yale University Press, 2000), p. 80.

Index